KDI STUDIES IN ECONOMICS

The Korea Development Institute was established on March 11, 1971 by President Park Chung Hee. K.D.I. systematically conducts research on policy matters concerning the overall national economy, helps develop the nation's five-year plans, and assists in policy making.

K.D.I. is a non-profit corporate organization operated on an endowment fund. For this reason, its autonomy and independence are guaranteed to the maximum possible extent in the performance of its policy-oriented research activities.

The results of research conducted by K.D.I. will be published and distributed. The contents of reports, however, will represent the opinion of the person in charge of the respective research, and shall not be construed as an official opinion of the Institute.

Trade and Development in Korea

Proceedings of a Conference held by the Korea Development Institute

Wontack Hong
and
Anne O. Krueger
Editors

1975

KOREA DEVELOPMENT INSTITUTE

Seoul, Korea

Distributed Outside Korea by
The University Press of Hawaii

ISBN 0-8248-0536-4

PREFACE

The papers brought together in this volume were presented at the Third KDI International Symposium on Trade and Development in Korea held in Seoul in June 1974. The conference was sponsored jointly by the Korea Development Institute and the Harvard International Institute of Development.

Most of the papers in this volume were written by economists affiliated with the Korea Development Institute, either as full-time fellows of the Institute, or as visiting fellows. These papers may be regarded as a part of the series of continuing KDI research on the general subject of the relationship between Korea's trade and Korea's growth. The interpretations and conclusions in each paper of this volume are those of the author or authors and do not represent the official views of the Korea Development Institute.

Among the policies adopted by the Korean Government to foster economic growth was the establishment of the Korea Development Institute in 1971. The Institute is an autonomous research body whose purpose is to increase understanding of the Korean economy, in the expectation that such knowledge will serve as a useful input into policy decisions. The Institute now has 18 full-time professional economists undertaking research, and in addition, finances academic economists to enable them to take leave from local universities in order to undertake research on specific topics.

I would like to take this opportunity to thank all those who did so much to ensure the success of the conference. Special gratitude is due to Professor Anne O. Krueger of the University of Minnesota and Wontack Hong of KDI, who assumed the demanding task of co-editorship of this volume.

Mahn Je Kim
President,
Korea Development Institute

TABLE OF CONTENTS

I

INTRODUCTION

I. INTRODUCTION

Korea achieved one of the highest growth rates in the world during the 1962–73 period. That rapid growth transformed the country from one of the poorest of the developing world, with bleak growth prospects, to one of the most dynamic. Over that period, per capita GNP in 1970 dollars rose from $150 to $343; Korea's commodity exports grew from $55 million to $3,225 million (for an average annual growth rate of 45 percent) with an increase in the share of exports in GNP from 1.8 to 25.0 percent. That change was accompanied by the cessation of new foreign aid, which had financed more than 70 percent of commodity imports during 1953–1961. Over the same period, Korea's domestic savings rate rose from 1.6 percent to 22.9 percent of GNP. By 1973, 28.4 percent of GNP originated in manufacturing and manufactured products constituted more than 90 percent of total commodity exports.

The entire Korean experience is therefore of great interest to all those interested in economic development, both because understanding what did happen will enable the design of policies to encourage further growth, and because it is natural to attempt to glean whatever lessons emerge from the Korean experience for application to other countries. In that regard, an important question is the extent to which Korea's success resulted from fortuitous circumstances, from the particular policies adopted, or from other factors.

In that regard, particular interest centers upon the fact that Korea's rapid growth was based upon an export-oriented growth strategy. Many questions arise: to what extent was the growth of exports responsible for the phenomenal growth of GNP? What policies were adopted to promote the growth of exports, and how efficient were they? What determined the composition of exports and their factor intensity? Finally, how does Korea's experience compare with other export-promotion oriented countries, especially Japan, Taiwan, Hong Kong, and Singapore?

The first two papers in the volume provide an introduction to the Korean experience during the 1962–73 decade. The first paper, by Kwang Suk Kim, analyzes Korea's economic growth in the context of her export oriented strategy, and introduces the reader to the incentives that were adopted to encourage export expansion. Kim traces the shift in the composition of Korea's exports (Table 3) and puts to rest one commonly heard, but empirically-unsupported, view: Japan's share of Korea's exports stood at 43 percent in 1962, and fell to 38.5 percent in 1973; it was thus not the fortuitous circumstance of being proximate to Japan with ready access to such a rapidly growing market that accounted for Korea's rapid export growth. Kim then proceeds to measure the extent to which exports and import-substituting industries contributed to Korea's growth rate. Whether looking at direct contributions, or direct plus indirect contributions to growth, domestic demand accounted for more than three fourths of the growth of output (for the period 1960–68), exports accounted for between 10 and 25 percent (depending upon the measure), while import substitution accounted for a negative fraction of total growth, and a negligible fraction of manufacturing growth.

The second paper, by Hak Yong Rhee, focuses more directly upon Korea's balance of payments and the changing nature of its components over time. In particular, Rhee is concerned with the relationship of current account and capital account transactions, and with the capital inflows that seem to have facilitated smooth adjustments to external shocks after the reforms of the early 1960's. Although Korean dependence on grant-in-aid ended in the mid-1960's, foreign capital inflows certainly enabled a higher rate of investment in Korea than would otherwise have been possible. Investigation into the determinants of that inflow is therefore of importance fo understadning future growth prospects. Some might argue that Korea's ability to borrow rendered the situation special; others, however, would contend that the reforms that were instituted in the early 1960's enabled realistic interest-rate policy and creditworthiness of the country. That question remains open, and of some importance for assessing future prospects.

The rapid expansion of Korea's exports raises a number of interesting questions. In many developing countries, the argument has been heard that concentration in primary commodity exports renders rapid expansion via export-promotion infeasible. In Korea's case, however, her initial concentration in primary commodities was unrelated to export expansion, which originated primarily in manufactured commodities.

The papers in Part III represent attempts to investigate aspects of the determinants of Korean comparative advantage. Wontack Hong's paper delves into the factor supply and factor intensity of trade, a subject of great interest in assessing prospects for other developing countries. There appears to be little doubt that Korea's manufactured exports are labor-intensive. However, Hong also investigates a second extremely important question. That is, even if a country's exports are labor intensive at an early stage of economic development, how will the factor intensity of its production and trade alter as its overall capital-labor endowment ratio grows and the real wage rate rises? The seven year period of 1966–72 seems to be especially suitable for this investigation, because total fixed capital stock in Korea increased by an average annual rate of about ten percent during this period. The capital intensity of Korea's commodity exports significantly increased during 1966–72, though no definite trend was established for the factor intensity of imports. Factor substitutions in a more capital intensive direction were also observed in production processes.

The next paper, by Cole and Westphal, investigates the employment generated by exports, contrasted with that from all sources. The Bank of Korea prepared input-output tables on a compatible 118 sector basis for a number of years, starting with 1960. Cole and Westphal used those tables to estimate the employment generated directly and indirectly by export sectors. Such an estimate does not attempt to attribute growth of the domestic economy to export-promotion policies; it simply estimates the employment generated directly by exporting, and indirectly by inputs used in export industries. They estimate that approximately 40 percent of the increase in employment between 1966 and 1970 was attributable to export expansion. In this connection, it is interesting to observe that Korea's rapid growth does not appear to have been accompanied by a worsening of income distribution; indeed, Korea is generally classified as one of the developing countries with small income inequality differentials.[1]

---

[1] Montek S. Ahluwalia "Income Inequality: Some Dimensions of the Problem", in Hollis Chenery *et al.*, *Redistribution with Growth,* Oxford University Press, London, 1974.

The paper by Sang Chul Suh, shifts to the microeconomic level for analysis of exports. Using the electronics industry as a case study, Suh traces government encouragement to the industry, its receipt of export incentives, and the role of multinational corporations in its growth. Production did not even start in Korea until 1958, and exports were only $1.4 million in 1965; by 1973, however, they had reached $311.8 million. He concludes that low labor costs were the chief factor providing Korea with a comparative advantage in electronics, and then raises some interesting questions with respect to the future: how long should it be before Korea moves from comparative advantage in labor-intensive commodities to developing her own potential in research and development and high technology industries? This is an important question, and one where little knowledge is available for guidance.

The paper by Chuk Kyo Kim attempts to estimate the growth rates of productivity in Korea's export and import substituting industries. He finds rather slow rates of growth in the productivity of export industries in comparison with other import substituting industries.

The final paper in Part III, by David Cole, attempts to investigate the way in which the exporting countries of the Far East increased their share of overseas markets. He finds that much of past export expansion was at the expense of established exporters' shares of the market. Such a conclusion is optimistic in two ways: it suggests that other developing countries can succeed through export promotion, perhaps by taking over Korean as well as other exporters' shares; and it also provides a basis for believing that, when development has proceeded far enough, Korea will be able to shift the composition of her exports toward more capital-intensive and technology-oriented goods as her comparative advantage changes.

In Part IV, analysis shifts from the determinants of comparative advantage to the optimality of the policies adopted for export promotion. The Korean Government intervened in a wide variety of ways to encourage exports; the range of effective exchange rates confronting Korean export industries was quite wide, as Kwang Suk Kim's paper demonstrated, and a natural question is whether the export-push went too far, or was too indiscriminate.

Charles R. Frank Jr. and Kwang Suk Kim try to investigate the optimality of Korean policies within the context of a macroeconomic model in which he simulates alternative exchange rate policies. In the simulation, they find that alternative policies might have yielded slightly higher real GNP, but never by more than 1 percent. Since the model is macroeconomic, and does not attempt to estimate the extent to which productivity growth and other sources of increase in output were attributable to export growth, their estimate suggests that the nonoptimality associated with bias toward exports may have been quite small. In most circumstances, one would judge policy to have been outstandingly successful if, over the period of a decade, the realization of target was within 1 percent of the maximum feasible performance!

Boum Jong Choe's paper proceeds along different lines. He attempts to examine concretely one particular export incentive policy: the development of the Masan Free Trade Zone in Korea. Although there are a number of difficulties surrounding an attempt at cost-benefit analysis within the context of an economy growing as rapidly as the Korean, Choe's data nonetheless are strongly suggestive that the development of the free trade zone probably did contribute enough to justify the investment.

As can be seen in a number of papers, there is argument among Korean economists that perhaps the "export-at-all-costs" policy has had some adverse resource allocation effects. It is clear that additional research on export policies and their effects is well warranted, and it is hoped that future Korea Development Institute research can fill in some of the missing pieces.

For readers interested in the economic development of Korea, these papers provide an introduction to the various aspects of Korea's trade policy that indicate directions in which future research should go. For those interested in the lessons to be learned from other countries, they provide a view of most of what has been important in the trade-growth relationship in Korea over the past decade and a half. As always, more research is needed, and it is hoped that these papers will provide a stimulus to that effort.

Korea Development Institute   **Wontack Hong**
University of Minnesota   **Anne O. Krueger**

February 1975

II

OVERVIEW OF KOREA'S GROWTH

Outward-Looking Industrialization Strategy: The Case of Korea

*Kwang Suk Kim**

I. INTRODUCTION

In the post-war period, many developing countries adopted a policy of import substitution as an industrialization strategy. In countries where this policy was emphasized, the domestic production of manufactured goods was protected by high tariffs, quantitative restrictions of imports and other controls. In such countries, exports were usually discouraged by an over-valued exchange rate, the prevalence of inefficient industries, the higher profitability of domestic sales relative to exports, etc.

The countries that emphasized import substitution actually made rapid progress in industrialization during the early stage of easy import substitution when domestic production replaced the imports of nondurable consumer goods and the intermediate goods used in their manufacture. However, once this stage of easy import substitution was over, the production of nondurable consumer goods and their inputs could not be expand-

* Senior fellow at the Korea Development Institute. This paper was presented at the Symposium on Asian Industrial Development sponsored by the Institute of Developing Economies, Tokyo, Japan, October 21–23, 1974. Although presented by the author alone, it is largely based on the results of two studies done in collaboration with Larry E. Westphal and Charles R. Frank, Jr. For a more complete and detailed discussion, the reader is therefore referred to Westphal and Kim (1974), and Frank, Kim and Westphal (1975).

ed rapidly due to the limited domestic market. These countries then turned to import substitution in durable consumer goods and machinery and in the intermediate inputs used in the production thereof. The industries producing these types of goods are generally more capital and technology intensive than the nondurable consumer goods industries and usually require high levels of output for efficient operation. In this stage, therefore, many countries encountered difficulties due to the small size of the domestic market and the technological and capital requirements of the industries in question.[1]

The Republic of Korea also started out with an industrialization strategy based on a policy of import substitution. She completed the easy import substitution in nondurable consumer goods and their inputs by around 1960. Instead of emphasizing further import substitution in machinery, durable consumer goods and their intermediate inputs, however, Korea changed its industrialization strategy from import substitution to export promotion in the early 1960's. The change in industrialization strategy was begun by the military government that came into power in 1961. The export-oriented industrialization strategy was then greatly strengthened by the exchange rate reform of 1964 and by subsequent major policy reforms.

Following this shift in industrialization strategy, Korea attained a remarkable rate of economic growth when compared with the previous period in which the policy of import substitution was emphasized. Commodity exports, which had been stagnant at a low level during the previous period, increased at a rapid rate, which averaged over 40 per cent a year during 1962–73. The growth rate of gross national product also accelerated from an average annual rate of 4 per cent during the earlier period to about 10 per cent during the latter period. The acceleration in the growth rate was mainly led by the rapid growth of the manufacturing sector. In view of the remarkable economic performance during 1962–73, it is no exaggeration to say that the export-oriented industrialization strategy of the period was largely successful.

This paper attempts to discuss the export-oriented industrialization strategy followed in Korea. The history of Korea's industry and trade policy is first outlined in Section II in order to show both the factors leading to the adoption of an export-oriented policy and the development of

---

[1] For this generalization regarding the industrialization strategies in developing countries, see B. Balassa and Associates (1971); Little, Scitovsky and Scott (1970); B. Balassa (1971).

that policy. Section III discusses the pattern of export expansion and its role in the growth of the Korean economy. Section IV attempts to evaluate the export-oriented industrialization performance by examining the factor intensity of Korea's exports and imports and the effective protection or subsidy rates. Finally, a summary of the discussion and concluding remarks are presented in Section V.

II. HISTORICAL DEVELOPMENT OF INDUSTRIAL POLICY

There are three distinct phases of Korean industrial policy over the period from 1945 to 1973. The first phase, which begins with Korea's liberation from Japan at the end of World War II and continues through 1960, may be characterized as the phase of easy import substitution. The second phase covered only a short period from 1960 to 1963, and was a transitional one between import substitution and export promotion. The period beginning in 1964 can be taken as the third phase, in which an export-oriented industrialization strategy was pursued in earnest.

At the conclusion of World War II, Korea was partitioned along the 38th parallel. This left South Korea with a majority of the peninsula's population, its most productive agricultural land, and the bulk of its light industry. On the other hand, most of the heavy industry and more than 90 per cent of the electricity generating capacity were in the North. The Korean War (1950–53) destroyed most of the industrial facilities located in South Korea. Between partition and approximately 1955, therefore, economic activity in the South was dominated by adjustments to partition and then to the dislocations caused by the war. During 1954–60, however, the post-Korean War reconstruction and industrialization programs were carried out with United States and United Nations assistance.

During the reconstruction period, the government controlled imports so as to favor import-substitution industries. In addition to high tariff walls, the government increasingly relied on quantitative restrictions in the late fifties in order to offset the progressive inflation of the "won" currency. A complex structure of multiple exchange rates was also developed to avoid balance of payments difficulties during this period. On balance, the structure of incentives during this period appears to have been biased against exports although there existed some promotional schemes.

The second phase covers the three years following the Student Revolution in April 1960. This was a period of social, political and economic instability notable for a number of attempts at liberalization and reform. The most successful of these was the establishment of a unified exchange rate. The military government that took control of the economy in 1961 completed the task of unifying the exchange rate began by the preceding civilian government.[2] The transition to a unified exchange rate in 1961 did not, however, appreciably increase export proceeds, for the new rate was somewhat lower than the earlier free market rate on export earnings. It did, however, raise the unit cost of imports by more than 40 per cent. Due to a decline in United States grant aid and the consequent balance of payments difficulties, the government generally tightened import controls by means of an import licencing mechanism and high tariffs. On the other hand, the government increased exporter incentives by means of preferential loans, income tax reductions, indirect tax exemptions on inputs and an export-import link system.

The "won" devaluation in 1964 and the subsequent policy reforms greatly strengthened the export-oriented industrialization strategy. The Korean "won" was devalued by almost 50 per cent from 130 won to the dollar to 255 won in May 1964, and a unitary floating exchange rate system was formally put into effect in March 1965. The "won" stabilized at 270 per dollar by the end of that year, and floated slowly upward under continued intervention by the Bank of Korea. Following this exchange rate reform, the government raised the interest rates on bank deposits and loans by almost 100 per cent in September 1965. The goal was to increase voluntary private savings. This interest rate reform significantly increased relative incentives to exporters since the preferential rates to exporters were not increased. Along with these reforms, the government also carried out price stabilization and tax reform programs to control inflation and raise the ratio of tax revenue to GNP.

Trade controls were gradually relaxed following the 1964 devaluation. The system was further liberalized in 1967 when a switch was made from the so-called "positive" list system (under which only those commodities listed in the trade program could be imported) to the "negative" system (under which all commodities not listed are automatically approved). Tariff reform was undertaken in the latter part of 1967 and again in early 1973 to reduce the average tariff rate on imports. Government supports

---

[2] Since then, Korea has had a unified exchange rate except briefly during 1963 and early 1964.

to exporters during this period thus included: preferential credit, indirect tax exemptions on inputs into export production and export sales, a 50 per cent reduction in income tax on export earnings (abolished in early 1973), tariff exemption on imported raw materials and equipment for export production, and wastage allowances on imported raw materials for export production. In addition, the government-subsidized Korea Trade Promotion Corporation (KOTRA) was established in 1964 to promote Korea's exports and conduct market research.

Table 1 summarizes the impact of many of the above policies in terms of purchasing-power-parity (PPP) adjusted exchange rates for exports and imports. The effective exchange rate for exports includes the effects of the following: the dollar premium due to multiple exchange rates (1955–61 and 1963–64), direct subsidy payments (1961–64 only), tariff and indirect tax exemptions, direct tax reductions and preferential rates.[3] The effective exchange rate for imports is a weighted average of the official rate and the free market rate (as applied to export earnings) and includes actual tariff collections and other tariff equivalents. The effective rate for imports does not, however, include the effect of quantitative restrictions on imports. The rate in the fifties and early sixties cannot, therefore, be compared directly with that in the subsequent period since the government relied heavily on non-price measures for import control in the earlier period. Nominal effective exchange rates on exports and imports have been adjusted for changes in domestic and world prices in order to obtain the PPP-adjusted effective exchange rates.

The most important policy measures favoring exports were taken by 1964, when the PPP-adjusted effective exchange rate reached 305 won per dollar in 1965 constant prices. The "won" became over-valued between 1965 and 1971 as the exchange rate floated upward less rapidly than the difference between inflation rates in Korea and abroad. Thus, increased export subsidies were required after 1965 to keep the PPP-adjusted effective exchange rate on exports roughly constant at around 300 won to the dollar during the period. On the other hand, the PPP-adjusted effective exchange rate on imports rose with the devaluations of 1961 and 1964, and fell subsequent to each of these realignments. Over the period 1965 to 1971, the rate declined from 293.1 to 266.2 won to the dollar. All in all, it appears that between 1964 and 1971, the relative incentive to export

---

[3] It does not include subsidies implicit in some imports linked to exports for 1964–73. Wastage allowance subsidies are considered to be largely covered in the exemptions of indirect taxes and tariffs.

Table 1

Nominal and Purchasing Power Parity Effective Exchange Rates for Korea

(Won per U.S. Dollar)

	Nominal Exchange Rate			Wholesale Price Index (1965 = 100)		Purchasing-Power-Parity Adjusted Exchange Rate[3]		
	Official	Effective Rates[1]		Major Trade		Official	Effective Rates	
	Rate	Exports	Imports	Korea	Partners[2]	Rate	Exports	Imports
1955	36.8	72.2	42.1	29.8	92.5	114.1	223.8	130.5
1956	50.0	102.8	57.3	36.6	95.4	130.5	268.3	149.6
1957	50.0	108.9	58.4	42.5	98.7	116.0	252.6	135.5
1958	50.0	115.2	64.0	39.9	97.2	121.8	280.6	155.9
1959	50.0	136.0	82.8	40.8	97.7	119.7	325.3	198.2
1960	62.5	147.6	100.2	45.2	97.9	135.4	319.6	216.9
1961	127.5	150.6	147.0	51.2	98.3	244.8	289.1	282.2
1962	130.0	151.5	146.4	56.0	97.6	226.6	264.0	255.1
1963	130.0	189.4	148.1	67.5	98.3	189.3	275.8	215.7
1964	214.3	281.4	247.0	90.9	98.5	232.2	305.0	267.6
1965	265.4	304.6	293.1	100.0	100.0	265.4	304.6	293.1
1966	271.3	322.9	296.4	108.8	102.8	256.3	305.1	280.0
1967	270.7	331.3	296.2	115.8	104.0	243.1	297.1	266.0
1968	276.6	354.3	302.5	125.2	105.6	233.3	298.8	255.1
1969	288.2	363.3	312.7	133.7	108.8	234.5	295.6	254.1
1970	310.7	397.4	336.4	145.9	112.8	240.2	307.3	260.1
1971	347.7	440.3[4]	369.5	158.5	114.2	250.5	317.2[4]	266.2
1972	391.8	n.a.	415.2	180.7	117.2	254.1[5]	n.a.	269.3
1973	398.3	n.a.	412.9	193.3	133.9	275.9[5]	n.a.	286.0

Source: Frank, Kim and Westphal (1974) and Westphal and Kim (1974)

[1] Effective rate on exports includes dollar premium due to multiple exchange rates during 1955–61 and 1963–64 and subsidies per dollar implicit in various incentives given to exporters (primarily after 1961), while that on imports includes actual tariffs and tariff equivalents per dollar.

[2] An average of wholesale price indices in the U.S. and Japan, weighted by Korea's annual trade volume with the respective countries.

[3] Nominal exchange rates adjusted by the price parity between Korea and its major trade partners.

[4] Export subsidies per dollar are assumed to have increased by the same percentage rate as estimated in Koo (1972).

[5] Due to the major foreign currency realignments, the Korean won was effectively devalued by about 7 per cent and 10 per cent in 1972 and 1973, respectively. When these effective devaluations are taken into account, Korea's official exchange rate at purchasing power parity rose to 271.9 to the dollar in 1972 and 303.5 in 1973.

expansion increased while that to import substitution fell due to over-valuation of the won. This provides evidence that increased incentives have been provided to exports relative to import substitution.

For the recent period, 1972–73, it was not possible to estimate the effective exchange rate on exports due to limitations of the available data. During this period, however, the official exchange rate was adjusted upward more rapidly than in the preceding period, so that the PPP-adjusted official rate might have reached 275.9 won to the dollar by 1973. In addition, the major foreign currency realignments in 1972 and 1973 resulted in an effective devaluation of the Korean won by 7 per cent and 10 per cent, respectively (taking into account Korea's trade volumes with the major currency countries). When these effective devaluations due to foreign currency realignments are included, the PPP-adjusted official rate was devalued to 271.9 to the dollar in 1972 and 303.5 won by 1973.

Since the PPP-adjusted official rate in 1973 was roughly equivalent to the PPP-adjusted effective exchange rate on exports during 1964–71, Korean industries became quite competitive in international markets, even without government support. In 1973, therefore, the government eliminated the system of income tax reductions for exporters, reduced the interest subsidies implicit in preferencial export credit and attempted to reduce the wastage allowances. In addition, the special tariff (used to soak up the excess profits arising from the large difference between domestic and world prices during 1962–72) was completely abolished in 1973.

We have thus far discussed the historical development of incentive policies relating to industrialization strategy. It should be clear from the discussion that the policies favoring export expansion began during 1961–63 and were fully implemented beginning in 1964. What were the reasons for adopting such an export-oriented strategy in Korea?

First, the economic growth performance in the late fifties and early sixties was frustrating to both policy-makers and the people, since the possibility of rapid growth through import substitution seemed nearly exhausted by that time. By around 1960, Korea had virtually completed import substitution in nondurable consumer goods and in the intermediate products used in their manufacture. A growth strategy concentrating on import substitution in machinery, consumer durables and their intermediate products did not seem to be an appropriate alternative because of the limitations imposed by the smallness of the domestic market and the large capital requirements. Secondly, Korea's natural resource endowment is so poor that an alternative development strategy based on domestic resource utilization was inconceivable. Thirdly, U.S. assistance, which financed most of the post-Korean war reconstruction, started to gradually decline in the early sixties. Faced with this reduction in foreign aid, Korean policy makers had to seriously consider an alternative source of foreign exchange to meet the balance of payments difficulties. Fourthly, the availability of a well-motivated labor force with a high educational level and relatively low wages provided the country with a comparative advantage in exporting labor-intensive goods. Lastly, one should mention the determination of the leadership to attain a high rate of growth, and a virtual lack of constraints on the ability to make decisions and to carry them out.

III. EXPORT EXPANSION AND ECONOMIC GROWTH

The Pattern of Export Expansion

Korean exports in the fifties were not only small in value but also fluctuated annually depending upon the supply and demand conditions of a small number of primary commodities. Although the export growth began in 1960, the total amount of exports was only about $55 million by 1962. Export expansion during 1962–73 was, however, very rapid, averaging 44.8 per cent annually. Exports in 1973 reached $3.2 billion, equivalent to about 25 per cent of gross national product (see Table 2).

As shown in Table 3, in the fifties and early sixties, most Korean exports were primary products—mainly tungsten, iron ore, fish, raw silk, agar-agar, rice, coal, etc. Manufactured exports were only a small fraction of total exports until 1962, but thereafter expanded more rapidly than the exports of primary products. By 1973, such manufactured goods as clothing, electrical machinery, plywood, textile fabrics, iron and steel sheets, footwear and wigs became the major components of Korean exports. According to an estimate made by the Ministry of Commerce and Industry, manufactured exports, which had been only 27 per cent of total exports in 1962, reached about 88 per cent by 1973 (see Table 2).[4]

---

[4] As the share of manufactured exports in total exports increased, the import content of Korean exports gradually increased in the sixties and very early seventies. The direct import content, estimated from the Ministry of Finance's Trade Statistics, increased from 40 to 46 per cent between 1967 and 1971 but declined to about 42 per cent by 1973. Ministry of Finance, *Foreign Trade of Korea* (annual), various issues.

Table 2

Major Indicators of Korea's Economic Growth

	1954	1962	1973	Annual Average Growth Rate (%) 1954–62	1962–73
1. **Population** (million)	21.8	26.1	32.9	2.3	2.1
2. **Gross National Product** (1970 constant billion won)					
Gross National Product	290	1,221	3,534	4.0	10.1 ⟵
Industrial Origin:					
Primary	434	512	838	2.1	4.6
(share in GNP, %)	(48.8)	(41.9)	(23.7)		
Manufacturing	61	142	1,002	11.1	19.4
(share in GNP, %)	(6.8)	(11.6)	(28.4)		
Social overhead & services	395	567	1,694	4.6	10.5
(share in GNP, %)	(44.4)	(46.4)	(47.9)		
Per capita GNP (1970 thousand won)	41	47	107	1.7	7.8
Per capita GNP (1970 dollar)	131	151	346	1.8	7.8
3. **Exports and Imports**					
Commodity exports ($ mil.)	24	55	3,255	10.9	44.8
Commodity imports ($ mil.)	243	422	4,240	7.1	23.3
Share of manufactured exports in total exports (%)[1]	n.a.	27.0	88.2		
Share of commodity exports in GNP (%)[2]	0.9	1.5	24.7		
Share of commodity imports in GNP (%)[2]	8.5	10.9	30.7		
4. **Investment and Saving**[3]					
Share of gross domestic investment in GNP (%)	11.6	13.0	26.4		
Share of manufacturing investment in gross fixed investment (%)	17.5	20.6	25.0		
Domestic saving rate (%)	4.7	1.6	21.0		
Foreign saving rate (%)	7.0	10.8	4.9		

Source: Bank of Korea, *Economic Statistics Yearbook* (various issues) and Economic Planning Board, *Major Economic Indicators* (various issues).

[1] The Ministry of Commerce and Industry's estimates given in EPB, *Major Economic Indicators*. The figures cannot be directly compared with the data given in Table 3.

[2] Based on 1970 constant price data given in the national income accounts.

[3] Based on current price data.

Table 3

Exports by Commodity Group and Major Commodities

(Percent of Total Exports)

SITC	Group & Commodities	1954	1962	1968	1973
0.	Food & Live Animals	12.1	39.8	9.8	7.6
	Fish & Fish Preparations	2.9	14.8	5.4	4.3
	Rice	0.0	16.2	—	—
	Dried Laver (Seaweed)	0.0	1.3	3.0	0.3
1.	Beverages & Tobacco	0.1	0.2	1.9	0.7
2.	Crude Materials except Fuel	76.7	35.4	13.5	6.1
	Raw silk	15.8	7.7	4.0	2.3
	Iron Ore & Concentrates	39.5	6.9	1.6	0.1
	Tungsten Ore & Concentrates		6.0	2.4	0.3
	Ginseng	0.4	0.4	1.0	0.4
	Agar-agar	5.7	2.4	0.4	0.1
3–5.	Mineral Fuel; Animal & Vegetable Oils & Fats; and Chemicals	0.0	5.1	1.2	2.6
	Anthracite Coal	0.0	4.9	0.5	0.1
6.	Manufactured Goods Classified chiefly by Material	4.6	11.3	31.5	34.2
	Plywood	0.0	4.2	14.4	8.4
	Textile Yarn	0.0	0.0	0.9	2.7
	Cotton Fabrics	0.0	3.3	2.9	1.8
	Other Textile Fabrics	0.0	0.0	7.7	8.1
	Sheet of Iron & Steel	0.0	0.9	0.2	4.0
7.	Machinery & Transport Equipment	0.3	2.6	5.4	12.3
	Electrical Machinery	0.0	n.a.	4.2	9.7
8.	Misc. Manufactures	0.2	3.7	36.7	36.3
	Clothing	0.0	n.a.	20.1	13.5
	Footwear	0.0	n.a.	9.0	3.3
	Wigs & False Beards	0.0	n.a.	7.7	2.5
9.	Unclassifiable	0.2	0.2	0.0	0.2
	Total Exports	100.0	100.0	100.0	100.0
	($ million)	(24)	(55)	(455)	(3225)

Source: Bank of Korea, *Economic Statistics Yearbook* (various issues)

Table 4

Exports by Country

(Percent of Total Exports)

	1954	1962	1965	1968	1973
United States	56.3	21.8	35.2	51.7	31.7
Japan	32.9	42.8	25.1	21.9	38.5
Other Asia	9.6	22.3	23.9	11.5	10.3
Europe	1.1	11.5	12.2	8.0	11.8
Rest of the World	0.1	1.5	3.6	7.0	7.8

Source: Bank of Korea, *Economic Statistics Yearbook* (various issues)

Table 4 presents the destination of Korean exports for selected years between 1954 and 1973. Throughout the period, more than half of Korean exports went to two rich countries: the United States and Japan. In 1954, about 90 per cent of Korean exports went to the two countries, but their share declined to about 60 per cent of total exports in the first half of the sixties before again increasing to roughly 70 per cent in the late sixties and early seventies. Although the share of Korean exports going to other Asian countries remained almost unchanged between 1954 and 1973, exports to Europe and the rest of the world increased substantially as a share of total exports during the same period.

As exports expanded rapidly during 1962–73, the growth rate of GNP amounted to an average annual rate of about 10 per cent during the period, compared to 4 per cent growth achieved in the earlier period (1954–62). In particular, the manufacturing sector grew by an average annual rate of 19.4 per cent during 1962–73, thus leading the growth of the overall economy. The growth rate of the manufacturing sector in the earlier period was about 11 per cent, despite the fact that the post-Korean War reconstruction programs were carried out with a large inflow of foreign assistance. The rapid growth in the economy was made possible by investing a greater share of GNP in productive activities during 1962–73. The share of gross domestic investment in GNP, which had been about 13 per cent until 1962, expanded to 26 per cent by 1973. Along with this increase in domestic investment, domestic saving also expanded rapidly from 1.6 per cent of GNP to 21 per cent between 1962 and 1973.

Contributions to Economic Growth

We now discuss the role of exports in the growth of the Korean economy, particularly in relation to the other sources of output growth, namely domestic demand expansion and import substitution. Our analysis is based on a series of five input-output tables: 1955, 1960, 1963, 1966 and 1968. The table for 1955 gives information at a 29 sector level[5] while those for the remaining observation years provide information in a 117 sector breakdown. Because of this difference, it is not possible to present the same information for all five observation years.

The input-output tables distinguish between competitive and non-competitive imports.[6] The list of items classified as non-competitive changes from table to table. Since much of Korea's import substitution has come through introducing the production of formerly non-competitive imports, we have adjusted the data so that virtually all imports are treated as competitive. In addition, the current price input-output statistics were deflated on the basis of a set of output deflators at the 117 sector level using independent time series on the general wholesale price level, the wholesale price level of imported commodities, the price level of exports and the exchange rate on imports and exports. The resulting constant price statistics were further deflated by the nominal protection rates[7] estimated for 1968 to yield a set of input-output statistics in constant world market prices. Deflation to constant world market prices was carried out only for commodities.

In order to estimate the relative contributions of exports, domestic demand expansion and import substitution to economic growth, we have to decompose the total output change between 1955 and 1968. There are a number of ways to do this but only one method of decomposition is presented below. The decomposition begins with the fundamental supply-demand balance equation of input-output analysis:

$$Q_{j,t} = W_{j,t} + C_{j,t} + Z_{j,t} + X_{j,t} - M_{j,t}$$

where $Q_{j,t}$ = gross output in sector j in period t,

$W_{j,t}$ = intermediate demand for the output of sector j in period t,

---

[5] The I-O table for 1955 was prepared especially for the Westphal and Kim (1974) study by the Inter-industry Research Section of the Bank of Korea with the financial support from the University Committee on Research in the Humanities and Soical Sciences and the Council on International and Regional Studies, Princeton Univ.

[6] Competitive imports are defined as items that are also produced domestically, while non-competitive imports are items not produced in Korea in the year for which the table was compiled.

[7] The nominal protection rate on each tradable commodity was measured as $P_d/P_w - 1$, where P_d is domestic producer's unit price and P_w, the world market unit price (see Section IV).

$C_{j,t}$ = private plus government consumption demand for the output of sector j in period t,

$Z_{j,t}$ = investment demand (including net stock accumulation) for the output of sector j in period t,

$X_{j,t}$ = export demand for the output of sector j in period t, and

$M_{j,t}$ = imports of items classified in sector j in period t.

We define import substitution as a change in the ratio of imports to domestic demand. Let $m_{j,t}$ be defined as $M_{j,t}/D_{j,t}$, where $D_{j,t} (= W_{j,t} + C_{j,t} + Z_{j,t})$ is total domestic demand. Letting $t = S$ denote the first period, we have

$$Q_{j,S} = (1 - m_{j,S})D_{j,S} + X_{j,S} .$$

For the second period (T), we write

$$Q_{j,T} = (1 - m_{j,S})D_{j,T} + X_{j,T} + m_{j,S}D_{j,T} - M_{j,T} ,$$

where we have both added and subtracted the term $m_{j,S}D_{j,T}$ on the right hand side of the equation. Subtracting the expression for $Q_{j,S}$ from that for $Q_{j,T}$ yields,

$$\Delta Q_{j,T} = [(1 - m_{j,S})\Delta D_{j,T}] + \Delta X_{j,T} + [m_{j,S}D_{j,T} - M_{j,T}] ,$$

where "Δ" is the first difference operator. The first term on the right (in square brackets) is the contribution of domestic demand expansion; the second is the contribution of export expansion; and the last (in square brackets) is the contribution of import substitution. Import substitution is thus measured as the difference between actual imports and the imports that would have been observed, had the first period's import ratio been realized in the second period.

This decomposition may yield biased estimates because of the arbitrary choice of the first period as the base period for defining the import ratio. Use of the second period is an equally arbitrary choice. The bias in both cases results from using values for two discrete points in time, which essentially means that we are confronted with an index number problem. The approach taken here to minimize this problem is the use of "chained" measures. Rather than applying the decomposition simply to the data for 1955 (or 1960) and 1968, we have separately decomposed the changes in output over each interval for which we have input-output data. The estimates for each interval are then summed to give the growth contributions between 1955 (or 1960) and 1968. In addition, since the measures of import substitution are also sensitive to the level of aggregation employed, the growth contributions are calculated by individual sectors (29 sector level for 1955 and 117 sector level for the remaining observation years).

The decomposition defined above yields the direct contribution of each source to each sector's output growth. The growth of intermediate demand for each sector's output may be traced back to import substitution, export expansion and final demand growth in the industries demanding the particular sector's output on intermediate account. The total (direct plus indirect) contributions were calculated through the use of the inverse input-output matrix. The estimates of both the direct and total growth contributions are given in Table 5.

The most striking result of this analysis is the predominance of export expansion over import substitution. Over the period 1955 to 1968, 20.2 per cent of total growth was attributable directly and indirectly to export expansion while –0.6 per cent was due to import substitution. Thus, on balance, there was negligible import substitution but substantial export expansion. As is to be expected, the expansion of domestic demand was the most important factor, accounting for more than eighty per cent of total growth. During the period 1960 to 1968, export expansion was relatively even more important, accounting for 22.4 per cent of growth compared to –1.4 per cent for import substitution.

Another striking conclusion which may be drawn from Table 5 is that export expansion generated considerable domestic backward linkages while import substitution did not. The average contribution of export expansion for either the 1955–1968 or 1960–1968 period is almost doubled when indirect effects are taken into account. That is, growth of exports generates substantial demand for domestically produced intermediate goods.

It is of interest to compare the relative importance of export expansion and import substitution in different time periods. The figures below show the *total* contribution of each to the growth of aggregate commodity output for each sub-interval:

	1955–60	1960–63	1963–66	1966–68
Export Expansion	12.9%	6.3%	31.4%	21.3%
Import Substitution	10.2%	–6.9%	8.9%	–6.6%

Export expansion contributed more to the growth of commodity output in each sub-period than did import substitution. The greatest contribution of export expansion and import substitution together was realized be-

Table 5

Direct and Indirect Contributions to Korean Economic Growth

(Percent of Total Growth of Sector)

	Domestic Demand Expansion		Export Expansion		Import Substitution	
	Direct	Total	Direct	Total	Direct	Total
Broad Sectors: 1955–1968						
1. Primary	109.2	94.7	4.0	19.4	−13.2	−14.2
2. Manufacturing	80.0	72.5	13.7	22.0	6.3	5.5
3. Social Overhead	91.4	86.7	8.8	12.3	−0.2	0.9
4. Services	96.4	86.7	5.0	14.9	−1.4	−1.6
Other	81.5	70.9	35.9	46.4	−17.4	−17.3
Total	88.9	80.3	11.2	20.2	−0.3	−0.6
Industrial Group: 1960–1968						
1. Agriculture, Forestry and Fishing	108.0	94.9	−0.1	15.9	−7.9	−10.8
2. Mining and Energy	88.0	70.6	15.9	28.2	−3.9	1.2
Primary	106.5	92.9	1.2	16.9	−7.6	−9.8
3. Processed Food	90.4	87.8	7.8	11.7	1.8	0.5
4. Beverages and Tobacco	93.8	88.9	4.0	9.9	2.2	1.1
5. Construction Materials	86.4	84.8	5.6	7.4	8.0	7.8
6. Intermediate Products I	68.2	54.0	17.0	32.3	14.8	13.6
7. Intermediate Products II	84.6	72.1	10.4	25.6	5.0	2.4
8. Nondurable Consumer Goods	57.0	53.0	36.2	40.2	6.8	6.8
9. Durable Consumer Goods	81.2	78.1	23.2	27.2	−4.4	−5.3
10. Machinery	141.0	149.5	8.0	12.2	−49.0	−51.8
11. Transport Equipment	141.7	144.6	0.2	4.2	−41.9	−48.8
Manufacturing	81.7	74.0	15.1	24.3	3.2	1.7
All commodities	88.2	79.0	11.4	22.4	0.3	−1.4

Source: Westphal and Kim (1974), p 107.

Note: All results are aggregated from 117 sector input-output data, except for 1955–60 which is from 29 sector data. Totals may not reconcile due to rounding errors.

tween 1963 and 1966, the same period in which the major policy reforms were carried out and in which Korea began its rapid growth. The growth of primary exports and import substitution in manufacturing characterized the earlier period. Manufactures dominated the growth of exports after 1960, and there was less import substitution in the sixties than there had been in the late fifties.

The figures below show the *direct* contributions of export expansion and import substitution to the growth of *manufactured* output alone:

	1955–60	1960–63	1963–66	1966–68
Export Expansion	5.1%	6.2%	29.4%	13.0%
Import Substitution	24.2%	0.9%	14.4%	–0.1%

The late fifties is seen to be a period of major import substitution in manufacturing during which exports played a relatively minor role in Korea's industrialization. Export growth is again seen to have made its major relative contribution in 1963–66. The negative coefficients for import substitution in the late 60's clearly reflect the effect of the high capital inflow which financed large imports of capital goods.

IV. EVALUATION OF THE EXPORT-ORIENTED GROWTH

It is difficult to present any conclusive evidence regarding the efficiency of Korea's export-oriented growth. In this section, however, I attempt to deal with the efficiency question on the basis of two partial measures: (1) the relative factor intensity of Korea's exports and imports, and (2) effective protection or subsidy rates. The effort is based on two assumptions. First, a poor country with a relatively abundant labor force such as Korea has a comparative advantage in the expansion of labor-intensive industries. Secondly, relative rates of effective protection (or subsidies) on industries indicate the relative efficiency of the industries concerned. That is, low rates allow less room for either excess profits or substantial inefficiency.

The Factor Intensity of Trade

This analysis of the factor intensity of Korea's trade follows the path-breaking work of Leontief. Using labor and capital input coefficients at the 117 sector level for 1968, we have calculated the direct as well as the total factor input requirements associated with Korea's exports and imports.[8] Total labor and capital requirements include both direct and in-

---

[8] For estimates of the sectoral labor coefficients, we have relied upon the labor input coefficient estimates provided along with the Bank of Korea's 1966 I-O Table (BOK, *Economic Statistics Yearbook,* 1969). Since these data are given at the 43 sector level

direct labor and capital requirements by sector per unit of production. The indirect factor requirements are determined by inverting the input-output table for 1966 at the 117 sector level.

Imports can be treated in two different ways. First, each import can be placed in one of the 117 sectors and capital and labor requirements calculated as if the imports were produced using the Korean sectoral coefficients. Second, clearly non-competitive imports, (i.e., imports not produced in Korea) can be excluded and the remaining imports classified by sector. The results reported here include non-competitive imports (except for a few primary products not found in Korea) in the bundle of imports that is considered to be replaced.[9] This procedure is followed so that comparisons over time can be made even though the composition of non-competitive imports changed from year to year.

In the calculation of the total factor input coefficients, the matrix of intermediate input coefficients includes the requirements for those inputs that were actually imported. It certainly does not make sense to calculate the factor requirements to replace some imports without also assuming that intermediate imports would also be replaced. To have consistent total factor input coefficients for imports and exports, one must use the same input-output matrix in both cases. This means, however, that the total factor input coefficients relating to exports are calculated on the assumption that *all* intermediate input requirements would be produced domestically. Given that there were imports of intermediate inputs related to export production, our calculations overstate the "actual" total factor usage associated with export activity.

For those years for which detailed input-output statistics are available, Table 6 gives the average direct and total labor to capital ratios for exports and imports of primary and manufactured products separately. In every

---

only, it was assumed that the same labor input coefficients pertain to all of the sectors at the 117 sector level that comprise a single sector at the 43 sector level. For estimates of the capital-output ratios, we have relied upon Han Kee Chun's exhaustive retabulation of the 1968 National Wealth Survey. Constant 1965 price input-output data on production, exports and imports were used to calculate factor input requirements. The 117 sector input-output matrix, for 1966, deflated to 1965 prices, was used to obtain total factor input requirements.

[9] Hong (1974) divided non-competitive imports into two groups; "non-competitive non-natural-resource-intensive imports," and "non-competitive natural-resource-intensive imports." He used the sectoral input coefficients taken from U.S. data for calculation of the factor intensity of "non-competitive non-natural-resource-intensive imports." His results concerning the relative factor intensities of exports and imports are consistent with ours although we used the domestic sectoral input coefficients.

Table 6

Factor Intensity of Korea's Trade

	Labor/Capital Ratios[1]			
	1960	1963	1966	1968
Direct Factor Requirements				
Primary Products				
Domestic Output	16.60	17.20	17.08	17.16
Exports	8.19	6.89	6.15	5.69
Imports	16.58	15.91	16.13	15.48
Manufacturing Products				
Domestic Output	2.97	2.89	2.67	2.64
Exports	2.72	3.02	3.24	3.55
Imports	2.09	1.93	1.98	2.33
Total Factor Requirements				
Primary Products				
Exports	6.55	5.75	5.13	4.81
Imports	11.99	11.50	11.90	11.30
Manufacturing Products				
Exports	3.74	3.71	4.09	4.29
Imports	2.77	2.40	2.40	2.74

Source: Westphal and Kim (1974), P. 123.

[1] Thousand man-years per billion won of capital in 1965 constant prices.

observation year, manufactured exports had higher direct and total labor/ capital ratios than did manufactured imports. On the other hand, primary exports were more capital intensive than primary imports. A large share of Korea's primary exports are capital-intensive minerals whereas primary imports include a large share of labor intensive agricultural products.

Even though there was a steady fall in the direct labor intensity of manufacturing production, the composition of Korea's manufactured exports shifted from 1960 to 1968 so as to increase the direct labor/capital ratio in manufactured exports by approximately 30 per cent. Korea's manufactured exports were less labor intensive than average manufacturing in 1960, but far more labor intensive by 1968. The direct labor intensity of manufactured imports was less than that of manufacturing production throughout the period. The total labor/capital ratio for Korea's manufactured imports declined slightly between 1960 and 1968. Thus, while Korea's manufactured exports were becoming more labor intensive, her manufactured imports were tending to become a bit more capital intensive.

The total labor intensity of exports was greater than the direct labor intensity. That is, intermediate products produced domestically for export industries have been even more labor intensive than the direct production of the exports themselves.

The results suggest that Korea's export-oriented growth was accomplished through the expansion of relatively labor-intensive manufactured exports. Apart from natural resource and labor skill considerations, Korea's comparative advantage, at least within manufacturing, should lie in exporting labor-intensive products and importing capital-intensive ones. In this sense, the evidence indicates that Korea has followed a fairly efficient growth path.

Effective Protection (or Subsidy) Rate

The industrial and trade policy of any country can have a substantial effect on the allocation of resources. However, it is difficult to know whether all the changes in the structure of prices and incentives caused by that policy lead to more efficient or less efficient resource allocation. The assumption in much static analysis of trade and development is that inefficient resource allocation results from any substantial deviation of the exchange rate from a unified equilibrium rate, large deviations in effective tariffs, and import controls. According to this view, world prices of tradable commodities reflect the true opportunity costs of production of those commodities. Thus, tariffs, controls, and multiple exchange rates, which distort world market prices, lead to inefficiencies.[10]

A simple measure of the divergence between world market and domestic prices is the legal tariff rate. In Korea, however, the legal tariff is generally not a good measure of such divergence for three reasons: First, some tariffs, though relatively low in absolute magnitude, are prohibitive; second, widespread exemptions and reductions of tariff levies are granted; and third, much of Korean industry is export-oriented even though domestic markets are protected by tariffs. For our study of protection in Korea, therefore, it was necessary to compare world market prices and domestic prices directly. The divergence between world market and domestic prices can be expressed as,

$$(1) \qquad t_n = \frac{P_d - P_w}{P_w},$$

---

[10] The most important argument that can be used to favor some divergence between world market and domestic prices may be the infant industry argument.

where p_d is the domestic price of a commodity and p_w is the world market price. We call t_n the rate of nominal protection or nominal tariff rate to distinguish it from the legal tariff rate.

Neither legal nor nominal tariff rates provide very good indicators of the resource diverting effects of tariffs and quantitative restrictions. A much better measure is the rate of effective protection, which takes into account the fact that intermediate goods are required for production along with primary factors. The general formulas for the effective rate of protection, t_{ej}, for activity j as:[11]

$$(2) \qquad t_{ej} = \frac{P_{dj} - \sum_i a_{ij}P_{di}}{P_{wj} - \sum_i a_{ij}P_{wi}} - 1, \text{ or}$$

$$(3) \qquad t_{ej} = \frac{P_{wj}(1 + t_{nj}) - \sum_i a_{ij}P_{wi}(1 + t_{ni})}{P_{wj} - \sum_i a_{ij}P_{wi}} - 1$$

$$= \frac{t_{nj} - \sum_i a_{ij}t_{ni}}{P_{wj} - \sum_i a_{ij}P_{wi}},$$

where P_{dj} is the domestic price of commodity j, P_{wj} is its world market price, a_{ij} is the input-output coefficient giving the input of commodity i per unit of output of j commodity, and t_{ni} is the nominal protection rate for commodity i. The effective rate of protection is the percentage difference between domestic value-added and the value-added in world market prices. The effective rate of protection may also be expressed in terms of the rates of nominal protection on commodity j and the rates of protection on all inputs into commodity j as in equation (3).

In addition to effective protection, we have to introduce the notion of effective subsidy. Subsidies in the form of income tax exemptions and special low interest loans to specific activities have not been taken into account in the usual measures of effective protection. Yet such subsidies may provide substantial incentives to particular sectors. Thus the rates

---

[11] This general formula assumes that all intermediate inputs are tradable, so that protection affects only factor rewards in a specific processing activity. There are two methods of computing effective protection where there are non-tradable inputs. The Balassa method, protected value-added includes only that in the specific processing activity(Balassa and Associates, 1971). The Corden method (1971) takes into account the indirectly generated value-added in those domestic industries which supply non-tradable commodities.

of effective subsidy were calculated as well as the rates of effective protection. For calculation of the rate of effective subsidy, total direct ta>
and interest subsidies were added to value-added in domestic prices. Thi:
adjusted value-added is divided by value-added at world market prices,
and the ratio (minus one) is the effective subsidy rate.

Since the data requirements and work loads for estimation of the effective protection and subsidy rates are formidable, we have done th
estimation only for 1968. Table 7 presents the average rates of variou:
incentive measures for major industries. The estimates given in the tabl
are based on 1968 domestic and world market prices,[12] 1968 trade an(

Table 7

Average Incentive Rates by Major Industrial Groups: 1968

Unit: Percent

	Legal Protection	Nominal Protection	Effective[1] Protection	Effective[1] Subsidy
Primary Sectors	**34.1**	**15.9**	**17.1**	**20.9**
Agriculture	36.0	16.6	18.1	22.1
Mining	9.6	6.9	2.9	4.7
Manufacturing Total	**58.8**	**10.7**	**−0.9**	**−6.5**
Export Industries[2]	53.7	5.2	−10.7	−13.4
Import-Competing Industries[3]	55.4	31.6	91.7	90.7
Export and Import Competing Industries[4]	46.3	23.1	45.2	37.9
Non-Import-Competing Industries[5]	64.1	5.0	−16.1	−23.7
All Tradables	49.4	12.6	9.9	10.0[6]

Source: Westphal and Kim (1974).

[1] Based on Balassa method.

[2] Exports greater than 10 per cent of total production.

[3] Imports greater than 10 per cent of total supply.

[4] Exports greater than 10 per cent of total production and imports greater than 10 per cent of total domestic supply.

[5] All other sectors.

[6] The average effective subsidy rate for all tradable commodities is almost identica:
to the average rate of effective protection, since the subsidies that directly affect value
added (direct tax and credit preferences) are treated in such a way that a weighted average for all sectors becomes zero.

---

[12] Of 2000 commodity groups, price comparisons were made for 365, accounting for
70.8 per cent of domestic sales and 78.2 per cent of exports. See Lee (1971).

output flows, and input-output coefficients from the 1966 input-output table. Effective rates of protection and subsidy were calculated separately for 150 tradable-goods sectors. The averages of legal and nominal protection are weighted by domestic sales volumes in world market prices, while those for effective protection and effective subsidy are weighted by value-added in world market prices.

The results are striking in a number of ways. First, the nominal rates of protection are substantially below legal tariff rates, indicating considerable tariff redundancy. Tariff redundancy is particularly great in manufacturing, where the average legal rate of protection was 58.8 per cent and the average nominal rate was 10.7 per cent, compared to agriculture and mining where the spread is much less. Tariff redundancy within manufacturing was greatest in the export industries and the non-import-competing industries. In the export and non-import-competing industries, the nominal tariff was only about one-tenth of the legal tariff, while in the import-competing sectors the implicit tariff was more than 50 per cent of the legal tariff. Since quantitative restrictions played a relatively minor role, tariff redundancy is what one would expect in industries where there were few imports.

Second, agriculture is much more highly protected than mining or manufacturing. Average nominal protection is 16.6 per cent in agriculture, 10.7 per cent in manufacturing, and only 6.9 per cent in mining. The difference between major industries is even larger in terms of effective protection. By the Balassa measure, for example, the average rate of effective protection of agriculture is 18.1 per cent, only 2.9 per cent in mining, and a negative 0.9 per cent in manufacturing. A situation in which agriculture receives much more protection than manufacturing is very unusual compared to other countries.[13]

Third, the average level of protection is quite low in Korea compared to other countries, reflecting the fact that the exchange rate in 1968 was not greatly over-valued. The level of protection in manufacturing is especially low. The Balassa measure of effective subsidy, for example, is a very low negative 6.5 per cent in manufacturing. The average level of effective protection for all sectors is only about 10 per cent. The low level of protection for manufacturing is partly influenced by the inclusion of processed food, beverages and tobacco in the manufacturing sector.[14] If

---

[13] See Balassa and Associates (1971) for comparison with other countries.

[14] The line dividing processed food, in particular, from primary production is quite arbitrary, for much of the food processing is in reality done in the primary sector.

these are excluded, the level of incentives to manufacturing increases. The average effective subsidy rate is no longer negative, but slightly positive (less than one per cent). It nonetheless remains well below the average for the primary, processed food, beverage and tobacco sectors taken together.

One may emphasize the resource-pull effect of effective protection or subsidy. However, as we stated at the beginning of this section, effective protection or subsidy rates may be indicators either of relative profitability or of relative inefficiency. If the rates are relatively low, however, they indicate little room for either excess profitability or substantial inefficiency. The low average incentive rates and their relatively small dispersion seem to provide some evidence that Korea's export-oriented growth and development have been relatively efficient.

V. SUMMARY AND CONCLUSIONS

Up until the early 1960's, the Republic of Korea followed a protectionist strategy of import substitution for the domestic production of nondurable consumer goods and their inputs. Upon the exhaustion of possibilities for further import substitution within these areas, Korea changed its industrialization strategy from import substitution to an "outward-looking" or export-oriented one. This shift in industrialization strategy is reflected in the incentive policies that the government adopted in the early sixties.

The outward-looking strategy of industrialization was firmly established by the "won" devaluation in 1964 and the subsequent policy reforms, although that strategy had been initiated in 1961. Beginning in 1964, the government tried to maintain the exchange rate near the free trade level and provided various types of export subsidies to further encourage exports and to offset the modest degree of progressive overvaluation that developed after each major devaluation. Importing was significantly liberalized as both quantitative restrictions and average tariffs on imports were gradually reduced following the 1964 devaluation.

Exports expanded rapidly in response to these policies. Korean exports, which had been stagnant at a low level in the fifties, started to increase very rapidly in the early sixties. Between 1962 and 1973, exports grew by an average annual rate of over 40 per cent. Manufactured exports increased from 27 per cent of total exports to nearly 90 per cent during the same period. As the rapid expansion of exports greatly stimulated the domestic economy, gross national product grew by an average annual rate of about 10 per cent during 1962–73, compared with the 4 per cent growth achieved in the earlier period, 1954–62. The manufacturing sector, in particular, grew by an average annual rate of 19.4 per cent between 1962 and 1973, thus leading the growth of the overall economy.

The outward-looking strategy of industrialization is also demonstrated by our analysis of structural changes in the Korean economy during the sixties. Although the expansion of domestic demand was the most important factor (accounting for about 80 per cent of total economic growth over the period 1960–68), export expansion was overwhelmingly more important as a source of growth than was import substitution in the same period. Export expansion accounted directly and indirectly for 22.4 per cent of total growth, while import substitution accounted for –1.4 per cent during the period. Comparing only the direct contributions of export expansion and import substitution to the growth of manufactured output, the relative contribution of import substitution was substantially greater than that of export expansion in the late fifties when exports played a relatively minor role in Korea's industrialization. During the period from 1960 to 1968, on the other hand, export growth was significantly more important than import substitution.

Export-oriented industrialization and growth resulted in the expansion of relatively labor-intensive manufactured exports. Our analysis of the factor intensity of Korea's exports and imports indicates that during 1960–68, the labor intensity of manufactured exports was significantly greater than that of manufactured imports. Since Korea's comparative advantage, at least within manufacturing, should lie in exporting labor-intensive products and in importing capital intensive ones, our analysis indicates that Korea's outward-looking strategy brought about a fairly efficient allocation of resources.

In addition, Korea's outward-looking strategy maintained incentive policies in such a way that the domestic prices of tradable commodities were not much higher than their world market prices. As a result, the average rates of effective protection or subsidy in Korea in 1968 were significantly lower than other developing countries and showed relatively small sectoral dispersion. If the effective protection or subsidy rates are indications either of relative profitability or relative inefficiency, the relatively low rates in Korea indicate that there is little room for either excess profitability or substantial inefficiency. The low average incentive rates and their relatively small dispersion seem to provide some evidence that

Korea's outward-looking industrialization and growth have been relatively efficient.

This discussion has summarized the development of Korea's outward-looking industrialization strategy in the sixties and early seventies, the industrialization and growth performances based on that strategy, and their efficiency aspects. We may conclude that Korea's outward-looking industrialization in the sixties and early seventies was largely successful on the whole, although there might have been some inefficiency in certain industries or sectors.

It is difficult to predict the future of Korea's industrialization and growth. In 1974, Korea began to face some difficulties in pursuing her outward-looking strategy. The recent increases in the prices of natural resources (particularly crude oil), and the economic slow-down and import controls in industrialized countries caused a sharp rise in the rate of domestic inflation and a slow-down in exports and other domestic economic activities. In view of Korea's poor natural resource base and her reliance on foreign trade, the future course of her industrialization and growth will largely depend upon the developments in international markets for natural resources and the growth and trade policies of major industrialized countries.

REFERENCES

Balassa, Bela, "Industrial policies in Taiwan and Korea," *Weltwirtschaftliches Arvhiv,* band 105, heft 1, 1971, 55–57.

Balassa, Bela, and Associates, *The Structure of Protection in Developing Countries,* Baltimore: The Johns Hopkins Press, 1971.

Balassa, B., and Associates, *Development Strategies in Semi-industrial Countries,* Washington: International Bank for Reconstruction and Development, forthcoming.

Bank of Korea, *Economic Statistics Yearbook,* Seoul, 1960 through 1973. (In both English and Korean)

Bank of Korea, Input-Output Tables and Supporting Materials for 1960, 1963, 1966 and 1968, Seoul: Research Department, various years.

Bank of Korea, *Monthly Statistical Review,* Seoul: Research Department, for selected months in 1960 through 1973.

Bank of Korea, *National Income Statistics Yearbook,* Seoul, 1968 through 1973.

Bank of Korea, *Review of the Korean Economy* (annual), Seoul, 1960 through 1973 (Both English and Korean editions available).

Bhagwati, Jagdish, and Krueger, A.O. (1973 a), *Exchange Control, Liberali-*

zation and Economic Development: Analytical Framework, New York: National Bureau of Economic Research, 1973. (mimeographed)

Bhagwati, Jagdish, and Krueger, A.O. (1973 b), "Exchange Control, Liberalization, and Economic Development," *American Economic Review,* May 1973, 419–27.

Bruno, Michael, "Domestic Resource Costs and Effective Protection: Clarification and Synthesis," *Journal of Political Economy,* January/February 1972, 16–33.

Cha, Byung Kwon, et. al., *Analysis of Korea's Import Substitution Industries,* Seoul: Seoul National University, 1967.

Chenery, Hollis B., "Comparative Advantage and Development Policy," *Surveys of Economic Theory,* Vol. II: Growth and Development, New York: St. Martin's Press, 1965.

Cole, David C. and Lyman, Princeton N., *Korean Development: The Interplay of Politics and Economics,* Cambridge: Harvard University Press, 1971.

Cole, David C. and Westphal, Larry E., "The Contribution of Exports to Employment in Korea," presented at KDI-Harvard IID Conference, Seoul, 1974.

Corden, Warner M., *The Theory of Protection,* Oxford: Clarendon Press, 1971.

Fane, George, "Import Substitution and Export Expansion: Their Measurement and an Example of their Application." *Economic Development Report No. 179,* Cambridge: Development Research Group, Harvard University, 1971.

Frank, Charles R., Jr., Kim, Kwang Suk and Westphal, Larry E., *Foreign Trade Regimes and Economic Development: South Korea,* National Bureau of Economic Research, N.Y., 1975.

Han, Kee Chun, *Estimates of Korean Capital and Inventory Coefficients in 1968,* Seoul: Yonsei University, 1970. (mimeographed)

Han, Kee Chun, *A Study on Export Promotion Measures in Korea,* Seoul: Yonsei University, 1967.

Hong, Wontack, "Factor Supply and Factor Intensity of Trade: The Case of Korea (1966–72)," Seoul: Korea Development Institute, 1974. (mimeographed)

Kim, Chuk Kyo, "Exports and Productivity Trends of Korean Manufacturing Industries," Seoul: Korea Development Institute, 1974. (mimeographed)

Kim, Kwang Suk, "Industrial Incentives for Export Promotion in Korea," in *Seminar on Korea's Foreign Trade and Balance of Payments in Economic Development,* Seoul: Korea University, International Management Institute, 1971 (In Korean).

Koo, Bonho, "Korea's Foreign Exchange Policies: An Evaluation and Proposals," Seoul: Korea Development Institute, 1972. (mimeographed)

Korea (Republic) (1967 a), *An Outline of Foreign Exchange System and Policy in Korea,* Seoul: Ministry of Finance (In Korean), 1967.

Korea (Republic) (1967 b), *The Structure and Policy of Korea's Foreign Trade,* Seoul: Ministry of Finance (In Korean), 1967.

Korea (Republic), *A Ten Year History of Korea's Trade and Industrial Policy, 1960–69,* Seoul: Ministry of Commerce and Industry (In Korean), 1970.

Korea Development Association, *Status and Outlook of Export Industry and Study of Export Promotion,* Seoul (In Korean), 1968.

Korea Development Bank, *Korean Industry,* Seoul (Both English and Korean editions available), 1970.

Korean Productivity Center, The Institute of Productivity Research, *The Analysis of Cost and Rate of Net Foreign Exchange Earnings of Korean Export Products,* Seoul, 1970.

Korean Productivity Center, *A Study of Export Supporting Measures through Cost Analysis,* Seoul (In Korean), 1968.

Korea Trade Research Center, *Measures to Increase Net Foreign Exchange Earning from Exports,* Seoul: Seoul National University (In Korean), 1969.

Korean Traders Association, *A Study of International Competitiveness of Korean Export Industries,* Seoul (In Korean), 1969.

Korean Traders Association, *A Study on the Promotion of Strategic Export Industries and Direction of Export Promotion Policy,* Seoul (In Korean), 1970.

Krueger, A.O., "Evaluating Restrictionist Trade Regimes: Theory and Measurement," *Journal of Political Economy,* January/February 1972.

Lee, S. Y., *A Study of Price Comparisons Between Domestic Producer's Unit Prices and International Prices,* Seoul: Sogang University, 1971.

Leontief, W., "Domestic Production and Foreign Trade: The American Capital Position Re-examined," *Input-Output Economics,* Oxford University Press, 1966.

Little, I., Scitovsky, T., and Scott, M., *Industry and Trade in Some Developing Countries: A Comparative Study,* London: Oxford University Press, 1970.

Park, Pil Soo, "Government Export Promotion Policy," in *Seminar on Korea's Foreign Trade and Balance of Payments in Economic Development,* Seoul: Korea University, International Management Institute (In Korean), 1971.

Westphal, Larry E., and Kim, Kwang Suk, "Industrial Policy and Development in Korea," (final draft) to be included in Balassa and Associates, *Development Strategies in Semi-industrial Countries,* 1974.

Structural Change in Korea's Balance of Payments: 1960-1973

*Hak Yong Rhee**

I. INTRODUCTION

The purpose of this study is to determine the trend of structural change in the Korea's balance of payments over the past decade. In particular, I would like to describe the phenomenal growth in certain major components of the balance of payments and then analyze the sources of the expansion in terms of government policies and other economic variables.

As Table 1 shows, the expansion of commodity exports has been extraordinary: its annual average growth rate during the First Five Year Plan (i.e., 1962–66) was almost 44%; during the Second Five Year Plan it was about 35%, and for the first two years of the Third Five Year Plan it was more than 70%.[1] Up to 1971, international price increases were minor, so that the general growth pattern does not change much even if we adjust for inflation. However, the nominal growth rate of exports

---

* Visiting fellow at the Korea Development Institute and assistant professor of economics at Yonsei University.

[1] The Korean balance of payments is prepared by the Bank of Korea, and one summary table is published in the *Economic Statistics Yearbook*. (Appendix 1) Detailed accounts are given in the so-called "Global Balance of Payments Summary" which is prepared by the Bank of Korea and submitted to the IMF. Since the "Global Balance of Payments Summary" contains the most detailed accounts, I used it as my data source. (Appendix 2)

Table 1.

Average Annual Rate of Changes in Principal Balance of Payments Indicators

Unit: Percent (%)

	1957–61	1962–66	1967–71	1972–73
Commodity Exports[1]	14.5	43.9	35.3	71.6
Commodity Imports	–2.6	23.1	26.8	36.9
Commodity Balance	4.1	–19.1	–20.9	23.3
Service Receipts	21.7	18.5	20.4	34.1
Service Payments	3.1	11.9	36.7	32.4
Service Balance	107.8	72.6	–8.9	61.0
Balance of Goods & Services	7.9	–18.5	–27.2	27.3
Transfer Receipts	–4.5	0.2	–2.5	14.5
(Grant in Aid)	(–8.4)	(–15.9)	(–22.0)	(–63.0)
Transfer Payments	–0.5	40.9	32.3	64.4
Net Transfer Receipts	–4.5	–0.1	–4.1	5.8
Receipts on Current Account	0.5	13.3	21.8	57.1
Payments on Current Account	–1.8	21.1	28.1	36.3
Net Capital Inflow[2]	—	—	24.9	16.7

Source: The Bank of Korea, *Economic Statistics Yearbook* and *Annual Report* (various issues).

[1] Includes nonmonetary gold.

[2] Net long-term capital inflow includes inter-branch account of the BOK, Cooly loan, DLF and PL 480 Title 1 trade credit. Net short-term capital inflow includes advance export receipts and export usance. (Total amount includes errors and omissions.)

for 1972–73 may be significantly different from the real growth rate because of the unusual inflation in that period. The export unit value index increased about 21% in 1973, meaning that the real growth rate of exports during 1972–73 is lower than the figures shown in Table 1. However, even if we discount the nominal growth rate by the change in the unit value index, the average growth rate of exports is still more than 50% for 1972–73.

Commodity imports have also been growing, but not as fast as exports. In fact, the import growth rate was almost half that of exports during 1962–66 and 1972–73. For the period 1967–71, it was somewhat higher, but still 10% below that of exports. As a result, the export-import ratio has been going up. In the 1957–61 period, exports were one-twelveth of imports, but during 1972–73, exports were five-sixths of imports. (See Appendix 1.) At the same time, the commodity trade deficit as a percentage of total imports has been going down. In 1957–61, the trade deficit was 92% of imports, but it came down to 75% in 1962–66, 55% in 1967–71, and 19% in 1972–73.

In the service sector, receipts grew by an average of about 20% through 1971, but in 1972–73 the growth rate went up to 34%. Payments in this sector grew by about 8% annually until 1966; thereafter, the growth rate went up to around 35%. However, Korea still maintains a small surplus in this sector.

Transfer receipts actually declined until 1971, while transfer payments grew rapidly, as shown in Table 1. As a result, the surplus in this sector has been declining. A notable fact is that AID grant-in-aid has been declining rapidly.

On current account (i.e., commodity, service, and transfer payments), Korea actually had a surplus in 1957–61. Since 1962, Korea has had deficits, and this deficit grew in such a way that the average annual deficit during 1967–71 was more than $500 million. If we look at the capital account, the net capital inflow has grown rapidly since 1962.[2] Thus the net capital inflow has been used to finance the current account deficits and to accumulate foreign currency reserves.

II. CHANGES IN CURRENT ACCOUNTS

The deficit in goods and services rose rapidly from 1965 until 1971, and most of this deficit resulted from commodity trade. In order to understand the details of this trend, we must look into the exchange rate and other trade policies of the Korean government as well as the variations in domestic and foreign prices.

The exchange rate was increased from 65 won to 100 won per dollar on January 1, 1961 and again to 130 won on February 2 of the same year. At the same time, the multiple exchange rate system was abolished and a

---

[2] There is an entry entitled "Bank Loans, Refinances and Others" in the balance of payment account of the Bank of Korea. These are mainly the changes in the accounts of commercial monetary institutions. Positive figures show net capital inflows, and negative figure shows net capital outflows. The reason that this item is not included under "Net Capital Inflow" is, I think, that these flows are more or less automatic results of trade and are for only a short term. Thus, they are not treated as capital borrowings even though, in a strict sense, they are also capital inflows.

single exchange rate system was adopted. Inflation rates in the U.S., Japan, and Korea were not significantly different from each other during 1960–62 although the inflation rate in Korea was a little bit higher than those of the U.S. and Japan.

In May, 1964, the exchange rate was increased to 225 won from 130 won and a floating exchange rate system was adopted. However, the Bank of Korea intervened in such a way that the exchange rate did not come down below 255 won. At the same time, as shown in Table 2, inflation was 16% in Korea, but insignificant in the U.S. and Japan. The increase in the exchange rate was almost 100%, and thus the difference in inflation was not enough to offset the effect of the change in the exchange rate. In 1964, total imports decreased by almost 30%. From 1965 on, the Bank of Korea continued to intervene in the foreign exchange market so that the exchange rate was maintained at around 270 won until 1967. Beside this exchange rate policy, the Korean government started to liberalize import restrictions from 1965. The number of prohibited commodites was 624 in 1965, but was reduced to 76 by 1968. At the same time, the number of commodities that were "regularly" imported was increased to 3,082 in 1967 from 1,124 in 1964. In 1967 the so-called "negative list system" was adopted;

Table 2

Exchange Rate and Wholesale Price Index: Korea, Japan and U.S.A.

	Wholesale Price Index (1970 = 100)			Exchange Rate of Won to U.S.
	U.S.A.	JAPAN	KOREA	Dollar (End of the Year)
1962	85.83	87.44	38.4	130.00
1963	85.62	88.95	46.3	130.00
1964	85.79	89.13	62.3	256.53
1965	87.50	89.84	68.5	272.06
1966	90.41	92.00	74.6	271.46
1967	90.59	93.68	79.4	274.60
1968	92.87	94.45	85.8	281.50
1969	96.49	96.49	91.6	304.45
1970	100.00	100.00	100.0	316.65
1971	103.23	99.24	108.6	373.30
1972	107.90	100.00	123.8	398.90
1973	122.80	115.83	132.4	397.50

Sources: U.S. Dept. of Commerce, *Survey of Current Business,* (various issues), The Bank of Japan, *Economic Statistics Monthly,* (various issues), and The Bank of Korea, *Economic Statistics Yearbook* (1973).

i.e., those commodities that were not on the list of restricted items were automatically allowed to be imported.

Besides the exchange rate policies, a number of export expansion policies have been implemented. From 1961, a direct subsidy of 25 won per dollar was paid on new export commodities, and imported raw materials used for export were exempted from tariffs. From 1965, business taxes were reduced by 31.6 won per dollar of export, and in 1970 the reduction was increased to 69.4 won. At the same time, various preferential loan programs have been used: loans of 200–220 won per dollar of export were made to exporting firms at 6% interest per annum for 90 days; special loans were made for purchasing raw materials for export industries; and loans for converting existing facilities into export production were granted at 12% per annum for 5 years. Considering the market interest rates in Korea as shown in Table 4, these loans have represented significant subsidies for export industries. In addition, export industries have been granted a 30% reduction in electricity and railroad charges, priority in import quota allocation, special stand-by credits, and subsidies for foreign market exploration. These various export expansion policies have certainly contributed to the rapid expansion of commodity exports.

The deficits in goods and services are largely attributed to the deficits in commodity trade as mentioned before. If we look at Table 3, however, we note that there are two additional items that contributed significantly to the deficit. The first item is investment income. Korea's investment income is mostly earnings from foreign exchange reserves, while its payments consist of interest on foreign loans, interest on short-term capital, and profit remittances. We can see that all of these payments are rapidly increasing. The second item is freight and insurance. As we can see from Table 3, Korea's receipts from this source are rising, but its payments are rising still faster. Furthermore, in 1972 Korea's receipts from freight and insurance were less than one-third of its payments. As the trade volume increases, the payments for freight and insurance are expected to rise.

Net earnings in the services sector consist primarily of travel and government transactions. From 1971 on, net travel earnings rose rapidly as indicated in Table 3. Government transactions reciepts are primarily military, and consist of: sales of goods and services to foreign military organizations (both in Korea and Vietnam) and remittances from dispatched soldiers. Government transactions are mostly diplomatic expenses and expenditures out of counterpart funds by various aid agencies. The net earnings from travel will rise in the future, as indicated by 1973 travel statistics, but there is no reason to expect an increase in net earnings from

Table 3

Balance of Payments: Goods & Services

Unit: In Million U.S. Dollars

	Merchandise	Freight & Insurance	Other Transportation	Travel	Investment Income	Government Transactions	Other Services	Total Goods & Services
1961	−242	−23	−5	−1	4	67	1	−198
1962	−335	−34	−5	1	5	80	−4	−292
1963	−410	−41	−4	0	3	55	−5	−403
1964	−246	−28	−5	0	2	62	−8	−221
1965	−245	−28	−7	6	1	75	−1	−199
1966	−430	−37	−7	13	1	123	14	−323
1967	−574	−52	−2	8	−2	190	16	−417
1968	−836	−73	−4	6	−5	233	12	−666
1969	−992	−85	−4	5	−5	274	11	−794
1970	−922	−95	−1	6	−37	246	0	−803
1971	−1,046	−122	−3	16	−91	211	16	−1,018
1972	−575	−125	15	62	−140	200	22	−541
1973	−567	−248	12	247	−173	141	87	−499

Source: Appendix 1.

government transactions. Indeed the latter may decrease significantly as Korea's involvement in Vietnam is curtailed and as its diplomatic expenses increase due to intensified economic and political activities abroad.

As we can see from Appendix 1, net earnings from transfer payments have been decreasing, from an average of a little over $200 million in the early sixties to a little over $150 million in the early seventies. If we look into the components of transfer payments, we find that the grants-in-aid component has been decreasing rapidly, while personal and institutional remittances have been increasing. In fact, grants-in-aid, (largely AID grants), was a mere $5 million in 1972, compared with more than $145 million in 1962. PL 480 Title I grants in 1972 were only $4.6 million, but over $54 million in 1962. One important component of transfer receipt is "imports without payment of foreign exchange". The most important transfer payment item is "exports without payment of foreign exchange".

III. CHANGES IN CAPITAL ACCOUNTS

Even with the rapid expansion in exports, Korea has had significant deficits as shown in Table 3, and of course these deficits in each year have necessarily been offset by net capital inflows. Without such inflows, the deficits could not have been incurred. In order to induce foreign capital, various incentive schemes have been used. From 1961, interest income from authorized foreign investments was exempted from all personal and corporate income taxes for the first five years, and from 50% of those taxes for the next five years. The income of foreigners who provide technical assistance is exempt from tax for the first five years and two-thirds exempt for the next two years. Dividends paid to foreigners from authori-

Table 4

Interest Rates

Unit: Percent per Annum

	U.S.A.[1]	JAPAN[2]	Weighted Averages of U.S. & JAPAN[3]	KOREA[4]
1962	2.78	5.50	—	15.0
1963	3.16	5.50	5.3	15.0
1964	3.55	5.50	5.5	15.0
1965	3.95	5.50	4.0	26.4
1966	4.88	5.50	5.3	26.4
1967	4.33	5.50	5.1	26.4
1968	5.35	5.50	5.4	25.2
1969	6.69	5.50	6.3	22.8
1970	6.44	5.69	6.2	22.8
1971	4.34	5.75	4.9	20.4
1972	4.32	5.50	5.0	12.0
1973	7.05	5.81	6.6	12.0

Sources: The U.S. Federal Reserve Bank, *Federal Reserve Bulletin,* and the Bank of Korea, *Economic Statistics Monthly* and *Economic Statistics Yearbook.*

[1] Treasury bill rate.

[2] One-year time deposit.

[3] Weighted by Korea's capital imports. (Commercial loans and direct investments only.)

[4] Actual rates on time deposit. (Over one year, but less than 2 years.)

Table 5

Balance of Payments: Capital Account

Unit: In Million U.S. Dollars

	Private Long-Term	Private Short-Term	Central Govern-ment	Central Monetary Institution	Other Monetary Institu-tion	Total Capital & Monetary Gold[1]
1961	8	-2	16	-46	..	-32
1962	3	-7	5	57	-1	57
1963	42	18	27	56	..	144
1964	12	-4	17	1	1	27
1965	40	-23	-8	-15	-1	-7
1966	177	6	34	-119	-1	99
1967	192	86	20	-64	-54	181
1968	402	13	19	-132	129	436
1969	391	57	192	-122	27	555
1970	292	122	191	-55	112	639
1971	293	135	233	69	104	834
1972	264	-16	226	81	-229	330
1973	690	84	236	-333	-116	290

Source: Appendix 2.

[1] Includes local government account.

zed corporations are also exempt from income tax for the first five years and 50% exempt for the following three years. Finally, for authorized foreign investment projects, capital goods may be imported free of tariffs.

Besides these various incentive schemes, the domestic interest rate was increased from 10% to 15% per annum in 1961, and raised again to 26.4% in 1965 as shown in Table 4. The differential between domestic and foreign interest rates was significant up to 1971. As Table 5 shows, the drastic increase in net capital inflow began in 1966, but decreased sharply in 1972. From Table 5, we can see that the net receipts from capital accounts consisted of private long-term borrowing, private short-term borrowing, the central government's borrowing, and central monentary institution's transactions. As Table 5 shows, net receipts of most of the components were increasing until 1971. Note that the trend of total net capital inflow up to 1967 was quite similar to that of private long-term capital inflow. After 1967, short-term capital inflows dominated the trend of total capital flows, whose increase more than offsetting the fall in private long-term capital inflow.

Net central monetary institution's transactions represents the change in the Bank of Korea's asset position, primarily the change in foreign exchange reserves. Thus a negative value represents the accumulation of foreign reserves, and a positive value represents a reduction. We can see from Table 5 that the central bank accumulated reserves from 1965 to 1970. Note that this figure only represents the foreign exchange held by the central bank, thus excluding that held by other monetary institutions.

In 1972, something different happened. Although capital inflow through private long-term borrowing and central government borrowing did not decrease very much, capital inflow through private short-term and non-central monetary institutions decreased drastically. This corresponded to the decrease in trade deficits on current account.

The decrease in private short-term inflows in 1972 was caused by a reduction in net export credits and net advance export proceeds, and by increased repayments of short-term loans. The reduction of "capital" inflows in 1972 was caused by increased bank acceptances abroad, reduction of foreign currency on hand by non-central monetary institutions, increased deposits abroad, and reduction of loans.

Some of the historical trends are very interesting. For example, the non-central monetary institutions repaid old loans rather than making new loans. Another interesting item is the deposits of these institutions. Up to 1971 deposits abroad were not significant (except in 1968), but in 1972 the deposits were over $180 million.

Thus, the drastic reduction in the trade deficit was matched by a reduction in short-term capital inflows including export credits, bank acceptances, short-term loans, and deposits abroad. The magnitude of the reduction in this short-term capital inflow in 1972 was well over $400 million. One interesting question is whether the direction of causality runs from reduction in trade deficits to the reduction of short-term capital inflows or vice versa.

IV.   CONCLUDING REMARKS

We have seen that the most important single characteristic of the Korean balance of payments between 1960 and 1973 was that commodity exports increased a hundred times, while imports increased only a little over ten times. One may argue that exports in 1960 were much lower than normal for a country like Korea, so that part of the enormous growth of exports was simply a "catching up". One may also say that the fantastic growth was based on nominal values, and we have to consider real values. Even if we take all these factors into account, the fact that for the past thirteen years the real average annual growth rate of exports has been close to forty percent is phenomenal by any standard. Another important thing is that this export expansion was combined with a relatively slower growth of imports. Also note that the huge deficits in commodity trade have been "financed" by inducements of foreign capital. The various trade policies that we mentioned were designed to accomplish exactly this: i.e., rapid expansion of exports, slower growth of imports, and successful "finance" of the deficits.

In the analysis of the growth patterns of individual accounts, we first observed that exports have grown consistently, perhaps due to the multitude of subsidy schemes. The second observation that we have made is that when the domestic currency was devalued in 1964 from 130 won per dollar to 256.53, total imports decreased by about 28% even though domestic inflation was significantly higher than that of the U.S. and Japan. Imports started to grow again when many trade liberalization policies were adopted from 1965. Imports grew more slowly during the 1970–72 period, while the domestic economy was generally sluggish and while the exchange rate was rising quite a bit.

A third interesting observation is that there is a clear correlation between interest rate differentials and capital inflows. Capital began to flow in from 1965 when the domestic interest rate was increased to 26.4%, resulting in a 14% real differential. When the interest rate differential disappeared in 1972 the capital inflow decreased sharply (see Table 5). At the same time, the sharp decrease in capital inflow was due to a decrease in short-term capital inflows (not long-term capital inflows), and to the decrease in the surpluses of the commercial banking institutions' accounts, which are primarily short-term capital transactions.

A fourth observation is that foreign reserves increased until they represented about 20% of total imports in 1973. The pattern of current account deficits before 1967 was closely related to the pattern of long-term capital inflows whereas after 1967 it was closely related to the pattern of short-term capital inflows, including the accounts of commercial banking institutions.

A final remark is partly observation and partly conjecture. We observed that the capital inflow (particularly short-term capital inflow including the accounts of commercial banking institutions) was sensitive to the real interest rate differential. Provided that the desired growth path of domestic GNP determines the expansion path of exports and imports and that the demand for foreign reserve is externally determined, it appears that the trade deficit is also determined by all those policy variables and it is met either by long-term or short-term capital inflow. Since capital inflow is sensitive to the real interest rate differential, the realized capital inflow or the availability of deficit financing may have something to do with the magnitude of trade deficits. Our conjecture, then, is that the actual size of the current account deficit is determined by the demand for foreign capital (both from the commodity trade side and the foreign reserve side) and by the availability of such foreign capital together.

Appendi

	1962 Credit	1962 Debit	1963 Credit	1963 Debit	1964 Credit	1964 Debit	1965 Credit	1965 Debit	19.. Credit
I. Goods & Services	163.2	455.2	175.5	578.3	211.0	432.0	289.8	488.4	454.7
Merchandise	54.8	390.1	86.8	497.0	119.1	364.9	175.1	420.3	250.3
Non-monetary gold	0.0		0.0		0.9		0.5		0.1
Freight & insurance	3.4	37.1	2.8	43.9	2.5	30.1	4.5	32.4	9.9
Other transportation	0.8	5.9	2.0	5.8	2.9	8.3	3.4	10.7	3.9
Travel	3.1	2.2	2.7	2.3	2.8	2.4	7.7	1.7	16.2
Investment income	5.2	0.3	3.4	0.7	3.8	1.7	3.7	2.3	5.6
Government, n.i.e.	90.5	10.2	72.1	17.5	75.7	13.6	88.1	12.8	136.5
Military transactions	84.7		58.3		63.7		74.0		114.1
Nonmilitary transactions	5.8	10.2	13.8	17.5	12.0	13.6	14.1	12.8	22.4
Other services	5.4	9.4	5.7	11.1	3.3	11.0	6.8	8.2	32.2
Net goods & services		292.0		402.8		221.0		198.6	
II. Transfer payments	238.7	2.2	266.3	6.8	198.6	3.7	210.2	6.9	227.3
Private	37.5	1.0	57.4	5.4	56.7	2.8	74.0	5.3	103.3
Central government	201.2	1.2	208.9	1.4	141.9	0.9	136.2	1.6	124.0
Net transfer payments	236.5		259.5		194.9		203.3		219.6
Net total (Item I + II)		55.5		143.3		26.1		4.7	
III. Capital & Monetary Gold	26.5	−30.8	114.9	−28.8	30.3	3.0	14.7	21.8	206.1
Private long-term capital	2.8		42.1		13.2	1.5	39.7		177.2
Private short-term capital		6.7	26.4	8.0	−3.3	1.1	−20.6	2.5	7.7
Local governments	—		—		—				0.2
Central governments	5.6	0.6	27.8	0.4	17.5	0.2	−7.5		37.4
Central monetary institutions	18.1	−39.2	18.6	−37.2	2.9	1.5	3.1	18.2	−16.4
To IMF							9.4	9.4	3.9
Foreign assets & liabilities		−45.3		−33.0		1.8		10.1	
Korea-Japan open account	5.2		−7.0		1.0		0.8		−7.5
Others	10.6		17.7		1.7	2.1	−7.2		−12.8
Monetary institutions						0.9		0.5	
Other monetary institutions						−1.3		1.1	
Net capital & monetary gold		57.3		143.7		27.3		7.1	99.0
IV. Net Errors & Omissions				0.4		1.2	2.4		4.4

Note: "Foreign assets & liabilities" is the sum of marketable assets, which consists of marke[t] securities and bank acceptance, deposits, and SDR holdings and SDR allocations of "… foreign assets and liabilities".

Balance of Payments

Unit: In Million U. S. Dollars

1967		1968		1969		1970		1971		1972		1973	
Credit	Debit	Credit	Debit	Credit	Debit	Credit	Debit	Credit	Debit	Credit	Debit	Credit	Debit
2.9	1,060.0	880.3	1,546.7	1,150.7	1,945.1	1,379.0	2,181.7	1,616.0	2,634.1	2,226.8	2,767.8	4,120.8	4,619.6
4.7	908.9	486.2	1,322.0	658.3	1,650.0	882.2	1,804.2	1,132.2	2,178.2	1,675.9	2,250.4	3,270.8	3,837.3
		0.1						0.1		0.6		0.5	
0.7	63.0	17.3	90.7	31.3	116.5	40.6	135.8	44.7	166.8	53.3	178.6	58.4	306.0
6.4	8.6	10.3	13.9	13.1	16.8	20.7	22.1	29.8	32.6	55.1	40.6	96.4	84.1
5.3	8.4	16.9	10.5	16.2	11.0	18.7	12.4	31.2	14.8	74.7	12.6	264.1	17.1
0.1	11.9	12.4	17.8	37.9	42.5	38.0	75.0	28.8	119.4	20.9	161.2	40.5	213.0
8.9	19.2	257.4	24.5	299.1	24.8	279.9	33.5	247.8	36.9	244.2	43.8	185.3	44.5
1.4		216.6		249.4		232.2		219.3		228.1		160.4	
7.5	19.2	40.8	24.5	49.7	24.8	47.7	33.5	28.5	36.9	16.1	43.8	24.9	44.5
5.8	40.0	79.7	67.3	94.8	83.5	98.9	98.7	101.4	85.4	102.1	80.6	204.7	117.6
417.1		666.4		794.4		802.7		1,018.1		541.0		498.9	
8.4	13.2	240.8	14.7	259.8	14.0	205.2	25.0	194.4	23.8	202.9	33.1	252.9	62.8
1.9	11.2	117.8	12.3	153.5	11.6	118.6	23.5	129.4	22.8	151.1	31.9	217.8	62.7
6.5	2.0	123.0	2.4	106.3	2.4	86.6	1.5	65.0	1.0	51.8	1.2	35.1	0.1
5.2		226.1		245.8		180.2		170.6		169.8		190.1	
191.9		440.3		548.6		622.5		847.5		371.2		308.8	
8.2	117.0	537.1	100.9	770.4	215.5	722.2	83.5	844.4	10.0	560.2	230.3	747.5	457.5
1.8		410.6	8.8	402.0	11.4	327.8	35.7	296.0	3.3	299.4	35.5	462.6	73.0
8.5	2.6	13.2		70.1	13.6	122.9	0.5	152.9	18.3	-0.5	15.8	103.5	19.5
1.1	4.9	10.7		6.7		2.5		3.7				28.9	
3.2	3.0	26.2	6.9	195.1	3.0	164.0	3.0	232.6		227.8	1.5	247.5	11.3
7.3	56.6	28.6	160.2	-3.1	118.6	1.2	56.3	26.3	-42.2	17.7	-63.5	-13.0	319.7
—	—	32.0	26.0	—	—	-12.5		30.0	30.0	5.8	6.9	-8.2	9.6
56.6		134.1				118.6	8.4	56.3	5.4	-72.3	10.3	-71.0	2.7
-4.6		-4.7		-4.6		-4.6		-4.6		—	—	-9.1	
-2.7		1.3		1.5		9.9		-4.5		1.6		1.6	
		0.1						0.1		0.6		0.5	
0.9	54.8	53.6	-75.0	95.6	68.9	99.6	-12.0	134.1	30.6	12.1	241.0	-82.0	34.0
31.2		436.2		554.9		638.7		834.4		329.9		290.8	
10.7	4.1			6.3		16.2		13.1		41.3		18.8	

Source: The Bank of Korea.

Hak Yong Rhee

	1962		1963		1964		1965		1966	
	Credit	Debit	Credit	Debit	Credit	Debit	Credit	Debit	Credit	Deb
Capital and Monetary Gold	26.5	−30.8	114.9	−28.8	30.3	3.0	14.7	21.8	206.1	107
1. Private long-term	2.8		42.1		13.2	1.5	39.7		177.2	
1.1 Direct investment	0.6		4.8		0.7	1.5	0.5		13.4	
1.6 Other loans & trade credits	2.2		37.3		12.5		39.2		163.8	
1.7 Other assets & liabilities										
2. Private short-term		6.7	26.4	8.0	−3.3	1.1	−20.6	2.5	7.7	1
2.3 Trade credits		6.7	26.4	8.0	−3.3	1.1	−20.6	2.5	4.9	
2.4 Other assets & liabilities									2.8	1
3. Local government									0.2	
3.3 Other assets & liabilities									0.2	
4. Central government	5.6	0.6	27.8	0.4	17.5	0.2	−7.5		37.4	3
4.4 Long-term loans	1.7		21.6		9.1		2.0		34.0	
4.5 Other long-term assets &		0.2	4.5	0.4	6.3	0.2	−7.6			3.
liabilities	3.9	0.4	1.7		2.1		−1.9		3.4	
4.6 Other short-term assets & liabilites										
5. Central monetary institutions	18.1	−39.2	18.6	−37.2	2.9	1.5	3.1	18.2	−16.4	102
5.1 Account with IMF							9.4	9.4	3.9	5.
5.2 Marketable assets		3.6		−6.5		1.2		10.1		2.
5.3 Deposits		−48.9		−26.5		−3.5	0.1	−6.7	−0.1	87.
5.5 Other foreign assets & liabilities	18.1	6.1	18.6	−4.2	2.9	2.9	−6.4	4.9	−20.2	6.
5.6 Gold						0.9		0.5		0.
6. Other monetary institutions		1.1				−1.3		1.1		0.
6.1 Marketable assets		1.1				−1.3		1.1		0.
6.2 Deposits										
6.3 Loans										
6.4 Other foreign assets & liabilities										
6.5 Gold										
Net capital & monetary gold	57.3		143.7		27.3			7.1	99.0	

Source: IMF Global Table prepared by the Bank of Korea.

Capital and Monetary Gold

Unit: In Million U.S. Dollars

1967 Credit	1967 Debit	1968 Credit	1968 Debit	1969 Credit	1969 Debit	1970 Credit	1970 Debit	1971 Credit	1971 Debit	1972 Credit	1972 Debit	1973 Credit	1973 Debit
	117.0	537.1	100.9	770.4	215.5	722.2	83.5	844.4	10.0	560.2	230.3	747.5	457.5
		410.6	8.8	402.0	11.4	327.8	35.7	296.0	3.3	299.4	35.5	462.6	73.0
		20.2	0.3	15.9		72.9	34.9	55.6	-0.2	75.2	28.4	188.7	73.0
		390.4	8.5	386.1	11.4	253.2		238.6	3.5	223.9		196.4	
						1.7		1.8		0.3	7.1	77.5	
	2.6	13.2		70.1	13.6	122.9	0.5	152.9	18.3	-0.5	15.8	103.5	19.5
		13.2		42.8	13.6	78.4	0.5	86.8	18.3	-26.0	15.8	138.3	19.5
	2.6			27.3		44.5		66.1		25.5		-34.8	
		4.9		10.7		6.7		2.5		3.7		28.9	
		4.9		10.7		6.7		2.5		3.7			
	3.0	26.2	6.9	195.1	3.0	164.0	3.0	232.6		227.8	1.5	247.5	11.3
		20.9		168.2		161.5		232.8		236.4		244.5	1.2
	3.0	-0.6	6.9	9.1	3.0	-2.4	3.0	-3.8		-5.1	1.5	3.0	10.1
		5.9		17.8		4.9		3.6		-3.5			
	56.6	28.6	160.2	-3.1	118.6	1.2	56.3	26.3	-42.2	17.7	-63.5	-13.0	319.7
		32.0	26.0			-12.5		30.0	30.0	5.8	6.9	-8.2	9.6
	1.4		-0.5				16.0		2.0		10.5		13.1
	55.2		134.6		118.6		30.0		-81.6		-92.2		293.3
		-3.4		-3.1		13.7	10.3	-3.7	7.3	11.9	10.7	-4.8	3.2
			0.1						0.1		0.6		0.5
	54.8	53.6	-75.0	95.6	68.9	99.6	-12.0	134.1	30.6	12.1	241.0	-82.0	34.0
	19.7		10.6		16.0	1.1	17.3	-1.5	10.5	-1.0	98.9	4.2	84.1
	26.8		-98.3		0.3	2.9	-20.2	0.4	9.7	19.4	182.9	-14.2	-59.8
		51.9		86.3		95.6		139.4		-9.5		-70.4	
	8.3	1.7	12.7	9.3	52.6		-9.1	-4.2	10.4	3.2	-40.8	-1.6	9.7
		436.2		554.9		638.7		834.4		329.9		290.0	

III

SOURCES OF COMPARATIVE ADVANTAGE

Capital Accumulation, Factor Substitution and the Changing Factor Intensity of Trade: The Case of Korea (1966-72)

*Wontack Hong**

I. INTRODUCTION

In the confusion following Leontief's finding that American exports are labor-intensive relative to American import-competing industries, an extremely important question has been neglected. That is, even if a country's exports are labor intensive at an early stage of economic development, how will the factor intensity of its trade alter as its overall capital-labor endowment ratio grows relative to that of other countries? The first purpose of this paper is to investigate the changes in the factor intensity of Korea's trade which followed increases in its overall capital-labor endowment ratio. The seven year period of 1966–72 seems to be especially suitable for our investigation, because total fixed capital stock in Korea increased by an average annual rate of as high as about ten percent during this period. This growth was accompanied by rapid expansion of exports of manufactured goods.[1] As there is less evidence of factor market dis-

* Senior fellow at the Korea Development Institute.

[1] Total commodity exports in 1966 amounted to only 5 percent of GNP, but they increased five times during 1966–72 and amounted to about 15 percent of GNP in 1972. Nearly 90 percent of these exports were manufactured products. Total commodity imports in 1966 amounted to about 15 percent of GNP, and these increased by almost three times during 1966–72, amounting to about 24 percent of GNP in 1972.

tortions to significantly offset comparative advantage in Korea than in most developing countries, there is a presumption that actual output moved in accordance with economic efficiency as the economy grew. The Korean experience over this period may then provide some clues as to the way comparative advantage may change (albeit at a slower rate in other, less rapidly growing, countries) with capital deepening for the economy as a whole.

On the other hand, we naturally expect changes in the factor-output ratios and inter-industry relationships in the course of economic growth. The second purpose of this paper is to examine the extent to which factor substitution occurred in Korea in association with the changing wage/ rental ratio, and its impact on the estimates of factor intensity of trade. In the analysis we rely on three sets of input-output tables (1966, 1968 and 1970) and corresponding sectoral capital and labor coefficients available for the period of 1966–72.

Leontief and his followers such as Wahl, Bharadwaj, Weiser and Baldwin excluded all non-competitive imports from their computation of factor intensities of trade. In the early stages of economic development, most developing countries import a wide range of goods which are not domestically produced. If one accepts any stylized version of the Heckscher-Ohlin model, the products produced and exported in the early stages of development are presumably labor intensive, while those imports not domestically produced are presumably those that would require the most capital intensive techniques of production. Therefore, a satisfactory estimate of the factor intensity of trade can only be made if the question of how to treat non-competitive imports is answered. The third purpose of this paper is to argue that, in a developing country like Korea, the factor intensity differential between non-competitive (non-natural-resource-intensive) imports and exports will be greater than that between competitive imports and exports.

The paper is organized as follows. The section II provides some basic data on the growth and structure of the Korean economy, with particular attention to Korea's changing factor endowment. Section III then addresses the question of the treatment of non-competitive, non-natural-resource-intensive imports, and discusses other computational procedures. A final section presents the empirical estimates of the factor intensity of Korea's trade and its changes over the period 1966–1972. The factor substitutions and their impact on factor intensity estimates will be discussed concurrently.

II. CHANGES IN FACTOR SUPPLY IN KOREA: 1953–1972

(1) Change in Supply of Labor

According to census data, the total population of Korea in 1955 was about 21.5 million and increased by an average annual rate of 3.02 percent during 1955–60, 2.63 percent during 1960–66, and by 1.90 percent during 1966–70, reaching about 32.5 million at the end of 1972. If we take the population aged 14 years and above to represent the potential labor force which can be engaged either in industrial production, education or house-keeping, then the supply was about 14.3 million in 1960, and increased by an average annual rate of 2.0 per cent during 1960–66, and by 4.1 percent during 1966–70, reaching 18.9 million in 1970. According to the sample surveys conducted in conjunction with 1960, 1966 and 1970 population censuses, the total number of employed persons was 6.9 million in 1960 and this increased at an average annual rate of 2.3 percent during 1960–66 and 6.3 percent during 1966–70, reaching 10.2 million in 1970.

(2) Domestic and Foreign Savings and Capital Formation

The growth rate of the Korean economy was rather moderate during 1953–65, and became very high only after 1965. That is, the GNP was a-bout $2.7 billion in 1953 (in 1970 dollars) and increased by an average annual rate of 4.7 percent during 1953–59, 5.6 percent during 1960–65, and 10.3 percent during 1966–72, reaching $9.7 billion in 1972.

These trends in growth rates were reflected in the aggregate investment rates: average annual gross investment for inventory and fixed capital formation was about 11.3 percent of GNP during 1953–65, and about 24.1 percent during 1966–72. A pertinent fact is that foreign savings played a (relatively) dominant role in the capital formation of Korea, especially during the 1953–65 period. If we take the difference between imports and exports in National Income Statistics of the Bank of Korea as foreign savings, then the average annual foreign saving was about 6.9 percent of GNP during 1953–65, and about 9.1 percent during 1966–72.

In order to measure the annual fixed capital stock since 1953, we used the net fixed capital stock data of 1968 as a bench mark and successfully

Wontack Hong

Table 1

Fixed Capital Stock, Population and Gross National Product: 1953–72

	Total Fixed Capital Stock (billion 1970 $)	Total Population (million persons)	Total Employed Persons (million persons)	Per Capita Capital Stock (1970 $)	Capital Per Employed Person (1970 $)	GNP (billion 1970 $)
1953	7.65	21.05		363		2.72
1954	7.74	21.27		364		2.87
1955	7.85	21.50		365		3.02
1956	7.99	22.15		361		3.03
1957	8.15	22.82		357		3.27
1958	8.29	23.51		353		3.44
1959	8.44	24.22		349		3.57
1960	8.60	24.95		345		3.64
1961	8.80	25.61		344		3.81
1962	9.06	26.28		345		3.93
1963	9.39	26.98	7.66	348	1,226	4.28
1964	9.66	27.69	7.80	349	1,239	4.64
1965	10.05	28.41	8.21	354	1,224	4.93
1966	10.73	29.16	8.42	368	1,274	5.54
1967	11.56	29.71	8.72	389	1,326	5.97
1968	12.78	30.28	9.16	422	1,395	6.72
1969	14.37	30.85	9.41	466	1,527	7.73
1970	15.95	31.44	9.75	507	1,636	8.34
1971	17.57	31.97	10.07	550	1,745	9.10
1972	18.94	32.51	10.56	583	1,794	9.74

Source: Kee Chun Han, *Estimates of Korean Captial and Inventory Coefficients in 1968* (Yonsei University, 1970); The Bank of Korea, *National Income Statistics Yearbook:* 1973; and Economic Planning Board, *Korea Statistical Yearbook:* 1972, *An Evaluation Study for the Accuracy of the 1960 Population and Housing Census of Korea, 1966 Population Census Report of Korea* (12–1, Whole Country), 1970 *Populalion and Housing Census Report: Vol 1, Complete Enumeration, and Annual Report on the Economically Active Population:* 1973.

Note: Population figures for the inter-census years were obtained by applying constant average annual growth rates: 1.075% for 1949–55, 3.02% for 1955–60, 2.63% for 1961–66, 1.90% for 1967–70, and 1.70% for 1971–72.

subtracted (or added) net annual fixed capital formation of each year.[2] We obtained about $7.7 billion (in 1970 dollar prices) for 1953 net fixed capital stock: a figure which increased by an average annual rate of 1.7 percent during 1953–59, 3.0 percent during 1960–65, and 9.5 percent annually during 1966–72 reaching $18.9 billion in 1972. We would expect that such remarkably high rates of capital accumulation during 1966–72 cannot but leave visible imprints on economic structure. This is the main reason why we selected the 1966–72 period for our analysis of the changing factor intensity of Korea's trade.

(3) Capital Accumulation, Capital Deepening and Rising Wage/Rental Ratio

The per capita capital stock in Korea fluctuated within a range of $344–365 during 1953–65 and has increased very rapidly only since 1966. There was about a 60 percent increase in per capita capital stock during 1966–72, but due to rapidly increasing employment, the fixed capital stock per employed person increased by only about 40 per cent. However, this still implies that a significant overall capital deepening occurred in Korea during 1966–72.

In order to examine the association between capital deepening and wage rates, we presented in Table 3 a set of data obtained from the Manufacturing Census. The value added per worker in manufacturing sector steadily increased throughout the period covered in Table 3 (1960–72). However, the wage rate in manufacturing sector started to rise only after 1966, thus paralleling the rapid increase in total fixed capital stock per employed person.[3]

---

[2] On the basis of the EPB's (Economic Planning Board) 1968 National Wealth Survey data, Professor Han computed the fixed capital stock employed in industrial production. Total gross (undepreciated) fixed capital stock in 1968 was estimated by Professor Han to be 4,836.4 billion won, and the total average (gross) capital-output ratio was derived to be 1.60103 for the 1968 Korean economy as a whole. He also estimated the same coefficient on a net (depreciated) basis which was 1.04721. We adopted this net figure of Professor Han (3,163.5 billion won) as the net fixed capital stock in 1968.

[3] We also computed the changes in per worker fixed capital stock for the manufacturing sector alone. Then we observed a very close association between the average wage rates and the fixed capital stock per worker in manufacturing. For instance, the per worker cpaital stock did not increase during 1960–66 and nor did the average wage rate; the former started to increase since 1967 and so did the latter; and the former decreased a little in 1972 and so did the latter.

Table 2

Total Domestic Loans and Weighted-Average Interest Rates: 1963–71

Unit: Billion Won & %

	Amount of Loans	Interest Rate	
		Nominal	Real
1963	101	18.9%	— 1.7%
1964	121	23.2%	—11.4%
1965	161	27.3%	17.3%
1966	229	30.1%	21.2%
1967	395	29.1%	22.7%
1968	604	26.9%	18.8%
1969	946	25.3%	18.5%
1970	1,282	24.8%	15.6%
1971	1,652	22.7%	14.1%

Source: B.K. Shim, et al., *A Study of Preferential Interest Rate Structure: The Korean Experience (1963–71), 1972.*

Note: We computed the real rates by subtracting the rate of changes in wholesale price index each year. Total loans consist of loans by individuals to incorporated firms and by financial institutions, loans by individuals to non-incorporated firms, and loans in curb markets.

Table 3

Capital Stock per Worker and Wage Rates
in Manufacturing Sector: 1960–72

Unit: In Thousand 1970 Dollars[1] & Persons

	Wages & Salaries	Number of Employees[2]	Wages Per Employee	Per Worker Value Added	Capital Per Worker[3]
1960	79,202	238,723	0.332	0.93	1.53
1963	118,698	352,223	0.337	1.13	..
1966	159,382	509,602	0.313	1.16	1.53
1967	220,512	620,753	0.355	1.32	1.43
1968	295,331	721,685	0.409	1.54	1.44
1969	377,394	800,680	0.471	1.82	1.56
1970	443,651	833,246	0.532	2.06	1.67
1971	500,584	819,673	0.611	2.52	1.76
1972	574,991	946,538	0.608	2.51	1.70

Source: Economic Planning Board (& The Korea Development Bank), *Report on*

Mining and Manufacturing Survey: 1967, 1969–1972, and Report on Mining and Manufacturing Census: 1960, 1963, 1966 & 1968, and Economic Planning Board, Annual Report on the Economically Active Population.

[1] We applied the implicit price deflator for manufacturing ouptut in order to get 1970 won values and then applied the exchange rate of 310.6 won per dollar to get 1970 dollar figures.

[2] Average number of employees during the 12 month period at the manufacturing establishments operating with five or more "workers" (which include working proprietor and unpaid family workers).

[3] Fixed capital stock data for manufacturing sector were estimated by using Han's net stock data of 1968 as the bench mark and subtracting (or adding) net annual fixed capital formation in manufacturing sector successively.

On the other hand, we can see from Table 2 that the average rates of interest were increasing up to 1966 but steadily declined after 1966. Hence, what we have observed so far is the rapid and significant capital accumulation and capital deepening in Korea since 1966 and the associated increase in the wage/rental ratio during 1966–72. Now we will examine the factor intensity of Korea's trade during 1966–72.

III. COMPUTATIONAL PROCEDURES

The balance equations of the Leontief type system can be written as:

$$[I - A]x = e - m + q$$

where I is the identity matrix, A the matrix of domestic and competitive import input coefficients, e a column vector of exports in thousand dollars, x a column vector of outputs, m a column vector of competitive imports, and q a column vector of final demands. We obtain;

$$k'x = k'[I - A]^{-1}(e - m + q)$$
$$n'x = n'[I - A]^{-1}(e - m + q)$$

where k and n represent column vector of capital and labor coefficients respectively.[4]

In computing domestic factor requirements for exports or for import replacement, the demand for non-competitive imports is assumed to be completely satisfied by foreign sources. For competitive imports, stepped-up domestic production can be an alternative to imports and vice versa. The final demand to replace imports or to export cannot be assumed to automatically result in demand for competitive imports. Especially when we want to compute the domestic factor requirements to "replace" current competitive imports, we logically have to assume that whatever the demand for competitive imports might be (to replace the competitive imports themselves), it will be satisfied entirely by domestic output. Hence for the computation of domestic capital and labor requirements to replace competitive imports, the use of the A matrix is justified.

However, when we want to compute the "domestic" factor requirements for current exports, we cannot arbitrarily assume that current export production does not use competitively imported inputs. Therefore, we have to use A^d (the matrix of domestic input coefficients) instead of A (the matrix of domestic and competitive import input coefficients) when we compute "domestic" capital and labor requirements for current exports.[5]

By using the A matrix instead of the A^d matrix in computation of factor requirements for exports, Leontief assumes that export production uses non-competitive imports but does not use competitive imports. However, A is the matrix of average sectoral input coefficients for the country as a whole and this includes the actual use of competitive imports in each industry. Hence it is absurd to use the average coefficients in order to compute the "domestic" capital and labor requirements as if the exported portion of production does not use competitive imports. Such an absurdity arose because Leontief is talking in terms of "reducing or increasing" exports by a million dollars and seeing how much capital and labor are

---

[4] Here, the expression $k'[I - A]^{-1}e$ may be interpreted as the amount of capital directly and indirectly required for exports and likewise $k'[I - A]^{-1}m$ as the amount of capital directly and indirectly required to replace the competitive imports by domestic production; $n'[I - A]^{-1}e$ and $n'[I-A]^{-1}m$ may be interpreted in a similar way.

[5] If we let A^m represent the matrix of competitive import input coefficients, we obtain separate balance equation for domestic output and competitive imports, i.e.,

$$A^m x + q^m = m \qquad\qquad A^d x + (q^d + e) = x$$

where q^d is a column vector of final demand for domestic products, and q^m is a column vector of final demand for competitive imports.

"released or required" thereby, while what is necessary for his test is, as Bhagwati says, to compute the total capital and labor requirements for current exports or import replacements.

The first problem we face is how to handle the non-competitive imports. The Bank of Korea (BOK) classified commodities whose domestic production was either absent or negligible (and expected to remain negligible in the near future) as non-competitive imports, and grouped them as one input item in its 1968 input-output table. As a result, about 1,600 items out of about 4,500 imported items (seven-digit SITC classification) including various kind of machineries and chemical products were classified as non-competitive imports. If we follow Leontief's method of computing factor requirements to replace imports, we have to exclude all those non-competitive imports from our computation.

It seems that Leontief treated natural resource intensive goods (which the U.S. does not possess) as non-competitive goods.[6] Since he assumed that their imports could not be replaced by domestic production, he excluded them from his computation of capital and labor requirements "to replace" imports.

In the U.S. there are very few things which cannot be produced because of scarcity of capital, and hence we may safely assume that anything not produced in the U.S. is natural-resource intensive. However, there are many things which are not produced in Korea because of scarcity of capital, and hence they are imported non-competitively. Since Korea is likely to be saving a large amount of capital through their imports, we cannot exclude them from our computation of the factor intensity of imports.

Therefore, we decided to divide the "non-competitive imports" into two groups, i.e., "non-competitive, non-natural-resource-intensive imports" and "non-competitive, natural-resource-intensive imports." Then the total factor intensity of imports is obtained by adding the factor requirements to replace "non-competitive, non-natural-resource-intensive imports" to the factor requirements to replace "competitive imports."

The factor requirements to replace competitive imports can be comput-

---

[6] Leontief (1956) himself defined the non-competitive imports in the following fashion: "With its present technology and a given endowment of labor, capital and natural resources, this country finds it advantageous to satisfy its entire demand for commodities such as coffee and other tropical products as well as certain minerals by imports from abroad. These are identified for purpose of the present study as non-competitive imports." He then defined the competitive imports as following: "The competivtive imports comprise all other goods which, although imported, are also produced in relatively substantial quantities at home."

ed using the A matrix and sectoral capital- and labor-output ratios. The factor requirements to replace non-competitive non-natural-resource-intensive imports may ideally be computed on the basis of "blue-prints" for their actual domestic production. However, since we do not have the necessary information, we decided to approximate their factor requirements using Leontief's data on the U.S. sectoral factor requirements in 1947.[7]

About 40 percent of total commodity imports in 1968 belong to the BOK's classification of non-competitive imports. We selected crude oil, crude rubber, raw cotton, raw sugar, wood and wool which together accounted for about 15 percent of total commodity imports in 1968 as "non-competitive natural-resource-intensive" goods. These were then excluded from our computation of the factor intensity of imports.[8] We then classified the remaining 25 percent (out of 40 percent) of what the BOK defined as non-competitive imports as "non-competitive, non-natural-resource-intensive" goods.

We further examined the 1968 trade data and found that there were large imports of rice and wheat (7 percent of total commodity imports, i.e., $106.2 million), about 43 percent of which was financed by aid and loans such as PL 480. In Korea, there have been large increases in imports of rice and wheat while there has been virtually no increase in their produc-

---

[7] So long as we are concerned with the "relative" factor intensity of "non-competitive, non-natural-resource-intensive" imports as a separate group, the use of the U.S. factor input coefficients would not give us a very distorted picture. Only in the unlikely event of large-scale factor intensity reversals would the conclusion based upon analysis using the U.S. factor input coefficients be considered invalid. However, when we add the absolute amount of capital and labor required to replace "non-competitive, non-natural-resource-intensive" imports to those required to replace "compeitive" imports, we may be adding very heterogeneous factors of production. Therefore, if we by any chance can get any reasonable information on "blue-print" factor requirements, we should try to improve our approximation on factor requirments. For the time being, we will make up the deficiency in our approximation by doing separated (i.e., exports vs. competitive *and* non-competitive imports) as well as aggregated (i.e., exports vs. competitive *plus* non-competitive imports) comparisons of the factor intensity of trade.

[8] For these goods, not even a drastic change in the domestic supply of capital and labor would lead to any significant amount of domestic production. That is, by "non-competitive, natural-resource-intensive" goods we imply those goods which use intensively those natural resources which Korea does not possess to a significant degree. There can be many other items with similar characteristics, but since there are difficulties in clear identification and classification and since their magnitude is rather small, we decided to limit the number to the six listed above.

tion or acreage under cultivation during 1961–72 period. Taking account of the fact that Korea's population density ranks second in the world, it does not seem likely that her imports could be replaced by the use of capital and labor in the proportions computed from 1968 sectoral capital-output and labor-output ratios.[9] Unless there is a really effective "green revolution", expansion of rice and wheat production via traditional methods would require tremendous amount of capital in the form of farm mechanization, irrigation systems, etc. This is all the more true because extra capital use in farming is more frequently labor-saving than output-increasing.[10] After giving some reflection to this subject, we eliminated rice and wheat from the BOK list of "competitive imports" and added them to our list of "non-competitive, natural-resource intensive goods."

The most significant differences between our approach and that of Leontief and his followers are: (1) use o the A matrix to compute the factor requirements for import replacement and the A^d matrix to compute the factor requirements for export production, and (2) the inclusion of non-competitive non-natural-resource-intensive imports in our computation of factor requirements to replace imports. From this on, we will simplify the exposition by referring to "non-competitive *non*-natural-resource-intensive" imports as "non-competitive" imports and to "non-competitive natural-resource-intensive" imports as "natural-resource-intensive" imports. we first intend to test the Leontief proposition for the year of 1968,

---

[9] In his Leontief type test, Bharadwaj found that Indian exports to the United States were capital intensive and imports from the United States were labor intensive. Hence he concluded his paper with the following comment. "Thus, large marginal factor requirements may induce a country to import certain commodities even though the prevalent (average) factor-input ratios for these commodities might suggest that the country enjoys comparative advantage in the production of these goods. This is especially so in land and natural resource intensive goods."

[10] Leontief (1956) himself made the following suggestion which seems to be a proper way to handle such cases: "The actual supply of a domestic natural resource . . . might be short and thus impose an effective limit on the output of . . . industries which use it as a direct input . . . if the product of these . . . industries are transportable, these products will probably be imported from abroad. Thus . . . the limited supply of domestic pulpwood is alleviated through the purchase of foreign pulp. This means that, although they seem to compete with corresponding domestic outputs in our economy, such imports might play the same role as obviously non-competitive imports, such as coffee, and consequently should be explained also in the same terms. For purpose our computations this would simply mean shifting an additional group of . . . imports from the list of competitive into that of non-competitive commodities."

and then to examine the changing factor intensity of trade for the 1966–72 period. Had a complete set of input-output matrices, with corresponding sets of labor and capital coefficients for the period of 1966–72 been available, it certainly would serve our purpose better. However, due to limited data availability, the internal structural relationships for the entire period must be based on the 1968 structural relationships. We will then apply the 1966 and 1970 sets of factor coefficients and input-output tables to the same series of trade data (1966–72) in order to investigate the impact of factor substitution on our factor requirement computations.[11]

IV. STATISTICAL RESULTS AND IMPLICATIONS

(1) Using the 117 sector 1968 A^d matrix, we computed the factor requirements for 1968 commodity exports. Total commodity exports in 1968 amounted to \$455 million. The amount of fixed capital directly and indirectly required was \$461 million (in 1970 dollar prices), while 413 thousand workers were needed.

In 1968, total commodity imports amounted to \$1,463 million, and about 70 percent of them were financed by foreign savings, non-commodity exports and factor income from abroad. Excluding about 25 percent of total imports which were defined as non-competitive imports plus the above listed six natural resource intensive imports (which took about 15 percent of total imports), we computed the factor requirements to replace the competitive imports (which, including rice and wheat amounted to about 60 percent of total commodity imports in 1968). The amount of fixed capital directly and indirectly required was \$1,088 million, while 750 thousand workers were needed.

If we compute the factor intensity ratio of trade (i.e., the amount of

---

[11] The basic data used in our study are 1966, 1968 and 1970 input-output tables (117 sector classification), sectoral capital coefficients, sectoral labor coefficients and foreign trade statistics. We obtained these data from: K.C. Han, *Estimates of Korean Capital and Inventory Coefficients in 1968*, Yonsei University, 1970; *Report on National Wealth Survey (1968)*, Economic Planning Board, 1972; *The Input-Output Table of Korea* (1966, 1968 & 1970), the Bank of Korea; *Report on Mining and Manufacturing Census (1966–70)*, the Korea Development Bank; *Statistical Yearbook of Foreign Trade* (1970–72), the Office of Customs Administration; and *Foreign Trade of Korea* (1966–69), Ministry of Finance.

Table 4

Factor Requirements (Direct and Indirect) Per $100 Million of Korea's Exports and Import Replacements: 1966–72

Unit: In Million 1970 Dollars & 1,000 Persons

	Applying 1966 Coefficients			Applying 1968 Coefficients			Applying 1970 Coefficients		
	Capital	Labor	C/L	Capital	Labor	C/L	Capital	Labor	C/L
I. Commodity Exports (A^a Matrix)									
1966	**86.2**	**97.6**	**883**	92.6	84.8	1,093	98.4	68.4	1,438
1967	89.8	99.1	906	94.0	84.1	1,117	100.6	68.1	1,478
1968	89.1	97.0	919	**91.6**	**82.0**	**1,117**	99.2	65.9	1,506
1969	90.6	97.0	934	93.3	82.6	1,130	98.5	65.5	1,503
1970	90.3	97.7	924	93.0	83.0	1,120	**96.6**	**65.1**	**1,485**
1971	89.9	93.4	963	93.2	79.2	1,177	98.3	62.1	1,583
1972	92.2	89.6	1,029	93.8	76.8	1,220	98.2	59.5	1,651
II. Competitive Import Replacements: Including Rice & Wheat (A Matrix)									
1966	**117.4**	**76.7**	**1,531**	139.3	68.0	2,048	146.2	65.6	2,230
1967	102.8	82.9	1,240	124.7	72.4	1,722	139.2	69.8	1,994
1968	97.4	90.3	1,079	**113.0**	**78.0**	**1,450**	131.7	73.7	1,786
1969	90.8	95.2	954	104.2	84.5	1,232	125.1	77.3	1,619
1970	88.0	96.3	914	101.5	84.9	1,195	**125.0**	**77.7**	**1,608**
1971	90.0	100.0	900	102.3	90.2	1,135	124.0	80.7	1,537
1972	94.0	99.1	949	105.1	89.0	1,181	126.8	80.0	1,585

	Applying 1966 Coefficients			Applying 1968 Coefficients			Applying 1970 Coefficients		
	Capital	Labor	C/L	Capital	Labor	C/L	Capital	Labor	C/L
III. Competitive Import Replacements: Excluding Rice & Wheat (*A* Matrix)									
1966	**124.3**	**71.6**	**1,736**	147.1	62.1	2,369	152.6	61.5	2,482
1967	109.3	77.5	1,410	132.4	65.6	2,017	146.1	65.4	2,235
1968	103.5	85.6	1,209	**119.5**	**71.6**	**1,669**	137.9	69.7	1,977
1969	100.1	88.1	1,136	113.6	74.8	1,519	135.1	70.7	1,910
1970	96.9	89.2	1,086	110.4	75.0	1,472	**135.1**	**71.1**	**1,900**
1971	99.6	93.7	1,063	111.7	81.4	1,373	134.2	74.5	1,801
1972	103.3	93.4	1,106	113.8	81.2	1,402	136.0	74.7	1,819
IV. Non-Competitive Import Replacements (U.S. Input Coefficients)									
1966	**163.5**	**8.5**	**19,236**	187.6	10.0	18,855	188.1	9.0	20,857
1967	177.2	10.3	17,167	175.3	10.4	16,848	172.2	9.8	17,530
1968	175.5	10.0	17,527	**173.1**	**10.1**	**17,151**	167.9	9.8	17,158
1969	174.0	10.1	17,167	172.2	10.2	16,889	170.8	10.0	17,118
1970	177.6	10.0	17,796	175.0	10.1	17,402	**178.2**	**9.8**	**18,240**
1971	178.6	10.1	17,634	176.6	10.2	17,297	181.3	10.0	18,226
1972	182.0	10.2	17,798	180.1	10.3	17,458	186.9	10.1	18,521
V. To Replace Total Non-Natural-Resource-Intensive Imports (III plus IV)									
1966	**135.8**	**53.1**	**2,557**	156.9	49.5	3,170	156.9	55.2	2,841
1967	129.8	57.1	2,273	144.6	49.9	2,901	149.9	57.4	2,614
1968	128.6	59.2	2,172	**36.9**	**51.6**	**2,654**	142.5	60.4	2,361
1969	127.8	58.9	2,170	134.3	52.0	2,580	142.3	58.4	2,438
1970	129.1	57.5	2,245	134.1	51.2	2,619	**144.6**	**57.6**	**2,511**
1971	132.4	59.0	2,244	136.9	53.7	2,549	145.9	58.5	2,494
1972	139.0	55.7	2,496	141.9	51.2	2,775	150.0	57.0	2,631

capital directly and indirectly required divided by the amount of labor needed), we get $1,117 per worker for exports and $1,450 per worker for competitive import replacements in 1968. Hence, Korea's competitive imports were more capital intensive than its exports, though the difference was rather small.

When we excluded rice and wheat (which took 7 percent of total commodity imports in 1968) from the list of competitive imports, the total requirements of capital and labor to replace competitive imports were $1,010 million and 605 thousand persons respectively. The factor intensity ratio of competitive imports became $1,669 per worker, which is much higher than that for exports ($ 1,117 per worker).

(2) On the basis of the direct and indirect factor requirements in the U.S. (1947), we then computed the factor requirements for that 25 percent of total 1968 imports which were defined as non-competitive. We got $705 million worth of fixed capital and 41 thousand workers, implying a very high capital intensity ratio of $17,151 per worker. As was expected, Korea was saving a large amount of capital through imports of non-competitive goods.

(3) If we compare the factor intensity of non-competitive imports ($17, 151 per worker) which was computed on the basis of the U.S. factor input coefficients with that of competitive imports ($1,450 per worker) which was computed on the basis of the Korean factor input coefficients, we might get an uneasy feeling at such an enormous difference. However, apart from the actual differences in the commodities included under identical I-O sector titles, it is only to be expected that the U.S. industries would use much more capital intensive methods due to the differences in relative factor abundance and the consequent factor substitutions. If we compare the factor intensity ratio of $17,151 with that of the U.S. exports in 1947 which was $25,258 (in 1970 prices), we can see that capital intensity of Korea's non-competitive imports in 1968 was lower than that of the average U.S. exports in 1947. (See Table 5.)

If we further examine the factor intensity of Japan's trade in 1951 ($710 per worker for competitive imports and $1,102 per worker for exports in 1970 prices as computed by Ichimura and Tatemoto), we first note the somewhat unexpected result that Japan's exports were relatively more capital intensive than its competitive imports. Aside from this, we can see that the factor intensities of Korea's trade in 1968 were not extremely different in "absolute" magnitude from the factor intensities of Japan's trade in 1951 and hence our statistical results are not unreasonable.

With factor intensity reversals, it is conceivable that the capital-rich

Table 5

Factor Requirements per $100 Million of Exports or Import Replacements: U.S. (1947), Japan (1951) & Korea (1968)

	Capital (K) (Million 1970 dollars)	Labor (N) (1,000 persons)	Factor Intensity (K)/(N) ($/person)
U.S., 1947			
Exports	255.1	10.1	25,258
Competitive Imports	309.1	9.4	32,883
Japan, 1951			
Exports	138.6	125.8	1,102
Competitive Imports	133.1	187.6	710
Korea, 1968			
Exports	91.6	82.0	1,117
Competitive Imports	113.0	78.0	1,450
Non-Competitive Imp.	173.1	10.1	17,151

Source: Leontief (1956), Ichimura & Tatemoto, and Table 4.
Note: The GNP deflator of the U.S. was applied to both Leontief's (1956) and Ichimura's data in order to get 1970 dollar figures. If we apply the GNP deflator of Japan and its official exchange rate of 360 yen per dollar in 1970 to Ichimura's data, we get about $1,400 for the capital intensity of Japan's exports and $900 for that of Japan's competitive imports in 1951.

country exports its labor-intensive good. However, as Jones says:

". . . no matter which commodity is exported from the capital-rich country, it must embody a higher proportion of capital than either commodity produced in the other country. . . . In concluding that America must be labor abundant, Leontief compared the capital/labor ratios in American exports and American import competing industries; no comparison was made with factor proportions abroad. If both American exports and import-competing products are produced with more capital intensive methods than abroad, Leontief's paradoxical conclusion is no longer valid."

Although Jones' proposition was stated within the framework of a two-country, two-good model, we can feel that what we observed from an international comparison here-- i.e., the Leontief paradox in the U.S. vs. the factor intensity of Korea's (or Japan's) trade as presented in Table 5--can be fit into the general theoretical framework of Heckscher-Ohlin (as understood by Jones).

(4) Even if we include rice and wheat in the list of competitive imports, import replacements require relatively more capital than export production ($1,117). This holds whether we compute the factor intensity of competitive imports ($1,450) and non-competitive imports ($17,151) separately or together ($2,265). However, if we take away rice and wheat from the BOK list of competitive imports and add them to our list of natural resource intensive goods, then as we can see in Table 4, the factor intensity ratio to replace competitive imports becomes $1,669 per worker. Further, if we add the non-competitive imports, the factor intensity ratio to replace the entire non-natural-resource-intensive imports becomes $2,654 which may look more consistent with Korea's per worker capital endowment ratio of $1,395 in 1968. This is also consistent with our hypothesis that Korea is a labor abundant country and has a comparative advantage in labor-intensive goods.

(5) According to the factor intensity computations based on 1968 coefficients, the capital intensity of Korea's exports was steadily increasing, and the capital intensity of competitive imports was steadily falling. That is, we observed a rapid increase in per capita fixed capital stock in a small, labor abundant country and the associated increase in the capital-intensity of the export commodity bundle and the decrease in the capital-intensity of the competitive import bundle.

(6) On the other hand, we can see that the factor intensity ratios of non-competitive imports were rather stable, i.e., around $17,000 per worker during 1966–72. Hence, we may say that, as far as these imports are concerned, there was no tendency towards continuously decreasing capital intensity. We may explain this phenomenon by the inherent difficulties in the import-substitution of new products and the unbiased (in terms of factor intensities) increasing domestic demand for the non-competitive goods.

In any case, the Korean experience seems to suggest that a developing country may save substantial amount of capital via trade in competitive exports vs. non-competitive imports, but save very small amount of capital in its trade in competitive goods. Leontief excluded all non-competitive imports from his computation of factor intensity of trade. Since the U.S. is the most capital abundant country, only goods intensive in natural resources (which the U.S. does not possess) were excluded. However, since a large portion of non-competitive imports in developing countries are non-natural-resource-intensive but highly capital intensive goods, if we exclude all non-competitive goods from our computation of factor intensity of trade, the test itself may become quite meaningless.[12]

(7) It seems reasonable to expect the sectoral capital- and labor-output ratios to decrease over time due to technical progress and economies of scale. Furthermore, with an increasing wage/rental raito (as well as with possible labor-saving technical progress), we may also expect factor substitution and resulting increases in sectoral capital-output ratios and/or increase in sectoral capital-labor ratios.

As a matter of fact, we could actually observe (see Appendix) very strongly biased changes in sectoral factor output ratios. That is, the sectoral capital-output ratios have mostly increased, and even when they decreased, the decreases in labor-output ratios were several times larger than the decreases in capital-output ratios, implying more rapid increases in labor productivities and also increases in capital intensities.

Since we applied the 1968 input-output table and 1968 factor-coefficients to the entire 1966–72 period, and since the degree of overestimation seems to be larger for labor requirements than for fixed capital in commodity sectors, we should expect a bias towards "less" capital intensive direction for all factor intensity figures computed for the period "after" 1968 and a bias in the opposite direction for the period "before" 1968. However, the existence of these biases does not weaken, but rather strengthens, our conclusion of increasing capital-intensity of exports. Of course, the opposite may be said for our preceding conclusion of increasing labor intensity of competitive imports.

In order to examine the combined effect of technical progress, economies of scale, factor substitution and changes in inter-industry relationships on factor requirements for export production or import substitu-

---

[12] Ichimura treated all the non-natural-resource-intensive imports as competitive imports and applied Japanese factor input coefficients when he computed the factor intensity of Japan's trade in 1951. However, Japan in 1951 was not one of the most capital abundant countries at that time, and hence there might have been enormous underestimation of the capital intensity of Japan's imports, and this enabled him to assert that Japan's exports were more capital intensive than its imports in 1951. If we apply the U.S. factor input coefficients to the non-competitive capital intensive imports of Korea (or Japan), we are assuming the homogeneity of both capital and labor among the countries. We know that Leontief himself argued the equivalence of three non-U.S. workers to one U.S. worker in terms of efficiency units. Similarly, U.S. capital may be more efficient than non-U.S. capital. Granted that our method of applying U.S. factor input coefficients to non-competitive, non-natural-resource-intensive imports will obviously result in a rather crude approximation, we may say that our approach will at least save us from grossly distorted results such as Ichimura's.

tion, we applied the 1966 and 1970 sets of factor coefficients and input-output tables to the trade data (classified according to 117 I-O sectors) during 1966–72. As we can see in Table 4, if we apply the 1968 set of coefficients to the 1970 commodity exports, for example, the capital requirements are 3.7 percent underestimated and the labor requirements are 27.5 percent overestimated in comparison with the results obtained by applying the 1970 set of coefficients. Hence the rate of increase in capital intensity of exports during 1968–70 becomes much higher when we apply the 1970 set of coefficients.

On the other hand, if we compare the capital intensity of 1968 competitive imports ("competitive" as of 1968) computed with the 1968 set of coefficients with the capital intensity of 1970 competitive imports ("competitive" as of 1970) computed with the 1970 set of coefficients, we can see that the capital intensity of competitive imports during 1968–70 has increased somewhat. Likewise, if we compare the capital intensity of 1968 non-competitive imports ("non-competitive" as of 1968) computed with the U.S. coefficients with the capital intensity of 1970 non-competitive imports ("non-competitive" as of 1970), we can see that the capital intensity of non-competitive imports has also increased during 1968–70. However, when we repeated the same type of comparison between 1966 and 1968, we could observe a decrease in capital intensity of both competitive and non-competitive imports, though the exports continued to show an increase in capital intensity.

Now we may say that the capital intensity of Korea's commodity exports consistently and significantly increased during 1966–72. However, it seems that we have to revise our preceding conclusion on the increasing labor intensity of competitive or non-competitive imports which was based on factor intensity estimates obtained by applying the fixed coefficients of 1968.

In sum, what we have observed is rapidly accumulating fixed capital stock, a rising wage/rental ratio, and the associated factor substitutions in production processes towards more capital intensive direction in Korea during 1966–72. We could observe not only the overall capital deepening of Korean industries, but we could further observe significantly increasing capital intensity of Korea's commodity exports. However, possibly due to difficulties in import substitution or to a changing demand pattern, we could not observe consistently increasing or decreasing capital intensity of imports.

Appendix

Changes in Industrial Structure and
Factor Requirements

In order to examine the extent of changes in factor-output ratios and inter-industry relationships, and their impact on factor requirement estimates, we computed the capital and labor requirements for export production during 1966–72 applying 1966, 1968 and 1970 sets of factor coefficients and input-output tables.

As we can see in Table 6, there were significant increases in sectoral capital-output ratios during the two-year periods of 1966–68 and 1968–70, and hence the application of the 1970 set of capital coefficients and the 1970 input-output table increased the capital requirement estimates by about 4–8 percent in comparison with those obtained by applying the 1968 set of capital coefficients and the 1968 input-output table. The latter, in turn, increased the capital requirement estimates by about 2–7 percent in comparison with those obtained by applying the 1966 set of capital coefficients and the 1966 input-output table.

On the other hand, not only were there large decreases in labor-output ratios during the two-year periods of 1966–68 and 1968–70, but, especially during 1968–70, there were also significant labor saving inter-industrial structural changes. As a result, the application of 1970 coefficients decreased the labor requirement estimates by as much as 19–23 percent in comparison with those obtained by applying the 1968 set of labor coefficients and the 1968 input-output table. The latter, in turn, decreased the labor requirement estimates by about 13–16 percent in comparison with those obtained by applying the 1966 set of labor coefficients and the 1966 input-output table.

We may speculate that such remarkably biased changes in factor uses, which were more pronounced during 1968–70, were due to biased technical progresses, economies of scale and the rising wage/rental ratio.

Table 6

Changes in Industrial Structure and Factor Requirements for Export Production: 1966–72

Unit: In Million 1970 Dollars, Thousand Persons & Percent (%)

	Estimated Capital Requirements Applying				Changes in Capital Requirements Due to Changes In			
	1968 Capital-Output Ratios & 1968 I-O	1968 Capital-Output Ratios & 1970 I-O	1970 Capital-Output Ratios & 1968 I-O	1970 Capital-Output Ratios & 1970 I-O	Input-Output Relationships	Capital-Output Ratios	Inter-action	All Coefficients
1966	272.1	277.4	282.2	289.1	2.0%	3.7%	0.6%	6.3%
1967	346.1	352.1	361.8	370.7	1.7%	4.5%	0.9%	7.1%
1968	460.9	467.8	486.3	499.6	1.5%	5.5%	1.4%	8.4%
1969	612.6	609.4	640.6	646.9	-0.5%	4.6%	1.5%	5.6%
1970	777.0	765.6	807.5	806.8	-1.5%	3.9%	1.4%	3.8%
1971	949.8	943.5	996.1	1,002.1	-0.7%	4.9%	1.3%	5.5%
1972	1,416.8	1,393.2	1,481.2	1,484.6	-1.7%	4.6%	1.9%	4.8%

	Estimated Labor Requirements Applying				Changes in Labor Requirements Due to Changes In			
	1968 Labor-Output Ratios & 1968 I-O	1968 Labor-Output Ratios & 1970 I-O	1970 Labor-Output Ratios & 1968 I-O	1970 Labor-Output Ratios & 1970 I-O	Input-Output Relationships	Labor-Output Ratios	Inter-action	All Coefficients
1966	249.1	241.7	209.4	201.1	-3.0%	-15.9%	-0.4%	-19.3%
1967	309.8	299.4	261.9	250.8	-3.4%	-15.5%	-0.1%	-19.0%
1968	412.8	399.1	346.0	331.7	-3.3%	-16.2%	-0.2%	-19.7%
1969	542.4	518.2	453.8	430.5	-4.5%	-16.3%	0.2%	-20.6%
1970	693.8	656.3	578.7	543.3	-5.4%	-16.6%	0.3%	-21.7%
1971	807.2	767.7	671.4	633.0	-4.9%	-16.8%	0.1%	-21.6%
1972	1,161.8	1,107.1	949.1	899.0	-4.7%	-18.3%	0.4%	-22.6%

Table 6

(Continued)

	Estimated Capital Requirements Applying				Changes in Capital Requirements Due to Changes In			
	1966 Capital-Output Ratios & 1966 I-O	1966 Capital-Output Ratios & 1968 I-O	1968 Capital-Output Ratios & 1966 I-O	1968 Capital-Output Ratios & 1968 I-O	Input-Output Relationships	Capital-Output Ratios	Interaction	All Coefficients
1966	253.3	256.5	264.4	272.1	1.3%	4.4%	1.7%	7.4%
1967	330.6	332.0	338.2	346.1	0.4%	2.3%	2.0%	4.7%
1968	448.5	445.8	452.3	460.9	-0.6%	0.9%	2.5%	2.8%
1969	595.3	595.7	595.5	612.6	0.1%	0.0%	2.8%	2.9%
1970	754.1	758.7	752.7	777.0	0.6%	-0.2%	2.6%	3.0%
1971	916.2	913.6	925.6	949.8	-0.3%	1.0%	3.0%	3.7%
1972	1,393.1	1,385.6	1,381.0	1,416.8	-0.5%	-0.9%	3.1%	1.7%

	Estimated Labor Requirements Applying				Changes in Labor Requirements Due to Changes In			
	1966 Labor-Output Ratios & 1966 I-O	1966 Labor-Output Ratios & 1968 I-O	1968 Labor-Output Ratios & 1966 I-O	1968 Labor-Output Ratios & 1968 I-O	Input-Output Relationships	Labor-Output Ratios	Interaction	All Coefficients
1966	287.0	292.4	245.7	249.1	1.9%	-14.4%	-0.7%	-13.2%
1967	364.9	371.2	306.1	309.8	1.7%	-16.1%	-0.7%	-15.1%
1968	488.3	494.5	410.0	412.8	1.3%	-16.0%	-0.8%	-15.5%
1969	636.9	649.0	535.9	542.4	1.9%	-15.9%	-0.8%	-14.8%
1970	815.9	835.2	682.1	693.8	2.4%	-16.4%	-1.0%	-15.0%
1971	952.5	968.3	799.7	807.2	1.7%	-16.0%	-0.9%	-15.2%
1972	1,353.4	1,369.5	1,156.1	1,161.8	1.2%	-14.6%	-0.8%	-14.2%

REFERENCES

Baldwin, R. E., "Determinants of the Commodity Structure of U.S. Trade," *American Economic Review*, Vol. LXI, No. 1 (March 1971)

Bank of Korea, *National Income Statistics Yearbook*, 1974.

Bhagwati, J., "The Pure Theory of International Trade: A Survey," *Economic Journal*, (March 1964)

Bharadwaj, R., "Factor Proportions and the Structure of Indo-U.S. Trade," *The Indian Economic Journal*, Vol. X., No. 2 (October 1962)

Economic Planning Board, *Annual Report on the Economically Active Population: 1973*, 1974

_____, *An Evaluation Study for the Accuracy of the 1960 Population and Housing Census of Korea*, 1963.

_____, *1966 Population Census Report of Korea*, 1969

_____, *1970 Population and Housing Census Report*, 1973

_____, *Korea Statistical Yearbook*, 1974

Economic Planning Board and the Korea Development Bank, *Report on Mining and Manufacturing Census (or Survey)*, 1960 through 1972

Han, K. C., *Estimates of Korean Capital and Inventory Coefficients in 1968*, Seoul: Yonsei University Press, 1970

Hong, Wontack, *Factor Supply and Factor Intensity of Trade: The Case of Korea*, Seoul: Korea Development Institute, 1973 (mimeographed)

Ichimura, S. and Tatemoto, M., "Factor Proportions and Foreign Trade: The Case of Japan," *Review of Economics and Statistics*, Vol. XII (November 1959)

Jones, R. W. "Factor Proportions and the Heckscher-Ohlin Theorem," *Review of Economic Studies* (January 1956)

Leontief, W., "Domestic Production and Foreign Trade: The American Capital Position Re-examined," *Proceedings of the American Philosophical Society*, XCVII (September 1953)

_____, "Factor Proportions and the Structure of American Trade: Further Theoretical and Empirical Analysis," *Review of Economics and Statistics*, XXXVIII, No. 4 (November 1956)

Shim, B. K., et al., *A Study of Preferential Interest Rate Structure: The Korean Experience (1963-71)*, Seoul: Seoul National University, 1972

Wahl, D. F., "Capital and Labor Requirements for Canada's Foreign Trade," *Canadian Journal of Economics and Political Science*, Vol. 27 (August 1961)

Weiser, L.A., "Changing Factor Requirements of United States Foreign Trade," *Review of Economics and Statistics*, Vol. 50 (August 1968)

The Contribution of Exports to Employment in Korea

David C. Cole and Larry E. Westphal*

I. INTRODUCTION

One of the most intriguing questions concerning South Korea's export-led development is the extent to which exports contribute to employment. Two approaches may be followed to examine this question. One is to obtain data from exporting firms regarding their employment and input purchases in order to build up estimates of total direct and indirect employment attributable to exports. The other is to employ input-output data and average labor-output coefficients for the various sectors to estimate the direct and indirect employment generated by exports. The first approach runs into difficulties when tracing through the multiple indirect effects, while the second generally fails to incorporate any special characteristics of production for exports which may affect factor proportions or the reliance upon different sources for intermediate inputs.

The first approach was recently followed by Watanabe to estimate total employment generated by South Korea's manufactured exports in 1969. In this paper, we follow the second approach to estimate employment generation from all exports in those years for which input-output tables and labor-output coefficients are available: 1960, 1963, 1966, and 1970. While our coverage is more complete than Watanabe's, a compari-

* The authors are respectively associate director, Institute for International Development and lecturer on economics, Harvard University, and senior economist at the Development Economics Department, World Bank.

son of the two sets of estimates indicates that the biases inherent in the two approaches are as expected and that the "truth" probably lies somewhere in between. In the following sections, we will first describe the methodology and data employed to obtain our estimates, then present the results, and finally compare them with Watanabe's.

II. METHODOLOGY

Following standard input-output methodology, we have estimated export employment generation by multiplying the vector of export demands by the vector of total (i.e., direct plus indirect) labor-output coefficients. The latter is derived by multiplying the vector of direct labor-output coefficients (L) times the inverse of the I-A^d matrix, where the A^d matrix includes only domestically produced intermediate inputs.[1] Imported intermediate inputs must be excluded as they do not generate domestic employment. The implicit assumption following from the use of input-output data is that input requirements for a particular sector's export production are the same as those for its production for domestic sale. The greater the degree of sectoral disaggregation, the less bias is likely to result from this assumption.[2]

If most producers used imported intermediate inputs in similar proportions to output whether exported or domestically sold, then the A^d matrix would yield a reasonable approximation of the indirect employment generated by exports. However, our estimates will overstate the indirect demand for labor if the import content of exports is significantly higher than that of production for domestic sale. There has long been a great deal of controversy about whether the import content of South Korea's exports, product by product, differs significantly from that of production supplied to the domestic market. On the one hand, easy access to imported

---

[1] Let A denote the matrix of intermediate input-output coefficients when both imported and domestically produced intermediate inputs are included, and A^m the matrix of intermediate input-output coefficients for imported inputs only. Then $A^d = A - A^m$.

[2] Because production for export and for domestic sale are not distinguished, input coefficients for a sector are weighted averages of those pertaining to exports and domestic sales. Without additional information, the two sets of input coefficients can not be separated.

intermediate inputs has functioned as a major export incentive.[3] On the other hand, generous wastage allowances have been given to many exporters with the understanding that the excess of duty free imports over the required inputs for export would be used to produce goods sold domestically. Since most enterprises produce for both the domestic and export markets, it is relatively easy to shift inputs imported ostensibly for export production over to production for domestic sale where this increases total profits. We know of no systematic studies of the relative import content of exports, but considering the ease of shifting imported inputs between production for the two markets and the difficulty of controlling it, we believe that the average import-output relations of the IO tables give more reliable estimates of import requirements for export than do estimates based on firms' requests or questionnaire responses. The latter are likely to be biased upwards by firms' desires to obtain as much duty free imports as possible.

III. DATA AND ADJUSTMENTS

The basic data used are the input-output tables published by the Bank of Korea for 1960, 1963, 1966, and 1970, and the labor-input coefficients corresponding to these tables. The original input-output tables have differing sectoral classifications. However, Westphal, in collaboration with the Bank of Korea and the Korea Development Institute, has reclassified these tables to a compatible 118 sector classification.[4] The employment data are at the 43 sector level for the first three tables and the 56 sector level for 1970. It was considered easiest to work at the 118 sector level since these data are available on computer tape. Thus, the compatible 118 sector classification was matched against those in which the labor data were given, and it was assumed that each sector at the 118 sector level had the same labor-output coefficient as the aggregated sector to which it belonged.[5]

---

[3] See Westphal, Larry E., and Kwang Suk Kim, "*Industrial Policy and Development in Korea*," World Bank, February 1974 (mimeographed).

[4] The compatible 118 sector tables are available on tape at the Korea Development Institute and are described in Westphal, Larry E., and Kyu Soo Kim,"*The KDI Input-Output Data Bank,*" 1974 (mimeographed).

[5] The labor-output coefficients were stated in workers (as opposed to employees,

The sector labeled "unclassifiable" accounts for a significant amount of exports, but shows no direct employment in the Bank of Korea estimates. To correct for this, we assumed that unclassifiables consist only of manufactures and distributed production, exports, and intermediate demand for unclassifiables among the manufacturing sectors in proportion respectively to the value of production, exports, and intermediate demand for each sector. Domestic final demand for unclassifiables was distributed residually in order to maintain the input-output accounting identities, and the labor-output coefficients for the manufacturing sectors were adjusted downward in order to maintain the same value of total employment when calculated by multiplying the labor-output coefficient times the value of gross output.

It was not possible to deduct imports from intermediate inputs to obtain the A^d matrices for 1960 and 1963 due to the lack of appropriately classified intermediate import data for these years. Thus for these years we had to base our estimates on the assumptions that all intermediate inputs are domestically produced and that all domestic final demands are met by domestic production.[6] To enable comparisons across the four years, we have also calculated estimates based on these assumptions for 1966 and 1970. These are the "A" estimates given in Table 1. The "B" estimates for 1966 and 1970 are the "correct" estimates, obtained by deducting imported intermediate inputs to get the Leontief matrix and subtracting final goods imports from domestic final demand to estimate the employment generated by domestic final demand.

IV. RESULTS

The principal results of our estimates are shown in Tables 1 and 2.[7]

---

which exclude workers on own account and family laborers) per million won of gross output. The estimates for all four years were derived from the Bank of Korea publications—1960: *Economic Statistics Yearbook*, 1965, p. 290; 1963: *Input-Output Analysis of the Korean Economy in* 1963 p. 67: 1966: *Economic Statistics Yearbook*, 1968, p. 383; 1970: *Economic Statistics Yearbook*, 1973, p. 361. The total coefficients were calculated as $L'(I-A^d)^{-1}$.

[6] That is, the A matrix was used rather than the A^d matrix, and imports of final goods were not deducted from domestic final demand to calculate the employment due to the latter.

[7] Additional details by disaggregated sectors available from the authors on request.

The first shows employment generated by domestic and export demand, while the second gives aggregate employment coefficients for manufacturing.

Estimates of total employment are shown in Table 1 for the primary and manufacturing sectors as well as for all sectors together. These are compared with the Bureau of Statistics' (BOS) estimates of employment for the last three years. According to the latter, which are believed more accurate, manufacturing employment doubled between 1963 and 1970, while primary sector employment was relatively constant. For the last two years, the input-output "B" estimates for the primary sectors are similar to the BOS figures. For the other sectors, our "B" estimates are somewhat below those of the BOS. But under alternative "A" for these years and for 1963, in which our estimates are overstated because of failure to deduct imports, the BOS estimates are lower, as expected. In any case, the differences are relatively minor and serve as a reassuring check on the overall magnitudes based on the input-output data.

The direct employment attributable to a sector's exports is shown in the table, as well as the total employment in the sector generated by the demand for all exports. In 1970 under alternative "B," for example, direct employment in exporting manufactures is estimated to be 225,000, while employment in manufacturing indirectly generated by all exports (including manufactures) was 83,000, giving total export-induced employment in manufacturing of 308,000. Thus exports generated slightly more than one-fourth of total manufacturing employment. Export-induced employment in the primary sector is estimated at 246,000 in 1970 (5 percent of total sectoral employment), while export-induced employment for all sectors is estimated to be 845,000 (9 percent of total employment).

The "A" estimates of total export employment generation are clearly too high, especially in manufacturing. Nonetheless, the *ratio* of export-induced employment to total employment in manufacturing appears to be understated by approximately 15 percent (compare "A" and "B" estimates for 1966 and 1970). Applying this correction to the 1960 and 1963 estimates, we find that the ratio of export-induced employment to total employment in manufacturing is estimated to have risen from 6 percent in 1960 to 8 percent in 1963, 19 percent in 1966, and 26 percent in 1970. A similar correction does not appear warranted with respect to the share of economy-wide employment due to exports. Thus, according to these estimates, export-induced employment increased from less than 4 percent of total employment in the 1960–63 period to about 9 percent in 1970.

Exports of manufactures accounted for roughly 30 percent of total ex-

David C. Cole & Larry E. Westphal

Table 1

Estimates of Export Employment Generation

Unit: In Thousands of Workers

	1960 (A)	1963 (A)	1966 (A)	1966 (B)	1970 (A)	1970 (B)
Primary Sectors						
Total Employment:						
BOS Estimate	n.a.	4,837	—	4,876	—	4,916
IO Estimate	6,320	6,597	5,369	5,095	5,595	4,912
Direct Employment						
in Exports	128	71	75	75	108	108
Total Employment						
Due to All Exports	214	181	237	222	279	246
Percent of Total						
Primary Employment	3.4%	2.7%	4.4%	4.4%	5.0%	5.0%
Manufacturing Sectors						
Total Employment:						
BOS Estimate	n.a.	610	—	833	—	1,284
IO Estimate	523	674	1,040	832	1,549	1,189
Direct Employment						
In Exports	12	23	113	113	225	225
Total Employment						
Due to All Exports	26	43	172	158	348	308
Percent of Total						
Manufacturing Employment	5.0%	6.4%	16.5%	19.0%	22.5%	25.9%
All Sectors						
Total Employment:						
BOS Estimate	n.a.	7,662	—	8,423	—	9,745
IO Estimate	8,147	8,764	8,726	8,107	10,534	9,291
Direct Employment						
in Exports	183	134	274	274	475	475
Total Employment						
in Exports	302	290	585	546	941	845
Percent of Total						
Employment	3.7%	3.3%	6.7%	6.7%	8.9%	9.1%

Notes:

1. BOS estimates of employment were taken from the *Annual Report of the Economically Active Population,* 1972, issued by the Bureau of Statistics. I-O estimates are derived from input-output data on production and labor-input coefficients. Percentages are calculated with respect to the I-O estimates.

2. "All sectors" includes the social overhead and service sectors in addition to the primary and manufacturing sectors.

3. Imports have not been deducted from final and intermediate demands under estimation method A. Imports have been subtracted under estimation method B, which yields the preferred estimates. See the discussion in the text for further explanation.

Table 2

Aggregate Employment Coefficients for Manufactured Products

	1960			1963			1966			1970		
	Do-mestic	Ex-port	Total	Do-mestic	Ex-port	Total	Do-mestic	Ex-port	Total	Do-mestic	Ex-port	Total
Value of Final Demand (billion won)	62	3	65	125	11	136	266	76	342	717	257	974
Percentage Distribution	95%	5%		92%	8%		78%	22%		74%	26%	
Direct Employment in Manu-facturing (thousand workers)	246	12	258	279	23	302	376	113	489	456	225	681
Percentage Distribution	95%	5%		92%	8%		77%	23%		67%	33%	
Total Employment in All Sectors (thousand workers)	n.a.	n.a.	n.a.	n.a.	n.a.	n.a.	1,387	343	1,730	1,633	518	2,151
Percentage Distribution	n.a.	n.a.		n.a.	n.a.		80%	20%		76%	24%	
Direct Employment Coefficient	4.0	4.0		2.2	2.1		1.4	1.5		0.6	0.9	
Total Employment Coefficient	n.a.	n.a.		n.a.	n.a.		5.2	4.5		2.3	2.0	

Note: Employment coefficients are in workers per million won of final demand, and are based on the "B" estimates.

ports in 1960, and for nearly 70 percent in 1970. Table 2 shows that the relative importance of exports in the final demand for manufactures also grew tremendously over the decade of the sixties. At the same time, the direct employment generated by a million won of exports increased in relation to that generated by an equal amount of domestic final demand, particularly in the latter half of the period. (No significance is to be attached to changes in the absolute magnitudes of the labor-output coefficients over time as output is measured in current prices without any adjustment having been made for inflation.) According to the estimates for 1966 and 1970, indirect employment generation by exports was relatively weak, so that the total employment coefficient for manufactured exports was significantly less than that for the domestic final demand for manufactures in both years. This suggests that manufactured exports were relatively labor-intensive, but that their linkages with other producing sectors were relatively limited or were with sectors having low labor-output coefficients.

V. COMPARISON WITH WATANABE'S STUDY

As stated at the outset, Watanabe estimated the employment effects of manufactured exports in 1969 only. He distinguished among four types of employment generation: 1) direct employment in the exporting sectors; 2) indirect employment generated by intermediate input purchases; 3) employment generated by the multiplier effect of increased consumption out of the wages of workers directly employed producing export goods; and, 4) employment expansion due to the increased production made possible by the rise in foreign exchange receipts. He makes quantitative estimates of only the first three, on the grounds that the fourth is employment-facilitating and therefore does not give rise to additional employment beyond that covered under the first three types, implying that net foreign exchange earnings from exports were used to reduce imports of foreign capital, which would otherwise have been greater.[8]

---

[8] Net foreign exchange earnings are equal to gross foreign exchange receipts less the foreign exchange required to import intermediate inputs for the production associated with the first three types of employment generation and induced imports of final consumption goods associated with the wages of workers employed.

This assumption is not particularly appealing, but short of using a simulation model, there does not appear to be any way to estimate the quantitative magnitude of the fourth type of employment generation without resort to excessively arbitrary assumptions.

Watanabe's estimate of direct employment generation is not based upon labor-output ratios, as he argues that these ratios are lower for export production than for goods sold on the domestic market due to the effects on export prices of various subsidies and tax incentives. He assumes that total raw material usage per worker is equal, product by product, for both exports and production for domestic sale, and applies this ratio to an estimate of raw materials consumed in export production to estimate direct employment due to exports in each of the major export industries. The assumption of equal raw material usage per worker biases the employment estimates downward, for equal usage in physical terms implies that the monetary value of raw materials per worker in exports must be less than that in production for domestic sale, since raw materials used in exporting are cheaper than those used to produce for domestic sale because of tax and tariff exemptions on the former. Estimates of raw material consumption per worker are taken from the Economic Planning Board's Mining and Manufacturing Survey for 1969, while raw material consumption estimates are taken from a sample survey of export producers conducted by the Korea Productivity Center (KPC). The latter are undoubtedly biased upwards, as exporters would appear to have an incentive to over-report raw material requirements for export in order to benefit from additional tax and tariff exempt imports. Watanabe does not seem to recognize this qualification.

With respect to indirect employment generation, Watanabe estimates that due only to the first round of purchases of domestically produced intermediate inputs. Watanabe relies upon the KPC survey for estimates of the latter. His estimates therefore presumably reflect actual purchases of domestically produced intermediate inputs for export and avoid the aggregation bias present in the use of input-output data. On the other hand, as we have noted previously, there is the distinct possibility of downward bias in the sample survey results. Furthermore, indirect employment generation is understated by limiting the estimate of the first round of intermediate purchases.

The multiplier effect is a Keynesian-type multiplier based on the assumption that aggregate demand rather than productive capacity was the primary determinant of the level of employment. While it may have been true that exports permitted a fuller and more rational use of existing industrial capacity, the evidence suggests that this was more a characteristic of the early sixties than of the last years of the decade. Regardless of the year, however, it seems unrealistic to assume that all of the income generated by direct export employment was a net increment to the income stream, particularly in view of the high inflation rates experienced during the period. Watanabe has to some extent anticipated this objection by including only the first round of additional consumption expenditure out of the wages of directly employed export workers alone. Nonetheless, his calculations of the multiplier effect estimate most of the increased employment to have been generated in the agricultural sector, where it seems fairly clear that the constraint on production was due to land, technology and weather rather than demand.

The two sets of estimates are compared in Table 3. Watanabe's estimate of direct employment generation in the manufacturing sector is substantially higher than ours, even though the latter pertains to 1970 when exports were appreciably greater than in 1969. On the other hand, our estimates of indirect employment generation in all sectors are a great deal higher than his, so much so in fact that the two sets of estimates are comparable only with the addition of multiplier-generated employment in Watanabe's estimate. With the off-setting differences, the two estimates of total employment generation due to manufactured exports are similar, in respect both to the percent of total employment (economy-wide) and the total employment coefficients.

While Watanabe does not explicitly estimate employment generation due to domestic demand, he tentatively concludes that the labor-intensity of manufactured exports is roughly twice that of production for domestic sale. Insofar as this conclusion is based on a comparison of average labor-output ratios, we can only point to the differences in sources of employment data and his use of raw material usage per worker in estimating export related employment to explain our lower estimate of the relative labor-intensity of exports. However, Watanabe also compares his estimate that 27 percent of manufacturing employment was due to direct export employment generation with the fact that exports were 14 percent of total manufactured output to reach this conclusion. This comparison is clearly invalid, for it is meaningless in the latter figure to focus on the proportion of exports, a component of final demand, to *gross* output, part of which includes intermediate inputs for export production. The correct comparison would be between the proportions of total export employment generation to total employment and that of total production (gross or, better, on a value added basis) due to exports, including indirect

Table 3

Comparison of Estimates

	Watanabe	Input-Output
	(1969)	(1970)
Manufactured Exports (million US$)	555	646
Export Employment Generation (thousand workers)		
Direct	331	225
Indirect	74	293
Primary	(47)	(120)
Manufacturing	(11)	(67)
All Other Sectors	(16)	(106)
Multiplier	98	—
Total	503	518
Percent of Economy-wide Employment	5.4%	5.6%
Employment Coefficients (per $1,000 of exports)		
Direct	0.60	0.35
Indirect	0.13	0.45
Multiplier	0.18	—
Total	0.91	0.80

Note: Watanabe's estimates derived from figures presented on page 514 of the article cited.

intermediate goods output, to total production. Alternatively, one may compare employment coefficients, as is done above in Table 2.

The difference between our estimates is equally brought out by looking at estimates of the percentage of employment growth in manufacturing due to manufactured exports. Watanabe estimates that 50 percent of the growth of manufacturing employment between 1963 and 1969 was due to the expansion of direct export employment generation alone.[9]

Our figure for the period 1963 to 1970 based on the "A" estimates in Table 1 is closer to 30 percent. When indirect employment generation is added, we estimate that 39 percent of the growth of manufacturing employment was due to manufactured export expansion. However, as this

---

[9] He bases this estimate on the assumption that "the labor intensity of exports relative to that of production as a whole" was the same in 1963 as in 1969. This implies constancy of the relative structure of labor-output coefficients and of the composition of exports.

estimate fails to adjust for imported intermediate inputs, it may be mis-leading. It is better in respect to total employment generation to look at the period between 1966 and 1970, where the percentage is estimated to be 40 percent.[10]

VI. CONCLUSION

We now have two sets of estimates of the growth of employment at-tributable to the growth of exports in South Korea. While the approaches and data sources are quite different, the overall estimates are roughly similar; the major differences are in the breakdown between direct and indirect effects and the extent to which employment effects are transmitted to other sectors. Both sets of estimates are subject to qualification due to the failure to remove the probable bias in the reported statistics resulting from the export incentive system which has in the past encouraged reliance upon imports to meet intermediate input requirements, or at least the use of export orders as the basis to obtain intermediate goods imports at low cost. In addition, neither study has effectively corrected the data for the price differentials introduced by the industrial policy system, though Watanabe does attempt a partial correction by using raw material con-sumption per worker rather than labor-output ratios. For many important export commodities, export prices are lower than domestic prices. Thus one million won of exports is not equal in physical quantity to one million won of domestic sales of the same commodity, when both are valued in actual prices. In turn, intermediate input prices are lower for exports (due to tariff and tax exemptions) than for production for domestic sales in most sectors. What is really needed on this account is a set of data, including labor-output and intermediate input-output coefficients and the com-position of final demand, in world market prices.[11]

The incentive structure and relative prices have changed in recent years in ways that have tended to reduce reliance on imported intermediate

---

[10] Indirect manufacturing employment due to manufactured exports was 36,000 in 1966 and 67,000 in 1970; the other figures needed are the "B" estimates given in Ta-ble 1.

[11] Such data were estimated for 1968 by Westphal and Kim, op. cit., but do not exist for any other year.

inputs. Particularly in view of the changes in export incentives introduced in 1973, it is also likely that export and domestic prices are more nearly equal, as are their respective input prices. It may therefore now be possible to obtain more reliable estimates of the import content of exports. A carefully conducted sample survey, using definitions comparable to those used in the input-output estimates, could be used to adjust the input-output matrix to yield input-output coefficients for exports and production for domestic sale, which would yield estimates of export employment generation presumably less subject to bias than those given here.[12] Further work along these lines is clearly needed to gain a clearer and more robust understanding of the current role of exports in employment generation. Because the required data do not exist, however, it is unlikely that much improvement in the estimates of direct and indirect employment generation for the 1960's will be possible. On the other hand, a complete understanding of the historical role of exports as a source of employment (and production) growth requires a more careful investigation of the multiplier effect of exports on aggregate demand and of the effects of net foreign exchange earnings on aggregate supply through relaxing

---

[12] The authors contemplated using the Korea Productivity Center's sample survey results to estimate separate input-output matrices for 1970, which could have been used to give some indication of the possible bias in our estimates. However, differences in levels of aggregation and apparent differences in definitions forced us to give up the attempt. One example may highlight these differences. According to the sample survey, 99.9 percent of the raw materials used to manufacture woolen fabric exports were imported. Just which inputs are considered to be raw materials, as opposed to other components of manufacturing cost, is not stated. (This in itself makes it a largely futile exercise to use the sample survey results in the way contemplated.) Assuming them to be either woolen yarn (42) only or the combined total of raw wool (10), all yarns (40 through 45) and chemical fibers (81), the input-output table for 1970 indicates that 22.0 and 26.6 percent respectively of these inputs used in the woolen fabrics sector (48) are imported. (The preceding numbers in parentheses refer to sector indexes at the 153 level.) The percentages imported are respectively 22.0 and 54.6 percent when indirect input requirements are included. (Again, the sample survey report does not indicate whether imported raw materials include indirect as well as direct inputs, though presumably they do not.) The sample survey estimate deviates so greatly from the input-output estimates, even in view of the fact that the latter are averages over all production that in our judgement the former simply can not be trusted as the basis to adjust the input-output average coefficients. Furthermore, the sample survey report freely admits that excess wastage allowances could not be estimated, so that the imported raw material estimates are biased upwards to an unknown degree.

the foreign exchange constraint.[13] The latter effect must surely have an important dynamic component, since a very high proportion of capital goods are imported. A simulation model is needed to properly assess these effects. Even without this more complete analysis, however, there can be no doubt that exports have contributed greatly to increased employment in South Korea.

REFERENCES

Economic Planning Board, *Annual Report of the Economically Active Population.*
The Bank of Korea, *Economic Statistics Yearbook.*
_____, *Input-Output Analysis of The Korean Economy.*
Watanabe, Susumu, "Exports and Employment: The Case of the Republic of Korea", *International Labor Review,* December, 1972, 495–526.

---

[13] Estimates of the growth of output due directly and indirectly to export growth are given in Westphal and Kim, *op. cit.,* Part 4.

Development of a New Industry through Exports: the Electronics Industry in Korea

*Sang Chul Suh**

I. INTRODUCTION

In a developing country where manufacturing for export is strategically used as the "engine of economic growth", policy decisions on industrial choice for international specialization have a critical impact on the development performance of the country. Industries to be promoted for export purposes must be selected properly if the country is to succeed in attaining modern economic growth through industrialization.[1]

Since developing countries generally lack sufficient capital, technology, and markets, the choice of export industries is often dictated by the availability of these factors from abroad. As a result, the developing countries are tempted to accept any type of foreign investment, often ignoring their long-term comparative advantages. Given the limitations of theoretical models, a case study of one export industry will be helpful in understanding the factors responsible for industrial choice, and the sources of comparative advantages in developing countries.

The primary purpose of this paper is to undertake a case study of an export industry with respect to the process of industrial choice, the sources

* Visiting fellow at the Korea Development Institute and professor of economics at the Korea University.
[1] See Chenery, Chenery & Hughes, Vernon, and Johnson.

of comparative advantage, and the impact of foreign direct investment. The Korean electronics industry is selected for our study because it is one of the most dynamic export-oriented industries that have developed in recent years.

Korean economic growth over the past 10 years was characterized by the strategic role of industrialization and exports. Lacking primary goods for export, the country had little choice but to pursue an outward-looking policy. Accordingly, export manufacturing was placed in the forefront of development strategy, and the electronics industry was actively promoted by public policy. The development strategy of the government plus the inflow of foreign direct investment are largely responsible for the rapid growth of this industry.

In order to place our analysis of Korean electronics in comparative perspective, we shall begin with on overview of the general characteristics of the electronics industry. The aim is to identify major patterns of development common to the advanced and developing countries alike. We shall then proceed to an analysis of the development pattern of electronics in advanced areas such as the United States, Europe and Japan. This will be followed by a detailed study of the current status and future prospects of the Korean electronics industry. Finally, the major characteristics and problems of "Korean type" development will be examined in the content of the developing countries in general.

II.   CHARACTERISTICS OF THE ELECTRONICS INDUSTRY

Let us first examine the general characteristics of the electronics industry from the standpoint of international specialization. The electronics industry produces both final goods and electronic components. The final goods are divided into consumer goods and industrial equipment. The industry was initially identified with consumer goods such as radio receivers, but over the past twenty years it has shown remarkable growth through technological innovations in the production of electronic parts and components (semiconductors in particular). New technologies have expanded the use of electronic products into almost all parts of modern society. The average annual growth of world electronics production during the 1950's was about 15 percent, and 12 percent during the 1960's.[2] The

---

[2] The estimates are based on EIA data which excludes the communist countries.

Table 1

Production of Electronics by Major Countries, 1970

	Rank	Total Production (Million Dollars)	Composition		
			Consumer Products	Industrial Equipment	Parts & Components
U.S.A.	1	28,679	13.7%	68.6%	17.6%
Japan	2	9,074	44.9%	27.7%	27.4%
West Germany	3	3,469	22.9%	51.5%	25.5%
United Kingdom	4	2,212	19.1%	52.8%	28.0%
France	5	2,066	19.8%	55.7%	24.5%

Source: Japan's Yearbook of Electronics Industry: 1973

Table 2

World Exports of Electronics by Major Countries

Unit: Billion Dollars

SITC Code	U.S.A.	Japan	EEC	EFTA
724	678.5	1,726.5	1,603.9	905.2
7262	24.7	9.8	178.9	33.9
7291	39.9	43.9	121.1	87.7
7293	477.4	107.6	553.2	105.0
7297	13.8	—	6.2	1.5
72991	5.4	12.9	49.3	14.3
72995	40.0	48.9	113.5	33.4
8911	220.3	662.0	637.9	264.4
Total	1,500.0	2,610.6	3,264.0	1,445.4

Source: OECD Data

electronics industry today is one of the world's most dynamic industries.

As shown in Table 1, the world's electronic industries are concentrated in a few developed countries. While the United States has long been a principal innovating country, the diffusion of innovation and technology to the other developed countries was rather swift in the electronics industry. World export of electronics products reflects a shifting pattern of comparative advantage from the innovating country to the latecomers among the developed countries. Today, Japan ranks first in the export of electronics products as shown in Table 2. It will be instructive for our

purpose to examine how comparative advantages in electronic products
has shifted between the advanced countries.

While the electronics industry in general is highly research-oriented
and technology-intensive, its production processes are now often separated
into a technology-intensive phase and a labor-intensive phase. For example, in the production of semiconductors, the chemical and testing processes correspond to the technology-intensive phase and the assembly
process to the labor-intensive phase. Since the mid 1960's the multinational
corporations have brought the labor-intensive phase to LDC's where the
labor costs are lower than in the advanced countries. The rapid expansion
of multinational corporations in such LDC's as Korea, Taiwan, Hong
Kong, and Singapore opened up new opportunities for the export of
electronics products. Needless to say, this type of international specialization is quite different from the development pattern of the electronics
industry in advanced countries.

Thus, we now have two distinctive patterns of international specialization in the electronics industry. One is the pattern of shifting comparative
advantage among the developed countries; the other is the pattern which
has prevailed in some LDC's since the mid 1960's. Let us call the first one
an "imitation pattern" to emphasize the process by which latecomers
(Like Japan) caught up with the principal innovating country (the U.S.).
The second pattern may be called the "LDC model" which represents the
common characteristics of LDC export of electronics products.

III. IMITATION PATTERN OF INTERNATIONAL SPECIALIZATION

In order to understand the process of diffusion of new technology from
innovating country to imitating countries, it is important to examine first
the product cycle of electronic products. Since the semiconductor industry constitutes the heart of the electronics industry today, it may be
taken to represent the electronics industry in this respect.[3]

Given a certain level of technology and financial resources, domestic
market conditions tend to stimulate innovations. The United States has
been the principal innovating country largely because the country has a

---

[3] This section draws heavily on Tilton's study of the semiconductor industry.

large government market for military and space programs, where performance is a more important than financial profitability. J. E. Tilton describes the product cycle of semiconductors as follows:

"Typically, a new semiconductor device is expensive, and consequently it is first used in military and other government equipment where performance takes priority over costs. As firms acquire production experience, costs fall. Several years after a device is first used in military equipment, its price is often low enough to permit significant penetration of the industrial market. After several more years, the device is often cheap enough to compete in the consumer market where the performance-cost trade-off is lowest."[4]

In this way, the product cycle of semiconductors is divided into the government market stage, the industrial market stage, and the consumer market stage. The average cost of production falls continuously over the product cycle due largely to the economies of learning (production experience). The declining trends in the average costs of transistors and integrated circuits over time in the U.S. conform to the above product cycle, as shown in Table 3.

We now consider the process of diffusion of a new product or technology from the innovating country to imitating countries, along with the shift of comparative advantage. Tilton again describes the diffusion process of

Table 3

U.S. Trends in the Average Costs of Transistors and Integrated Circuits

Unit: Dollar

	Transistors	Integrated Circuits
1954	3.89	
1956	2.91	
1958	2.40	
1960	2.36	
1962	1.21	
1964	0.83	18.50
1966	0.56	5.05
1968	0.43	2.33
1970	0.38	1.49

Source: U.S. EIA.

---

4 Ibid, pp. 35–36.

emiconductors between the United States and Europe as follows:

"Despite the initial cost disadvantages, European firms will undertake production once sufficient demand arises in their home markets for two reasons. First, in domestic markets trade barriers partly offset the lower cost of American firms. Second, the relative advantage that the latter derives from learning economics tends to diminish as European firms acquire production experience, and at some point this advantage is completely offset by the lower wage rates in Europe. Comparative advantage then shifts to the European firms (unless it has already shifted to firms in another country like Japan with even lower wage rates)."[5]

In the above analysis of the diffusion process, the major sources of comparative advantage appear to include technical resources to imitate new technology, economies due to learning acquired through production experience, and low wage rates. The essence of the imitation pattern may be found in that the condition of low labor cost was strategically used to offset the initially higher cost of new technology in the diffusion process. However, there are certain prerequisites for the success of the imitation pattern. These are shown by the Japanese experience, which we now examine in some detail.

The Japanese electronics industry has a rather long history. In the late 1920's the nation started producing radio sets, and actively promoted the borrowing of technology from the United States during the 1930's. The national demand for electronics products for military use jumped during World War II. In order to meet the war-period demand, the electronics firms had to bring their technology up to date and carried out a rationalization program so that all the small firms became subcontractors to the major producers. In this way, the electronics industry of Japan was able to accumulate sufficient resources and establish a technological base to be used later for the full-scale diffusion process.

During the post-war period Japan had a large domestic market for consumer electronics product arising from rapid income growth and a large population base. Coupled with the technological base built during the war period, the market conditions provided incentives for innovation and diffusion. Development of new products or new designs in electronics also required a domestic market for testing marketability before moving to foreign markets. The government also helped to enlarge the domestic market by restricting foreign imports and by regulating the conditions of foreign investments in the electronics industry.

---

[5] Ibid, pp. 40–41.

The international competitiveness of the Japanese electronics industry was further enhanced by the fact that labor costs were low relative to other advanced countries. The cost advantages in electronics production led Japan to become one of the world's major exporting countries.

In short, the full-scale difussion process required a technological base, a domestic market large enough to provide incentives, and favorable cost conditions. With the imitation pattern of international specialization as our background, we now proceed to the analysis of the Korean electronics industry.

IV. GROWTH AND STRUCTURE OF THE KOREAN ELECTRONICS INDUSTRY

The Korean electronics industry has a rather short history of development. Its beginning may be identified with the domestic production of transistor radios starting in 1958. Export of the radio receivers in 1962 marked the beginning of Korean electronics exports.

During the second half of the 1960's, the multinational corporations began to invest in the Korean electronics industry.[6] These corporations, with the associated technology and marketing facilities, introduced a new opportunity for exports. Since the development strategy of the Government was also to promote industrialization for exports, the electronics industry promised great potential for further growth. The electronics industry was designated by the Government as a "strategic export industry", and the industry was entitled to receive government subsidies to foster development.[7] The Government was active in inducing foreign capital into the electronics field, with a variety of incentives and privileges offered to foreign investors and special privileges offered to the electronics industry.

Thus, from the early years of its development, the Korean electronics industry was promoted as an export industry. The rapid growth of this industry from the late 1960's was largely attributable to the investment of

---

[6] The multinational corporations which invested in Korea during this period include Komy Corp., Fairchild, Motorola, Signetics, Control Data, etc.

[7] The benefits associated with being a "strategic export industry" were largely limited to local producers.

Table 4

Growth of Electronics Industry Production and Exports

Unit: In Million U.S. Dollars

	1965	1966	1967	1968	1969	1970	1971	1972	1973
Electronics Industry									
Production (a)	10.6	21.9	36.8	51.2	79.9	106.2	138.1	195.0	435.0
Exports (b)	1.8	3.6	6.5	19.4	41.9	55.0	88.6	142.0	322.0
Ratio: b/a	17.0%	16.4%	17.7%	37.9%	52.4%	51.8%	64.2%	72.8%	74.0%
Total Exports (c)	175.1	250.3	320.2	455.4	622.5	835.2	1,067.6	1,624.1	3,220.6
Ratio: b/c	1.0%	1.4%	2.0%	4.3%	6.7%	6.6%	8.3%	8.7%	10.0%

Sources: Fine Instruments Center, *Korea Electronics Industry Year Book*, 1972; *The Electronics News*, April 1974, and Bank of Korea, *Monthly Economic Statistics*, April, 1974.

multinational corporations and the export-oriented development policy of the Government. As Table 4 indicates, the share of exports in total e-lectronics production rose rapidly from 17 per cent in 1965 to 74 per cent in 1973. The percentage share of electronics exports in total exports increased from 1 per cent in 1965 to 10 per cent in 1973. In less than 10 years the electronics industry in Korea has developed into a dynamic export industry.

The output composition of the Korean electronics industry is characterized by the large share of electronic parts and components in total production. During the period of rapid growth, the percentage share of parts and components increased steadily, reaching to 62 per cent in 1973. This figure is substantially higher than the corresponding shares in the advanced countries which were below 30 per cent in the countries listed in Table 1.

Being developed as an export industry, the composition of industry output is determined largely by its export composition. As expected, e-lectronic parts and components accounted for about four-fifths of Korean electronics exports as shown in Table 5. The importance of foreign markets in the development of the Korean electronics may be seen once again in Table 6. The share of exports in total production in 1972 was over 80 per cent for electronic parts, 51 per cent for consumer electronics, and 39 per cent for industrial equipment.

The composition of electronic firms by nationality shows the predominance of foreign firms with respect to sales and size of operation (Table 7).

Table 5

Composition of Electronics Industry

	1968	1970	1973
Production			
Consumer Goods	29%	29%	29%
Industrial Equipment	15%	16%	9%
Components	56%	55%	62%
Exports			
Consumer Goods	18%	16%	22%*
Industrial Equipment	1%	1%	1%
Components	81%	83%	77%

Sources: Same as Table 4.
* 1972 data

Table 6

Production and Exports of Electronic Products by Commodity: 1970 & 1972

Unit: In Thousand U.S. Dollars

Selected Items	1970			1972		
	Production (A)	Export (B)	B/A (%)	Production (A)	Export (B)	B/A (%)
(I) Consumer Electronics: Total	30,382	8,973	29.53	55,253	28,207	51.05
Radio Receivers	7,483	5,230	69.89	12,096	9,829	81.26
Car Radios	926	—	—	320	128	40.00
B/W T.V. Receiver	20,471	3,084	15.07	32,997	8,165	24.74
Tape Recorder, Cassette	853	647	75.85	7,410	7,660	103.37
(II) Industrial Equipment: Total	17,470	351	2.01	25,318	9,783	38.64
Transceiver	565	—	—	1,953	457	23.40
Telephone Exchanger	9,842	124	1.26	13,462	1,058	7.86
Desk Top Calculator	—	—	—	2,123	1,894	89.21
Carrier Equipment	555	216	38.92	1,383	109	7.88
Telephone	3,690	—	—	2,546	350	13.75
(III) Parts, Components & Raw Materials: Total	58,484	45,640	78.04	127,034	104,143	81.98
Resistor, Fixed	601	219	36.44	680	539	79.26
Resistor, Variable	712	278	39.04	1,979	1,879	94.95
Capacitor, Fixed	2,542	1,301	51.18	4,431	2,003	45.20
Capacitor, Variable	750	541	72.13	1,594	1,886	118.32
IFT & Coil	1,015	39	3.84	1,969	3,091	156.98
Transistor	12,422	12,909	103.92	26,568	25,824	97.20
I.C.	17,735	17,295	97.52	48,819	38,959	79.80
Memory Plane	2,523	2,347	93.02	8,189	8,202	100.16
Receiving Tube & Cathode Ray Tube	1,664	311	18.69	7,190	751	10.45
Speaker	2,017	345	17.10	4,176	2,420	57.95
Mag. Head	571	1,076	188.44	1,243	3,584	288.33
Dry Battery	3,965	405	10.21	7,135	811	11.37
Diode	772	740	95.85	339	188	55.46

Sources: Fine Instruments Center, *Korea Electronic Industry Data Book*, 1973.

Table 7

Number and Size of Firms by Nationality (1972)

	Local Firms	Joint Ventures	Foreign Firms
Number of Firms	253	27	8
Average Number of Employees	167	411	1,383
Percentage Share of Production	46%	20%	34%
Percentage Share of Exports	28%	18%	54%
Percentage Share of Capital Stock	43%	14%	43%

Sources: Korea Development Bank, *Korean Industry Survey* (in Korean), 1973.

While there were only 8 foreign firms, compared to 253 local firms and 27 joint ventures in 1972, they accounted for 34 per cent of total production and 54 per cent of electronics exports. The size of firm measured by the average number of employees also confirms the predominant position of the foreign firms: the average number of employees per foreign firm was 1,383, compared with only 167 for local firms. It should be noted in Table 7 that the average size of joint-venture firms is not too different from the average size of local firms.

Table 8 lists the ten largest firms with foreign capital (including joint ventures), as measured by sales. They account for over 40 percent of total sales and 59 percent of electronics exports. Nine of the ten firms listed produce electronic parts and components. As for the national origin of foreign capital, Japan and the United States dominated as shown in Table 9. Japan accounted for 65.8 per cent of the total, and the U.S. for 30.7 per cent. While the U.S. investment took place mainly through wholly owned subsidiaries, the Japanese investment was quite active in both subsidiaries and joint ventures.

The export markets for Korean electronics are geographically very concentrated. In 1973, 62 per cent of total exports went to the U.S., 15.6 per cent to Hong Kong, and 13 percent to Japan. This pattern is closely related to the above pattern of foreign direct investment. Many American and Japanese firms established foreign subsidiaries and joint ventures in Korea to cope with the swift rise in wages at home. Accordingly, the products of these subsidiaries and joint ventures were channeled either to their home markets or to their main customers which, in the case of Japanese electronics firms, are in the U.S.

Table 8

Ten Largest Foreign Firms in Korean Electronics Industry (1972)

Name	Sales in 1972 (Million Won)	Percentage Share in Total Sales	Exports (Thousand Dollar)	Percentage Share in Total Exports	Nationality	Type of Products*
Motorola Korea, Ltd	9,348	11.3	23,200	16.3	U.S.A.	P
Signetics Korea Co., Ltd	4,814	5.8	12,011	8.5	U.S.A.	P
Korea Micro System, Inc	4,087	4.9	10,217	7.2	U.S.A.	P
Fairchild Semi Conductors, Ltd (Korea)	4,042	4.9	9,748	6.9	U.S.A.	P
Sam Sung-Sanyo Electronic Co., Ltd.	4,023	4.8	9,955	7.0	Japan	P
Control Data, Korea, Inc	3,152	3.8	7,896	5.6	U.S.A.	P
Applied Magnetics Co., Ltd	1,496	1.8	3,233	2.3	U.S.A.	P
Crown Radio Corp.	1,201	1.5	3,002	2.1	Japan	C
Toshiba Korea Co, Ltd	1,195	1.4	2,894	2.0	Japan	P
Gold-Star Alps Electronic Co, Ltd	962	1.2	1,555	1.1	Japan	P
Sub Total	34,320	41.3	83,711	59.0		
Other Firms	48,722	58.7	58,289	41.0		
Total	83,042	100.0	142,000	100.0		

* C . . . . . Consumer Products. P . . . . . Parts and Components.

Sources: Fine Instruments Center, *Korea Electronics Industry Data Book*, 1973.

Table 9

Foreign Direct Investment in Korean Electronics (1973)

Unit: In Thousand U.S. Dollars

	Foreign Subsidiaries	Joint Ventures	Total
U.S.	26,895	5,020	31,915 (30.7%)
Japan	35,521	32,948	68,469 (65.8%)
Others	839	2,856	3,695 (3.5%)

Source: Korea Fine Instruments Center.

Table 10

Five Largest Local Firms (1972)

	Sales (Million Won)	Number of Employee	Exports ($1,000)	Main Product*
Gold Star Co.	7,805	3,410	6,349	C
Gold Star Tele-Electric Co.	3,650	1,683	1,048	I
Tai Han Electric Wire Co.	2,973	3,450	3,871	C
Ho Nam Electric Co.	2,276	1,962	697	C
Dong Nam Electric Co.	2,174	822	1,388	C
Percent of Total for Local Frms	48%		40%	

Sources: Korea Development Bank, *Industry Survey*, 1973 and FIC, *Buyers Guide: Korea Electronics Product*, 1973.

    * C. . . . . . Consumer electronics products.

     I. . . . . . Industrial equipments.

In response to the public policy of promoting electronics the number of local firms increased from 115 in 1968 to 253 in 1972. However, most of the local firms tend to be extremely small-scale operations. Let us consider first the five largest local firms listed in Table 10. They accounted for about 48 per cent of total production, and 40 per cent of exports, by all local firms in 1972. This means that the remaining 248 local firms shared 51 per cent of the total product produced by local firms. It is quite evident that the impact of the public policy was largely limited to small-scale operations. Unlike the ten largest foreign firms, the giant local firms primarily produce consumer electronic products.

The main characteristics of the Korean electronics industry may now be summarized. The industry consists of a few large firms and a large number of small-scale local firms and joint-ventures. However, the rapid development of the industry as an exporter must be attributed mainly to the former group. Among the large firms, the multinational corporations, with international capital, technology, and market facilities, are mainly responsible for the booming exports of Korean electronics.

V. KOREAN ELECTRONICS IN COMPARATIVE PERSPECTIVE

Let us now evaluate the characteristics of the Korean electronics industry in light of our discussion of the imitation pattern of international specialization and the experiences of other Asian countries. The imitation pattern involved a nation's borrowing technology from, and imitating the new products of, other countries. Also, domestic market conditions provided incentives for technological diffusion. However, if a country lacks these prerequisites as in many developing nations in Asia, we simply cannot expect the imitative pattern to work. In this case, we must find a substitute appropriate to the developing countries.

Indeed, foreign direct investment in many Asian countries have substituted for domestic firms in the development of the electronics industry. For example, new technologies were brought in by foreign subsidiaries through their special access to the know-how of the innovating countries. This development is quite evident in the Asian countries which have made substantial progress in exporting the electronics products. These countries are Taiwan, Hong Kong, Singapore, and Korea, listed in order of the export value as shown in Table 11. Taiwan ranked higher than Korea in terms of export value, but the share of foreign capital in total electronics investment was also higher. (See Table 12.)

In these countries, the prime force behind the export expansion of electronics products was provided by the multinational corporations. Since these corporations brought with them the capital, technology, production experience, and market facilities, the only remaining source of comparative advantage was labor cost. The most attractive feature of Korea for foreign investors was the abundant supply of relatively skilled workers with low

Table 11

Major Exports of Electronics by Asian Countries (1972)

Unit: In Million U.S. Dollars

	Korea	Taiwan	Hong Kong	Singapore
Radio	9.9	83.6	163.0	31.3
B-W T.V.	8.2	140.2	12.5	8.4
Color T.V.	—	33.7	—	—
Tape Recorder	7.6	7.4	3.4	14.2
Calculator	1.9	32.7	3.7	4.8
Transistor	25.8	15.9	48.8	46.3
I. C.	39.4	25.0	23.7	72.4
Others	49.3	160.1	46.0	106.9
Total	142.1	498.6	301.1	284.3

Sources: *Korea Electronics Industry Data Book*, 1973 and *Electronics*, August 1973.

Table 12

Capital and Employment by Type of Investment (1973)

	Korea			Taiwan		
	Number of Firms	Investment ($1,000)	Persons Employed	Number of Firms	Investment ($1,000)	Persons Employed
Domestic Firms	202	48,947	44,006	254	31,424	28,993
Joint Ventures	42	19,183	22,558	57	52,972	19,093
Foreign Subsidiaries	12	26,112	19,221	54	47,558	50,473

Sources: Korea Electronic Industries Association, *Electronics Industry,* September, 1974.

wage rates and high productivity.[8] Furthermore, until recently the increase in wage rates lagged far behind the labor productivity increase, as shown in Table 13.

---

[8] A top manager of the leading multinational corporation privately admitted that the average productivity of the Korean workers is about 20–25 per cent higher than similar workers in the U.S. But, the wage rate in Korea is less than one-tenth the U.S. rate.

Table 13

*Labor Productivity and Wage Level in the Korean
Electronics Industry**

Unit: In Thousand Won

		1969	1970	1971	1972
a)	Value Added Per Worker (annual)	275	517	685	572
b)	Wage Per Worker (annual)	149	233	274	294
c)	Ratio: b/a	54.2%	45.1%	40.0%	51.4%
d)	Ratio of Value Added to Total Capital	31.0%	33.0%	30.0%	32.9%

Source: Bank of Korea, *Financial Statements Analysis.*
*Samples taken from radio, T.V. and communication apparatus producers.

Table 14

Supply of Raw Material (1972)

	Value (Million Won)		Percentage Share	
	Domestic Production	Imports	Domestic Supply	Imports
Local Firms	15,698	14,620	52%	48%
Joint Venture	2,688	8,904	23%	77%
Foreign Firms	—	16,208	—	100%

Source: Korea Development Bank, *Korean Industry Survey,* 1973.

As pointed out already, comparative advantage in the electronics industry shifted among the advanced countries over the product cycle, stemming from a combination of technological diffusion, economics of learning and low wages. When multinational corporations move to LDCs, however, low wages are exploited as the only source of comparative advantage. This is so because the multinational corporations are merely setting up a base in low-wage countries to supply markets in developed countries. Typically, they bring semi-finished products for assembly in the labor-intensive segment of the production process. Data in Table 14 confirms this effect by showing the foreign firms importing almost all the raw materials needed in 1972. In this way, the foreign firms maintain a mini-

Table 15

Number of Inventions and New Devices in the Electronics Industry: Korea and Japan

	Korea			Japan		
	Innovations	New Devices	Total	Innovations	New Devices	Total
1968	2	8	10	1,371	1,944	2,415
1969	6	5	11	2,739	1,899	4,638
1970	13	9	22	3,052	1,642	4,694
1971	10	30	40	2,804	2,043	4,847
Total	31	52	83	9,966	6,628	16,594

Source: KIST Data.

mum of interindustry relations with local firms. The local producers of finished electronic products often import electronic parts and components instead of using similar products made by foreign firms in Korea.[9] When the already developed technologies are brought in for predetermined markets, there is unlikely to be any incentive for technological innovation. Compared to Japan, which went through the imitation pattern of industrialization, the conspicuous lack of such innovations and new devices in the Korean electronics industry bears testimony to the serious shortcomings of the LDC model (See Table 15).[10]

The relationship between the product cycle and the shift of comparative advantage among nations becomes meaningless to those countries where the international specialization of electronics is based only on labor cost advantages. If electronics firms in advanced countries secure low-wage advantages by moving a part of their production process to an LDC, they will be able to maintain the comparative advantages which might otherwise be offset by the higher wage rates. Herein lies the major shortcoming of the development pattern characterizing the electronics industries in many developing countries, including Korea.

Needless to say, the development of the electronics industry has made

---

[9] In the consumer electronics industry, technology inducement contracts with foreign firms often precludes the use of parts other than the brand of the foreign firms.

[10] We are fully aware that the different levels of science and technology between the two countries will produce different rate of innovation & new devices. Yet, the differences seem too large to be explained by the different level of development alone.

a significant contribution to the over-all growth of the economy and to the development of Korean electronic firms. However, this pattern is not likely to accomplish a full-scale diffusion of modern technology. Yet, the diffusion process is essential if a country is to catch up with the advanced countries. If the past Korean pattern of development is allowed to persist into the future, there is a real danger that the Korean electronics industry may develop into a permanent satellite of a few advanced countries under the disguise of the international division of labor. In the extreme case, the Korean pattern of international specialization may suddenly be discontinued when the country no longer commands low-wage advantages.

In spite of the weakness inherent in the "Korean type" development, the official growth targets of the Korean electronics industry for 1980 seem to imply the pursuit of the same old growth pattern. The plan seems to lack a definite strategy designed to facilitate the diffusion process while maintaining comparative advantage. Table 16 summarizes the growth targets for 1980. It is said that the Japanese experience was taken as a model in setting up these targets. The exports of $2.5 billion (one-fourth of the total Korean exports in 1980) will be achieved mainly through the rapid expansion of consumer electronics as was the case in Japan around 1972. It is argued that Japan had comparative advantages in the production of consumer goods due to low wages. With the increasing labor costs expected in Japan, their comparative advantage in this field will shift to Korea. However, what is overlooked in this type of argument is the process and economies of learning as sources of comparative advantage. By the time Japan attained $2.5 billion exports in the electronics, it had developed the scientific and technological capacity to innovate and pioneer as shown in Table 15. The target-oriented approaches to planning for Korean electronics are not adequate to remedy the shortcomings of the past development pattern. Goals and strategies should be designed to fully utilize comparative advantage and, at the same time, to secure the full-scale technological diffusion effects of a modern electronics industry.

VI. SUMMARY AND POLICY IMPLICATIONS

In this paper we pointed out the two distinctive patterns of development in the electronics industry. The developed countries show a shifting pattern of comparative advantage over the product cycle. Initially, the in-

Table 16

Growth Targets of the Korean Electronics Industry

	1974		1976		1980	
	Value	Composition	Value	Composition	Value	Composition
1. Production (Million Won)	258,104	100.0%	553,708	100.0%	1,770,574	100.0%
Consumer Products	96,268	37.3%	232,997	42.1%	959,720	54.2%
Industrial Products	28,941	11.2%	54,409	9.8%	198,352	11.2%
Components and Parts	132,895	51.5%	266,302	48.1%	612,502	34.6%
2. Exports (Million Dollars)	431		837		2,506	

Source: FIC Data.

novating country exports the new product. Then, the latecomers quickly imitate the new product (or technology) as long as domestic demand warrants it. Along with the technological diffusion, the comparative advantages shift from the innovating country to the latecomers as the latter gain production experience and benefit from lower wage rates. The prerequisites for this pattern of development are a scientific and technological base for as imitating the new technology and a large enough domestic market to justify the diffusion process.

When we turn to developing countries such as Korea, these prerequisites are absent. During the 1960's, the multinational corporations opened up a new opportunity for the developing countries to export electronic products. However, this pattern of specialization tended to exploit only the labor cost advantages without the full-scale diffusion of innovation and technology. If the aim of developing the electronics industry is eventually to catch up with the more advanced countries, the "Korean type" of development should be modified by public policy to build up the technological base for diffusion while still exploiting labor cost advantages. Herein lies the significant role of public policy to foster the modern electronics industry.

It would be presumptuous to suggest any specific policy recommendations based on this study alone. What we propose to do, therefore, is to outline the broad policy consideration which might be elaborated on by a team of electronic engineers and economic planners.

The "Korean type" of international specialization should be modified by shifting emphasis from export expansion to the establishment of a technological base and improved market conditions. The first requirement for technological diffusion is a technology base. The government should take specific measures to encourage the expansion and accumulation of this base. Specifically, the scale of production must be enlarged to realize cost advantages. A rationalization program must be carried out in order to facilitate the specialization of small producers centered around the major producers. This would allow them to benefit from the economics of learning and from technical diffusion from major producers to small producers. The government should also maintain the competitive market structure most conducive to imitating new technology from the more advanced countries.

In building up the technology base for a full-scale diffusion process in later years, the most important element is the training of skilled workers. According to the manpower projections of the government, skilled workers in the electronics industry must increase from 40 thousand in 1972 to

370 thousand in 1980 in order to achieve $2.5 billion in exports. Thus, the training of skilled workers should command top priority, both in public investment and in the regulation of foreign direct investment.

The technological diffusion process also requires marketing activities. As pointed out already, marketing activities are important not only for selling new products, but also for gathering necessary information for innovation and developing new technology. The diffusion process takes place only when the market conditions justify. Of special importance in this connection is the role of the domestic market. The adaptation of new techniques to production often require a domestic market where the products are tested commercially before competing with foreign producers. For example, when Japan exported $2.5 billion of electronics products, the export market accounted for only 25 per cent of total domestic production. However, Korean exports will be over 60 per cent of domestic production when the exports reach $2.5 billion in the 1980's. Marketing activities, especially in the domestic market, should be reexamined to improve the development of Korean electronics.

REFERENCES

Chenery, H. B., "Comparative Advantage and Development Policy" in *Surveys of Economic Theory: Vol. II* (New York: St. Martin's, 1965).

Chenery, H. B. and Hughes, H., *The International Division of Labor: The Case of Industry,* IBRD, Staff Working Paper No. 123 (1972).

Johnson, H. G., *Comparative Cost and Commercial Policy Theory for a Developing World Economy* (Stockholm: Almqvist and Wiksell, 1968).

Tilton, J. E., *International Diffusion of Technology: The Case of Semiconductors* (Brookings Institute, 1971).

Vernon, R., "International Investment and International Trade in the Product Cycle", *Quarterly Journal of Economics* (May 1966).

Exports and Productivity Trends of the Korean Manufacturing Industries

*Chuk Kyo Kim**

I. INTRODUCTION

One of the most significant features of the economic growth of Korea since 1961 has been an extremely rapid expansion in exports. During the period 1961–72, Korea's exports, as shown in Table 1, rose at an average annual rate of 38.8 percent, far exceeding the growth rates of GNP (8.6 percent) and of manufacturing production (16.7 percent). particularly notable was the sharp increase in merchandise exports which grew at the rate of 62.4 percent per annum during the same period. As exports grew rapidly, the commodity composition of exports also changed very drastically. The share of manufactured goods, for example, which comprised only 22 percent of total exports in 1961, accounted for almost 90 percent of total exports in 1972.

Numerous factors are responsible for this unusual expansion in exports, although the high growth rate was to some extent attributable to an initially low level of exports in the early sixties. As far as policy measures responsible for this unusual expansion in both output and exports are concerned, one cannot fail to indicate the outward-looking strategies which characterized the basic policy lines of the Korean government during the sixties.[1]

---

*Senior fellow at the Korea Development Institute.
[1] See Balassa (1971).

Table 1

Growth Rates of GNP, Manufacturing, and Exports

Unit: In Percentage Changes[1]

| Year | GNP | Manu-facturing | Exports | | | | |
			Total	Manu-factured goods	Share (%)	Others	Share (%)
1961	4.9	3.1	24.5	51.4	22.0	18.6	78.0
1962	3.1	13.2	34.1	64.6	27.0	25.5	73.0
1963	8.8	17.3	58.4	203.2	51.7	4.8	48.3
1964	8.6	6.5	37.2	36.9	51.6	37.5	48.4
1965	6.1	20.0	47.1	77.6	62.3	14.6	37.7
1966	12.4	17.1	43.0	43.2	62.4	42.6	37.6
1967	7.8	22.8	27.9	43.7	70.1	1.7	29.9
1968	12.6	27.0	42.2	56.8	77.3	8.0	22.7
1969	15.0	21.4	36.7	39.7	79.0	26.5	21.0
1970	7.9	18.4	34.2	42.0	83.6	4.8	16.4
1971	9.2	17.7	27.8	34.0	87.0	-2.3	13.0
1972	7.0	15.7	52.1	55.8	89.0	27.9	11.0
1961–66	7.3	12.9	40.7	79.5	46.2	23.9	53.8
1967–72	9.9	20.5	36.8	45.3	81.0	11.1	19.0
1961–72	8.6	16.7	38.8	62.4	63.6	17.5	36.4

Sources: Bank of Korea, *Economic Statistics Year book,* 1973.
[1]In 1970 constant market prices except exports.

The present paper is intended (1) to examine the growth performance of individual export industries by means of total factor productivity analysis, (2) to make productivity comparisons among export, import-substitution, and domestic sectors, and (3) to investigate the possible implications of our observations in terms of efficiency of resource allocation.

The scope of the study and the method of productivity measurement is outlined in Section II. The statistical findings on total factor productivities of export industries are given in Section III and productivity trends are examined in connection with the export performance of individual industries. Section IV deals with the relationship between factor prices, factor intensity, and productivity growth. Productivity comparisons among export, import-substitution, and domestic sectors are made in the next section. Finally, Section VI tries to draw some policy implications for future export promotion.

II. SCOPE AND METHOD OF PRODUCTIVITY MEASUREMENT

(1) Scope of Study

Using the Korean Standard Industrial Classification (KSIC), we have classified whole manufacturing industries at the 4-digit level into three categories; export, import substitution, and domestic industries. The classification of whole manufacturing industries into three different categories is a fairly arbitrary one; there is no ideal way of defining export and import substitution industries, since most of the Korean manufacturing industries are exporting some of their products while importing raw materials and intermediate goods either for their exports or for domestic production. Therefore, we simply used the ratio of exports as well as imports to total production as criteria of classification. Export industries are defined as those manufacturing industries whose average export ratio exceeds 10 percent, while import substitution industries defined as those industries showing an average import ratio higher than 30 percent.[2] All other industries are classified as domestic industries.

Since the Report on *Mining and Manufacturing Census and Surveys* in successive years is available only from 1966 through 1972, we confine our study to the period 1966–72.

(2) Method of Productivity Measurement

Total factor productivity suggested by John W. Kendrick has the general form of

$$\frac{V}{\alpha L + (1 - \alpha)K}. \tag{1}$$

V is value added in constant prices, L is labor input, K is capital input, and α is labor share of income. On the basis of equation (1), we may construct the total factor productivity index for an individual industry as

---

[2] We apply an import ratio which is higher than the export ratio because in Korea most industries are initially import substitution industries which are transformed into either export or domestic industries. Accordingly, the application of an import ratio as low as the export ratio might lead to an exaggeration of import substitution industries.

follows:

$$T_{t/oij} = \frac{V_{ij,t}/V_{ij,o}}{\alpha_{ij,o}\dfrac{L_{ij,t}}{L_{ij,o}} + (1-\alpha)_{ij,o}\dfrac{K_{ij,t}}{K_{ij,o}}} \tag{2}$$

where $T_{t/oij}$ is the total factor productivity index for the jth 4-digit industry in the ith 2-digit industry and subscript o denotes the base year.

Since all inputs are weighted by their base year prices, the total factor productivity index measures the change in output per combined factor input changes between two periods, had the prices of factors of production in the base year prevailed. In other words, it measures efficiency change in the use of resources, reflecting the "Residual".[3]

All inputs are supposed to represent services of individual factors which are directly utilized in production. Labor input should be measured in terms of man-hours and capital input in terms of capital services which take into account the degree of capacity utilization. Unfortunately, no data is available for man-hours in the *Report of Manufacturing Census*. Hence, we have simply used average number of employees as labor input. As far as capital input is concerned, we have calculated capacity utilization ratio by means of peak-to-peak method,[4] and this was used to estimate capital input.

Equation (2) is in principle appropriate to measure the total factor productivity of an individual, homogeneous industry. For the economy as a whole or an industry at an aggregate level, labor and capital in different industries should be weighted by their respective prices, because the productivities of labor and capital are different in different industries. The

---

[3] The numerical result of "Residual" measured by the total factor productivity index does not differ much from the one measured by a Cobb-Douglas production function. It differs only in that the former combines changes in output, labor, and capital multiplicatively, whereas the latter used the additive combination of three factors, namely, $R = \dot{V}/V - \alpha\dot{L}/L - (1-\alpha)\dot{K}/K$, where R is the resiudual. Because of this difference, the total factor productivity index tends to underestimate the Residual as compared with the Cobb-Douglas production function. The difference is, however, negligible for the short period. Total factor productivity of the Kendrick type seems in general preferable to a Cobb-Douglas function, since the former does not necessarily assume an elasticity of substitution of one and constant returns to scale as the latter does. See, Riese, Brown, Domar.

[4] Capacity utilization ratio is obtained when we divide the actual output by capacity output. I am indebted to Dr. Y.H. Kim at KDI for suggesting and providing capacity output figures for manufacturing industries.

weighted total productivity index for the ith 2-digit level industry can be expressed as

$$
T_{t/oi}^{*} = \frac{\dfrac{\sum V_{ij,t}}{\sum V_{ij,o}}}{\alpha_{i,o} \dfrac{\sum m_{ij,o} L_{ij,t}}{\sum m_{ij,o} L_{ij,o}} + (1 - \alpha)_{i,o} \dfrac{\sum n_{ij,o} K_{ij,t}}{\sum n_{ij,o} K_{ij,o}}} \tag{3}
$$

where mij, o is the real labor compensation per employee in the jth 4-digit industry in the ith 2-digit industry in the base year and nij, o is the base year rate of return on capital[5] in the jth 4-digit industry in the ith 2-digit industry. Since labor and capital in different industries are weighted by their prices in the base year, the weighted productivity index measures the efficiency change in production within the individual industries. In other words, productivity changes due to the structural changes are eliminated in the weighted total productivity index.

(3) Statistical Data

The data used in the present study are all taken from the *Report on Mining and Manufacturing Census and Surveys* from 1966 through 1972. The basic data we need, such as output, value-added, tangible fixed assets, number of employees, employees' remuneration, etc., are all given in the Report, and are classified by KSIC 2–digit and 4–digit levels. As far as tangible fixed assets are concerned, the data are available only for 1966 and 1968. The capital stock figures for the remaining years are estimated by means of the bench-mark year method as follows:

$$
K_{t+1} = K_t + I_{t+1} - D_{t+1},
$$

where

    K_t = Fixed tangible assets excluding land in year t;
    I_{t+1} = Investment in tangible fixed assets excluding land in year t + 1;
    D_{t+1} = Disposal of tangible fixed assets excluding land in year t + 1.

The estimated capital stocks based on the 1966 benchmark year do not, however, coincide with the one based on the 1968 benchmark year. In general the former rises faster than the latter. In view of the relatively small yearly fluctuations at the industrial level, the capital stock series

---

[5] Rate of return on capital is defined as (V−W)/K where V, W, and K denote value added in constant prices, real labor compensation and real capital stock, respectively.

based on the 1968 benchmark year seem much more preferable for productivity analysis. Therefore, the 1968 capital stock series are used in the
measurement of total factor productivity. Since information on depreciation is available only for one year (1968), no attempt is made to measure
net capital stock. Hence, capital stock is on gross terms. It may be true
that new industries have less depreciation than old industries, and this
might create a bias when the capital stock is estimated in gross terms. But
this may be not so important, given Korea's rapid growth. Capital stock
in current prices is deflated by using a GNP deflator for fixed capital
formation in manufacturing sector. We have constructed a price index for
each industry at the 4–digit level, and this is used to deflate value added in
individual industries.

III. EXPORTS AND PRODUCTIVITY GROWTH

Table 2 shows the average annual percentage changes of output (value
added), exports and total factor productivity of export industries during
the period 1966–72. We have shown only the productivity changes using
the 1968 capital input series. For the convenience of the discussion, however, figures are given only at 2–digit industrial level.

We find that exports grew much faster than output in the export industries, implying that an increasing portion of output has been exported
between 1966 and 1972. Exports grew at an average annual rate of 38.0
percent[6] as against the 27.2 percent growth rate of output (value added).

In spite of this rapid expansion of both output and exports, the productivity growth of the export industries as a whole was relatively low as compared with import substitution and domestic industries.[7] The unweighted
total factor productivity showed an average annual growth rate of 6.9
percent[8] between 1966 and 1972, suggesting that about 25 percent of out-

---

[6]Exports are in current dollar prices and not deflated because unit value index of exports has been very stable between 1966 and 1972.

[7] Import substitution and domestic industries show the growth rates of 8.8 % and 12.
5 % in the case of unweighted total factor productivity and 0.5 % and 7.9 % in the case
of weighted total factor productivity. See Table 8 in page 140.

[8] The productivity increase of 6.9 % per annum is a high growth rate in international
comparison. In the United States, the total factor productivity of manufacturing sector
rose at an average annual rate of 2.5 % during 1948–66 and it was 3.6 % in West Germany during 1951–6? and 7.1 % in Japan between 1953 and 1965. See Kendrick, Willy
and Yoshihara.

Table 2

*Growth Rates of Output, Exports, and Total Factor Productivity
of Export Industries, 1966–72*[1]

Unit: Percent

Industrial Group	Output	Exports	Total Factor Productivity	
			Unweighted	Weighted
Food	20.8	11.8	5.3	6.8
Textiles	26.0	39.3	12.4	10.9
Footwear & wearing apparel	25.4	48.7	–0.3	–1.9
Wood products	41.0	34.2	7.8	7.7
Leather products	51.9	80.4	29.1	29.1
Rubber products	26.5	52.3	7.0	1.9
Clay, glass & stone products	46.1	217.6	23.2	21.9
Basic metal industries	24.9	57.7	3.0	3.0
Metal products	24.4	28.7	13.0	9.7
Machinery	4.2	73.4	–7.6	–8.0
Electrical machinery, & appliances	70.4	49.7	29.8	28.2
Other manufacturing industries	26.3	79.1	3.4	18.3
Total export industries	27.2	38.0	6.9	5.2

[1] Growth rates are simple arithmetic annual averages.

put growth can be explained by productivity increase.

The weighted total factor productivity growth is, as expected, somewhat lower than the unweighted, indicating 5.2 percent per annum between 1966 and 1972.[9] Since the weighted total factor productivity excludes productivity changes due to inter-industry resources shift in export sector, a small growth differential between weighted and unweighted total factor productivity implies that the major portion of productivity gains in export sector is attributable to increase in efficiency within individual export industries, so that structural changes in export sector account for only small

[9] The total factor productivity based on the 1966 capital stock series shows much less growth rates, indicating 4.7% in the case of unweighted and −0.6% in the case of weighted total factor productivity.

portion of productivity growth. As shown in Table 2, there is little growth differentials between weighted and unweighted total factor productivity except rubber products and other manufacturing industries.

Although the productivity gains of export sector as a whole was not significant as compared with its output and exports performance, there are a number of industries indicating a remarkable productivity growth between 1966 and 1972. (See Table 2). These industries are textiles (10.9 %), leather products (29.1%), clay and stone products (21.9%), metal products (9.7%), electrical machinery and apparatus (28.2%) and other manufacturing (19.3%).[10]

Particularly notable in this connection is the fact that in these industries the productivity growth accounts for almost 50 percent of output growth, indicating a substantial efficiency improvement of these industries, and it seems that this has certainly contributed to strengthen the international competitiveness of these export industries. Therefore, we may contend that exports are closely associated with productivity improvement or vice versa, as far as these industries are concerned.

All other industries, on the other hand, show either a low or negative productivity growth, even though exports expanded very rapidly between 1966 and 1972. The relatively low productivity growth is observed in such industries as basic metal industries (3%), rubber products (1.9%), food manufacturing (6.8%) and wood products (7.7%). Footwear and made-up textile goods, and machinery indicate a negative productivity growth implying that factor cost has increased faster than output growth. The low or negative productivity growth associated with high export growth seems to suggest that in many of these industries productivity changes did not play any important role in the export performance. Although the observation period is too short to reach any conclusion regarding the relationship between exports and productivity trends, it seems that in major export industries productivity gain did play an important role in export performance.

---

[10] The rapid productivity growth of these labor intensive industries seems, to some extent, due to underestimate of labor input, since labor input is measured in terms of number of employees rather than man-hours. Multiple shifts have been common practice in many export industries, especially during the booming period of later sixties. Therefore, if the labor input were measured in terms of man-hours, the productivity growth would have been much less than presented in Table. 2 The rapid rise in wages relative to the price of capital stock, as will be shown later, might also have led to more intensive use of the labor input, resulting in a higher productivity growth in the labor intensive industries than otherwise.

IV. FACTOR PRICES, FACTOR INTENSITY, AND PRODUCTIVITY GROWTH

(1) Relative Factor Prices and Factor Intensity

In this Section, we shall attempt to investigate the impact of factor price changes on factor intensity and productivity growth. Table 3 shows changes in factor prices and capital intensity of export industries during the period 1966–72. Factor prices are defined as a ratio of current-price factor compensation to real factor input, as suggested by J. W. Kendrick.

As shown in Table 3, the price of labor has almost tripled between 1966 and 1972, while the price of capital (fixed capital stock) increased by only 86.5 percent during the same period. Since the price of labor rose faster than that of capital, there should have been factor substitution in favor of capital.[11] This is confirmed by our empirical finding on the change in

Table 3

Changes in Factor Prices and Factor Intensity in Export Sector

Year	Price of Labor[1]	Price of Capital[2]	Capital Intensity
1966	100.0	100.0	100.0
1967	125.8 (25.8)	127.6 (27.6)	91.0 (–9.0)
1968	161.0 (28.0)	119.2 (–6.6)	106.0 (16.5)
1969	195.1 (21.2)	127.1 (6.6)	127.0 (19.8)
1970	234.5 (20.2)	137.7 (8.3)	152.0 (19.7)
1971	279.1 (19.0)	154.6 (12.3)	175.0 (15.1)
1972	307.0 (10.0)	186.5 (20.6)	172.0 (–1.7)
Average Rate of Changes, 1966–72	20.7%	11.6%	10.1%

[1] Current price labor compensation divided by average number of employees.

[2] Current price capital compensation divided by real capital stock. Current price capital compensation is obtained when we subtract current price labor compensation from value added in current price.

*Figures in parenthesis are rates of percentage changes.

---

[11]In view of the situation in Korea where labor is relatively redundant in relation to capital, one may wonder why the price of labor rose much faster than that of capital. The increasing demand for labor, particularly the demand for skilled and semi-skilled labor, which accompanied rapid growth, seems to have resulted in a relatively rapid rise in the labor price. The imperfect labor market might also have contributed to the rapid

Table 4

Factor Intensity and Productivity Growth, 1966–72

Unit: In Percentage Changes

Industrial Group	Capital-Labor Ratio	Total Factor Productivity (unweighted)	Labor Productivity	Capital Productivity
Food	8.4	5.3	8.8	5.0
Textiles	8.2	12.4	17.4	10.2
Footwear & wearing apparel	19.3	–0.3	6.9	–1.7
Wood products	17.5	7.8	20.1	4.9
Leather products	–0.5	29.1	17.6	35.8
Rubber products	24.2	7.0	18.0	3.3
Clay, glass, & stone products	21.0	23.2	14.5	31.2
Basic metal industries	72.9	3.0	8.1	4.6
Metal products	2.8	13.0	9.8	16.3
Machinery	31.5	–7.6	9.0	–11.9
Electrical machinery, & appliances	–1.7	29.8	24.5	42.2
Other manufacturing industries	50.1	3.4	8.2	3.1
Total exports industries	10.1	6.9	14.6	4.8

capital intensity. As shown in Table 3, the capital-labor ratio of the export sector as a whole rose by 72.1 percent between 1966 and 1972. A relatively rapid increase in the price of labor in relation to the price of capital and a resultant increase in capital intensity are found in all export industries except leather products and electrical machinery and apparatus in which a decline in capital intensity is observed (See Table 4).

---

increase in the price of labor relative to that of capital. The other reason seems to be easy access to relatively cheap foreign capital which has been the major source of financing during this period. The massive inflow of foreign capital has resulted in capital deepening, since imported technology is likely to be more cpaital intensive than the existing one. The preferential interest rate for loans for export industry may also have contributed to the capital deepening process. See Shim, et. al.

(2) Factor Intensity and Productivity Growth

We shall now investigate the relationship between factor intensity and productivity growth. As Table 4 exhibits, the capital intensity of the export sectors rose at an average annual rate of 10.1 percent during the period 1966–72, while labor and capital productivity during the same period grew at average annual rates of 14.6 and 3.8 percent, respectively. In general, the growth rate of labor productivity is higher, while that of capital productivity is lower, than total factor productivity growth in most export industries.

Looking at the industrial level, we find considerable variation in the changes in capital intensity among different industries. Heavy industries such as basic metal industries and machinery show a sharp increase in capital intensity, whereas such light consumer goods industries as food manufacturing, textiles, leather products, and electrical machinery and apparatus indicate either a small or negative increase in the capital-labor ratio.

In this connection, it is interesting to observe that industries with a relatively low increase in capital intensity tend to be associated with a relatively high total productivity gorwth. This seems partly due to the fact that because of a relatively high share of capital income, as will be shown later, the relatively rapid increase in capital input relative to labor input led to a much greater increase in the total factor inputs, and this resulted in the relative downward trend in total productivity growth. In other words, total productivity growth is strongly affected by the movements of capital input rather than that of labor input because of the high weight of capital input.

On the other hand, the growth of labor productivity is very high in almost all export industries. It is interesting to find that the growth of labor productivity is not so highly associated with the growth of capital intensity. In other words, industries showing rapid growth of labor productivity indicates relatively lower growth of capital intensity, and vice versa. This can be interpreted to suggest that the Korean export industries have been economizing on labor rather than capital. The trends of capital productivity seems to support this reasoning. As Table 4 indicates, the growth of capital productivity is much lower than that of labor productivity except in several industries in which capital intensity shows either a very low or negative growth rate.

(3) Factor Shares of Income

We shall now examine how the productivity gains of export industries which we have so far discussed are distributed among the owners of factors of production. We can easily identify changes in factor shares of income, once we know the factor prices and the factor productivities. Factor shares will remain constant if the real price of each factor rises in proportion to the increase in the corresponding partial factor productivity. For example, if the price of labor, i.e., labor compensation per employee rises in proportion to labor productivity, the labor share of income will remain unchanged, since employees receive exactly so much as they contributed to the increase in output. But if the price of labor rises less than its productivity increase, then the labor share of income will decrease, while the capital share of income will increase.

As shwon in Table 5, the real price of labor (real labor compensation per employee) rose slightly less than labor productivity (real output per employee) in export sector during the period 1966–72. This implies that the labor share of income in export sector would have slightly decreased during the same period. The slightly downward trend of labor share is confirmed by our estimate.[12] In Table 5, we have shown two series of

Table 5

Labor Productivity, Real Price of Labor and
Labor Share of Income in Export Sector

	Labor Productivity	Real Price of Labor	Ratio of Labor Share to	
			Value Added	Net Factor Cost[1]
1966	100.0	100.0	34.6%	39.7%
1967	107.9	113.8	36.5%	42.3%
1968	124.8	138.6	38.6%	45.7%
1969	145.6	163.7	38.9%	46.1%
1970	172.7	197.4	37.2%	44.3%
1971	208.4	212.2	35.4%	41.9%
1972	225.1	208.9	32.5%	38.7%

[1] Data on depreciation and indirect taxes are not available in the Report on Manufacturing Census. Therefore, the net factor cost is indirectly estimated by using the ratio of NNP at factor cost to GNP.

---

[12] The labor share of income is estimated in the following way. The labor compen-

labor share; the first one is the ratio of labor share to gross value added, while the second one is the ratio of labor share to value added net of depreciation and indirect taxes. In both series, we find that the share of labor income is slightly lower in 1972 than in 1966, although it has been increasing up to 1969 and then slightly falling thereafter.

The falling labor share of income[13] in export sector in 1972 seems to be largely affected by the movement of labor share in textile industries which play a dominant role in terms of both output and labor compensation in export sector. (See Table 6). It is, however, noted that except several other industries such as wood and rubber products, the falling labor share of income is not observed between 1966 and 1972. On the contrary, most export industries demonstrate a steadily rising trend of labor share, implying rising unit labor cost during this period.

We have further estimated the labor share of income for import substitution, domestic and total manufacturing industries. (See Table 7). The import substitution sector indicates a slightly upward trend of labor share while the labor share in domestic sector has slightly decreased between 1966 and 1972. On the other hand, the total labor share of income in manufacturing industries as a whole has remained fairly stable between 1966 and 1972. It remained almost constant at the level of 29 percent in 1966 and 1972, although it indicates a slightly rising trend until 1970. In all sectors, labor share has been rising up to 1970 and then falling thereafter.

---

sation for employees is given in the Manufacturing Census. The labor compensation for an unpaid family worker or a proprietor is imputed on the assumption that these people are paid the average compensation per employee. This may not be very realistic. But in view of the fact that the productivity of an unpaid family worker is likely to be lower while that of a proprietor higher than the average productivity of employee, our estimate seems to provide a good approximation. The sum of employee compensation and the imputed compensation for unpaid family workers and proprietors gives total labor compensation. The ratio of total labor compensation to value added gives labor share of income.

[13] The slightly falling labor share of income implies that the elasticity of substitution between capital and labor is not unitary. In order to test this, we have calculated the elasticity of substitution as follows:

$$\delta = \frac{G_K - G_L}{G_W - G_\pi} = \frac{22.3 - 11.4}{20.7 - 11.6} = 1.197$$

G_π and G_L indicate growth rates of capital and labor while G_W and G_π growth rates of real prices of labor and capital, respectively.

Table 6

Labor Share of Income In Export Industries

Unit: Percent

Industrial Group	1966	1967	1968	1969	1970	1971	1972
Food	29.6	37.3	32.6	32.1	33.0	46.4	31.4
Textiles	36.4	35.5	48.4	38.1	37.7	36.9	33.0
Footwear & wearing apparel	34.8	35.8	37.9	44.7	42.6	37.4	36.5
Wood products	29.5	32.3	24.6	43.1	34.3	22.9	19.4
Leather products	25.8	39.2	28.3	44.4	46.1	30.7	36.7
Rubber products	46.7	41.9	38.9	38.9	38.7	39.5	37.6
Clay, glass & stone products	17.7	36.0	45.9	45.2	44.9	44.3	32.3
Basic metal industries	16.9	42.1	35.6	26.4	29.3	22.3	28.5
Metal products	34.4	49.8	39.4	66.6	52.2	53.3	49.5
Machinery	28.4	39.6	46.3	35.4	41.8	39.7	43.0
Electrical machinery & appliances	30.8	41.2	38.8	29.4	28.2	32.9	32.1
Other manufacturing industries	27.8	45.2	46.3	47.5	41.4	50.1	38.6
Total exports industries	34.6	36.5	38.6	38.9	37.2	35.4	32.5

Table 7

Labor Share of Income[1] in Export, Import Substitution and Domestic Sectors

Unit: Percent

	Export Sector	Import Substitution Sector	Domestic Sector	Total Manufacturing
1966	39.7	30.6	25.7	29.5
1967	42.3	37.3	30.6	34.6
1968	45.7	35.2	25.7	31.2
1969	46.1	34.2	27.4	32.5
1970	44.3	36.8	27.6	32.8
1971	41.9	33.4	24.2	29.7
1972	38.7	31.4	24.5	29.1

[1] Ratio of labor compensation to value added net of depreciation and indirect taxes.

V. INTER-SECTORAL PRODUCTIVITY COMPARISON

We shall now turn to a comparison of productivity among export, import substitution and domestic sectors during the period 1966–72. (See Table 8).

In the case of unweighted productivity, we find that the growth rate of total factor productivity is much lower in the export sector than in the import substitution and the domestic sectors. The highest productivity growth is observed in the domestic sector, showing an average annual growth rate of 12.5 percent between 1966 and 1972. Relatively rapid productivity gains (8.8%) are also registered in the import substitution sector, while the export sector, as already indicated, shows a growth rate of 6.9 percent between 1966 and 1972.

In this connection, it is interesting to note that output growth of the domestic as well as the import substitution sectors is lower than that of export sector, showing average annual growth rates of 24.6 percent and 26.6 percent, respectively. In other words, this implies that in these two sectors productivity increase has played a more important role in output growth than in the export sector: productivity increase accounts for 50 percent of output growth in the domestic sector and 33 percent in the im-

Table 8

Total Factor Productivity Index for Export, Import Substitution, and Domestic Sectors

	Export Sector			Import Substitution Sector			Domestic Sector		
	Output	P¹	wp²	Output	P¹	wp²	Output	P¹	wp²
1966	100.0	100.0	100.0	100.0	100.0	100.0	100.0	100.0	100.0
1967	125.9	115.5	104.4	125.6	111.3	107.1	104.1	102.0	90.2
1968	158.4	123.1	108.5	186.1	144.7	123.4	157.5	142.7	119.8
1969	210.6	126.2	114.7	268.3	188.9	150.7	217.7	162.6	132.9
1970	279.2	130.9	117.8	320.6	203.6	159.3	253.8	178.8	135.3
1971	323.5	134.3	127.5	310.9	179.9	120.7	302.5	185.5	134.3
1972	420.8	147.5	135.4	389.3	152.7	93.0	357.6	195.5	150.5
Average Rate of Changes(%)	27.2	6.9	5.2	26.6	8.8	0.5	24.6	12.5	7.9

¹ Unweighted total factor productivity.
² Weighted total factor productivity.

port substitution sector, while it accounts for about 25 percent of output growth in the export sector.

The productivity trends of the three sectors change substantially when we look at weighted total factor productivity. The domestic and export sectors show a higher productivity growth than the import substitution sector. Even in this case, the domestic sector shows the highest productivity growth of 7.9 percent per annum. Import substitution sector shows, on the other hand, no significant productivity gains: the annual average rate of change is only 0.5%. This is due to the fact that the import substitution sector has undergone rapid structural changes, whereas in the export sector no such structural changes took place between 1966 and 1972. In other words, the productivity gains of 8.8% in the import substitution sector are to a large extent attributable to the shift of resources from low to high productivity industries, while in the domestic as well as export sectors the productivity gains are to a large extent due to an increase in efficiency within the individual industries.

As shown in Table 9, the lower productivity gorwth in export industries is observed in most industries except the major export industries such as wood and leather products, clay and stone products, and electrical machinery and apparatus. In the case of textiles, a leading export industry in Korea, we find a very small differential in productivity growth between export and domestic industries. Therefore, we may conclude that the productivity gains of the major export industries were higher than that of the industries oriented toward the domestic market.

As far as productivity comparisons between the import substitution and domestic industries are concerned, we find that in a given 2 digit industry the domestic industries show a higher productivity growth than the import substitution industries except in the case of metal products, transport equipment and electrical machinery and apparatus. The higher productivity growth of the domestic sectors seems largely attributable to substantial productivity gains in such industries as tobacco manufacture (18.5%), rubber products (16.2%), chemical products (18.5%), glass and stone products (20.3%), and other manufacturing (30.9%).[14]

---

[14] The reason why these industries show such a high productivity growth seems to some extent attributable to underestimate of labor input which is measured in terms of number of employees rather than man-hours as already noted. Therefore, the actual productivity growth would be much less than indicated, implying a lower productivity growth of the domestic sector as a whole than obesrved in Table 8.

Table 9.

Growth Rate of Total Factor Productivity by Industries in Export,
Import Substitution, and Domestic Sectors

Unit: In Percentage Changes

Industrial Group	Export Sector		Import Substitution Sector		Domestic Sector	
	p^1	wp^2	p^1	wp^2	p^1	wp^2
Food	5.3	6.8	13.9	13.9	15.6	13.1
Beverage	—	—	—	—	9.4	10.9
Tobacco	—	—	—	—	18.5	18.5
Textiles	12.4	10.9	—	—	13.7	15.4
Footwear & wearing apparel	−0.3	−1.9	—	—	—	—
Wood & cork	7.8	7.7	—	—	7.0	7.0
Furniture & fixtures	—	—	—	—	13.8	13.5
Paper & paper products	—	—	—	—	3.7	1.1
Printing & publishing	—	—	—	—	5.6	1.8
Leather & leather products	29.1	29.1	—	—	9.6	6.5
Rubber products	7.0	1.9	—	—	16.2	14.1
Chemicals & chemical products	—	—	18.9	17.2	18.5	12.9
Petroleum & coal products	—	—	—	—	4.6	10.5
Clay, glass & stone products	23.2	21.9	4.6	4.6	20.3	20.7
Basic metal industries	3.1	3.0	−4.4	−6.9	−1.3	−1.9
Metal products	13.0	9.7	19.8	19.8	8.3	5.6
Machinery	−7.6	−8.0	3.4	3.8	11.1	11.6
Electrical machinery & appliances	29.8	28.2	21.3	18.6	20.6	6.3
Transport equipment	—	—	9.7	8.9	7.5	8.7
Other manufacturing industries	3.4	18.3	26.6	26.6	30.9	28.5
Total	6.9	5.2	8.8	0.5	12.5	7.9

[1] Unweighted total factor productivity.
[2] Weighted total factor productivity.

VI. CONCLUDING REMARKS

We have demonstrated that the productivity growth of export industries as a whole was quite low when compared with their output and export performance. This is due to the fact that the export sector did not undergo rapid structural change as did the import substitution sector, so that the productivity growth in the export sector is to a large extent attributable to an increase in efficiency within the individual industries. Looking at the individual industries, poor productivity gains are observed in such industries as footwear and made-up textiles, food manufacturing, rubber and basic metal products, and machinery.

The reason why these export industries show a low productivity growth seems to be that they are mostly small in scale and are equiped with traditional technologies, which are not likely to allow any substantial productivity improvement. Furthermore, a variety of direct and indirect subsidies extended to export industries should have, to some extent, distorted investment decision, resulting in inefficient management and excessive investment in these industries. A particularly rapid increase in capital intensity in these industries seems to reflect this phenomenon.

On the other hand, the major export industries such as textiles, wood and leather products, clay and stone products, and electrical machinery and apparatus show a remarkable productivity increase explaining almost 50 percent of their output growth, although there are slight deviations in some of these industries. The economies of scale and modern technology with which these industries are equiped seem to be the major sources of productivity growth in these industries. Since the major export industries are mostly labor intensive, it seems that at the moment comparative advantage works for Korea's labor intensive industries, with the implication that a Heckscher-Ohlin type of factor intensity theroem is quite tenable.

As far as inter-sectoral productivity comparisons among the export, import substitution and domestic sectors are concerned, we find that the domestic sector shows the highest productivity gorwth. This seems largely due to an increased efficiency stemming from competition, economies of scale, and better management.

However, it is noted that even in this case a number of export industries such as wood and leather products, clay and stone products, and electrical machinery and apparatus show a higher productivity growth than the same industries oriented toward the domestic market. This seems to suggest that as far as these industries are concerned, the outward-looking strategy of the government policy was successful in terms of efficiency of resource allocation.

REFERENCES

B. Balassa, "Industrial Policies in Taiwan and Korea," *Welt-wirtschaftliches Archiv,* Band 106, Heft 1 1971.

Murry Brown, *On the Theory and Measurement of Technological Change,* Cambridge University Press, 1968.

E. V. Domar, "On Total Productivity and All That," *American Economic Review,* December 1962.

John W. Kendrick, *Productivity Trends in the United States,* Princeton University Press, Princeton 1961.

John W. Kendrick, *Postwar Productivity Trends in the United States,* 1948–1969, NBER, 1973.

H. Riese, *Struckturprobleme des wirtschaftlichen Wachstums,* Basel 1959.

H. David Willey, "Growth Patterns and Export Performance: Britain and Germany," in P. Kenen and R. Lawrence, eds., *The Open Economy: Essays on International Trade and Finance,* Columbia University Press, 1968.

K. Yoshihara, "Productivity Change in the Manufacturing Sector, 1906–65", in Kazushi Okkawa and Yuziro Hayami, eds., *Economic Growth: The Japanese Experience since the Meiji Era,* The Japan Economic Research Center, Tokyo 1973.

B. K. Shim, et al., *A Study of Preferential Interest Rate Structure: The Korean Experience* (1963–71), Seoul 1972.

Market Penetration by Asia's Super Exporters

David C. Cole[*]

I. INTRODUCTION

Korea, Taiwan and Hong Kong are three Asian countries which have pursued export-oriented development strategies over the past decade. The rate of growth of exports from these countries has been remarkable as has the resulting growth of their incomes and living standards. Before these countries had demonstrated that it was possible, there had been considerable skepticism about the potential for expanding exports from less developed countries. The raw material exporters had experienced slow growth of demand and declining prices for their products. Manufactured goods were expected to flow from the developed to the developing countries, not the reverse, and Japan had already re-established its dominance as the main Asian exporter of manufactures. The objective of this paper is to see how Korea, Taiwan and Hong Kong managed to push their way into the world markets for manufactured exports, looking particulary at the kinds of commodities that they exported, the major countries to which those exports flowed and the extent to which they took over the markets of other exporting countries, especially the more developed countries.

This study covers the period from 1962 to 1972, the latest year for which comprehensive statistics were available. Preliminary statistics for 1973 in-

---

[*] Associate director, Institute for International Development and lecturer on economics, Harvard University.

dicate a sharp break from the pattern of the preceding decade, largely as a consequence of the realignment of exchange rates, particularly between the Yen and the dollar, that took place in 1972. Thus this study may have more historical value than as an indicator of future trends. Even so it helps to understand the first phase of export expansion during which the Yen was undervalued which had the effect of making export expansion that much more difficult for the three countries which we are studying.

II. EXPORT GROWTH

For the decade from 1962–72, exports increased at an average annual rate of about 40 per cent for Korea, 30 per cent for Taiwan and 15 per cent for Hong Kong. The rate o increase is inversley related to the initial base in that both Hong Kong and Taiwan had substantial exports at the beginning of the decade while Korea's export level was very low. As shown in Table 1, Korea's exports rose from 5 per cent of GNP in 1962, to 21 per cent by 1972, while the ratio in Taiwan went from 13 per cent to 40 per cent.

Comparable ratios for Hong Kong in the 1960's are not readily available, but in 1972 Hong Kong's export ratio (excluding reexports) was 66 per cent. An alternative measure is in terms of the U.S. dollar value of exports per capita which shows that Hong Kong with the smaller population has a significantly higher ratio over the past decade.

Table 1
Ratio of Goods and Services Exports to GNP

	1962	1967	1972	1973
Korea	5.2%	11.4%	21.1%	31.8%
Taiwan	13.1%	21.9%	44.8%	51.6%
Hong Kong			66.0% est.	

Source: Korea and Taiwan estimates based on GNP and export figures from *IFS* (*International Financial Statistics*, IMF).
Note: Hong Kong estimate based on GNP and export-excluding reexport-figures from *Hong Kong '73 Focus*.

Table 2.

U.S. Dollar Value of Goods Exports per Capita

	Exports (Millions of US$)		Population (Millions)		Exports per Capita (US$)	
	1962	1972	1962	1972	1962	1972
Korea	55	1,629	26.1	32.4	2.1	50.3
Taiwan	218	2,908	11.3	15.1	19.2	192.0
Hong Kong	580	2,800	3.3	4.1	176.0	682.0

Source: Export figures for Korea and Taiwan are from *Direction of Trade*, IMF. Exports figure for Hong Kong is from *Commodity Trade Statistics*, UN. Population figures are from *IFS*.

Note: Hong Kong figures exclude reexports.

III. MAJOR MARKETS

Two countries, the U.S. and Japan, have been the major markets for exports from Korea and Taiwan, and the U.S. also has accounted for about 35 per cent of Hong Kong's exports in recent years. In the early 1960's Japan was the more important market for both Korea and Taiwan, but by the early 1970's the U.S. market was nearly twice as big as the Japanese market for Korea and three times as big for Taiwan. In 1973, however, the substantial devaluation of the won relative to the yen raised the Japanese share of Korea's exports above U.S. share for the first time in nearly a decade. The Japanese market has not been very significant for Hong Kong throughout this period.

Viewed from the other perspective of their importance as suppliers of imports to the U.S. and Japan, it is clear that these three countries still account for a relatively small share of total imports. By 1972 only 6 per cent of U.S. imports and 4 per cent of Japanese imports came from Korea, Taiwan and Hong Kong. All three had increased their shares in the U.S. market, but only Korea had achieved a significant increase in its share of the Japanese market, i.e. from 0.5 per cent in 1962 to 1.8 per cent in 1972. Taiwan's share of the Japanese market oscillated around 1.5 per cent and the Hong Kong share was less than 0.5 per cent.

During this period Japan had a high growth rate of GNP (averaging 10 per cent in real terms), and a marginal propensity to import of .09. The

Table 3.

Share of Total Commodity Exports Going to the U.S. and Japan from Korea, Taiwan and Hong Kong

	From Korea to			From Taiwan to			From Hong Kong to		
	U.S.	Japan	Both	U.S.	Japan	Both	U.S.	Japan	Both
1962	21.9	42.8	64.7	24.4	23.9	48.3	20.7	5.0	25.7
1963	28.0	28.6	56.6	16.3	31.7	47.9	20.3	6.1	26.4
1964	29.9	32.0	61.9	18.7	30.9	49.6	22.0	5.5	27.5
1965	35.2	25.1	60.4	22.0	31.1	53.1	27.6	6.0	33.6
1966	38.3	26.5	64.8	22.3	24.4	46.6	28.3	5.8	34.1
1967	42.9	26.5	69.4	24.5	17.5	42.0	29.9	5.7	35.7
1968	51.7	21.9	73.2	35.5	15.8	51.3	34.3	5.5	39.8
1969	50.7	21.4	72.1	38.0	15.0	53.0	35.1	6.5	41.6
1970	47.3	28.1	75.4	39.7	15.1	54.8	42.0	4.0	46.0
1971	49.8	24.5	74.4	43.4	12.3	55.7	35.0	6.6	41.6
1972	46.8	25.2	71.9	43.9	13.0	56.9	33.5	6.8	40.2
1973	31.4	38.6	70.0						

Source: 1973 figures for Korea are from the Bank of Korea. All others are based on IMF trade statistics.

Table 4.

Shares of Korea, Taiwan and Hong Kong in Total Imports of the U.S. and Japan

	Share of U.S. Imports from				Share of Japanese Imports from			
	Korea	Taiwan	H.K.	Total	Korea	Taiwan	H.K.	Total
1962	0.06	0.3	1.0	1.36	0.5	1.1	0.3	1.9
1963	0.1	0.3	1.1	1.5	0.4	1.8	0.4	2.6
1964	0.2	0.4	1.3	1.9	0.5	1.8	0.4	2.7
1965	0.3	0.4	1.6	2.3	0.5	1.9	0.4	2.8
1966	0.3	0.5	1.6	2.4	0.8	1.6	0.5	2.9
1967	0.4	0.6	1.9	2.9	0.8	1.2	0.5	2.5
1968	0.6	0.8	1.9	3.3	0.8	1.2	0.4	2.4
1969	0.8	1.1	2.3	4.2	0.9	1.2	0.5	2.6
1970	0.9	1.4	2.4	4.7	1.3	1.2	0.5	3.0
1971	1.1	1.8	2.2	5.1	1.4	1.5	0.5	3.4
1972	1.3	2.3	2.3	5.9	1.8	1.8	0.5	4.1

Source: International Monetary Fund, *Direction of Trade.*

U.S. had both a much lower growth rate (3.5 per cent) and lower import propensity of .075. For the decade 1962–72 Japanese imports increased from $5.6 billion to $23.5 billion in current prices, or roughly 4 fold, while U.S. imports went from $16.5 billion to $58.8 billion, or 3.6 times. Achieving increasing shares of two such rapidly growing markets contributed significantly to the success of the export–oriented strategies of Korea, Taiwan and Hong Kong.

IV. MAJOR EXPORTS

The ten major exports of the three countries in 1971 or 1972 are listed in Table 5. Textiles and clothing are high on the lists of all three countries, as are electronic or electrical appliances. Plywood and footwear were important for both Korea and Taiwan, while Taiwan and Hong Kong lists both include toys and plastic articles. Only Taiwan had several agricultural items among its top ten exports.

V. SUPPLYING EXPANDING MARKETS

One way of assessing the market potential of these major exports is in terms of the relative rates of increase of demand in the main buying countries. We have calculated ratios of rates of increase in imports in terms of both GNP and total imports of the U.S. and Japan for all of the items on the lists of major exports from Korea, Taiwan and Hong Kong. The results are shown in Tables 6 and 7.[1] Of the major export items from Korea, Taiwan and Hong Kong, only bleached cotton cloth had a low growth of demand in the U.S., while raw sugar was the only such item in Japan.

The impression gained from these measures is that the major exports from the three countries are items for which import demand in the importing countries is clearly growing relative to income and relative to total imports, so these should continue to be rapidly expanding markets. We have not attempted to determine whether these high import propensities

---

[1] The ratio of the rate of increase of total imports to the increase of GNP for the U.S. was 1.6 between 1962–64 and 1969–71. For Japan it was 0.94.

Table 5.

Main Exports of Korea, Hong Kong and Taiwan

Unit: In Thousand U.S. Dollars

	SITC	Korea 1971	
1.	8414	Clothes and Accessories	132,921
2.	8411	Textile Clothes not Knit	129,135
3.	6312	Plywood	126,823
4.	899	Other Manufactured Goods	73,088
5.	7293	Transistors and Tubes	48,472
6.	2613	Raw Silk not Thrown	39,273
7.	8510	Footwear	37,217
8.	8412	Textile Clothing Acsry non Knit	36,205
9.	6521	Grey Woven Cotton Fabric	20,716
10.	0311	Fish, Fresh, Chilled or Frozen	20,016
		Hong Kong 1972	
1.	8411	Textile Clothes not Knit	552,699
2.	8414	Clothing Acsry Knit	454,522
3.	8942	Toys, Indoor Games	248,995
4.	7242	Radio Broadcast Receivers	174,196
5.	899	Other Manufactured Goods	168,336
6.	6521	Grey Woven Cotton Fabric	80,034
7.	7299	Oth. Electrical Machinery	73,218
8.	8930	Articles of Plastic Nes	63,583
9.	7293	Transistor, Valves etc.	58,060
10.	6522	Woven Cotton Blchd. etc.	57,101
		Taiwan 1971	
1.	8412	Textile Clothing Acsry non Knit	371,614
2.	7249	Telecommunication Equip.	223,553
3.	8930	Articles of Plastic Nes	109,044
4.	6312	Plywood	95,261
5.	0548	Edible Veg. Nes Fresh, Dry	62,277
6.	0611	Raw Beet and Cane Sugar	61,511
7.	6521	Grey Woven Cotton Fabric	59,149
8.	8510	Footwear	50,055
9.	6535	Woven Synthetic Fabric	43,984
10.	8942	Toys, Indoor Games	42,448

Source: United Nations, *Commodity Trade Statistics:* 1971 & 1972, and The Statistical Department Inspectorate General of Customs, Taipei, Republic of China, *The Trade of China,* 1971.

Table 6.

Ratio of Rates of Increase for Selected United States Imports Relative to Rates of Increase of GNP and Total Imports (1962–1964 *to* 1969–1971)

SITC		Ratio to GNP	Ratio to Total Imports
0311	Fish Fresh, Chilled, Frozen	1.60	1.01
0548	Edible Veg. Nes Fresh, Dry	1.22	0.77
0611[1]	Raw Beet and Cane Sugar	2.84	1.80
2613	Silk not Thrown	2.15	1.36
6312	Plywood	1.47	0.93
6521	Grey Woven Cotton Fabric	1.18	0.75
6522	Woven Cotton Blchd etc	0.67	0.43
6535	Woven Synthetic Fabrics	3.32	2.10
7242	Radio Broadcast Receivers	2.33	1.47
7249[2]	Telecommunication Equip	2.62	1.66
7293	Transistors, Valves. etc	3.00	1.90
7299	Oth. Electrical Machinery	1.78	1.13
8411	Textile Clothes not Knit	2.11	1.33
8412	Textile Clothing Acsry non Knit	1.13	0.72
8414	Clothing Accessorys Knit	2.31	1.46
8510	Footwear	2.56	1.62
8930	Articles of Plastic Nes	3.06	1.94
8942	Toys Indoors Games	1.85	1.17
899	Other Manufactured Goods	1.79	1.13

Source: Total import figures are from *Direction of Trade*, IMF; GNP figures are from *IFS*; and other figures are from *Commodity Trade Statistics*, UN.

[1] 1964–66 to 1969–71.
[2] 1963–65 to 1969–71.

reflect high income elasticities of demand for the commodities, or whether the imports are taking the place of domestic production, because of the difficulty of matching the import classification with production statistics.

VI. INCREASING MARKET SHARES

In addition to exporting commodities which faced high demand growth from the main importing countries, Korea, Taiwan and Hong Kong have

Table 7.

Ratios of Rates of Increase for Selected Japanese Imports Relative to Rates of Increase of GNP and Total Imports (1962–64 to 1969–71)

SITC		Ratio to GNP	Ratio to Total Imports
0311	Fish Fresh, Chilled, Frozen	1.59	1.69
0313[1]	Shell Fish, Fresh, Frozen	1.43	1.52
0513	Bananas, Plantains, Fresh	1.23	1.30
0548	Edible Veg. Nes Fresh, Dry	1.26	1.33
0611	Raw Beet and Cane Sugar	0.37	0.39
2432	Lumber Shaped Conifer	1.14	1.21
2613	Raw Silk not Thrown	2.06	2.19
6312[2]	Plywood	2.01	2.13
6521[1]	Grey Woven Cotton Fabric	1.84	1.95
6522	Woven Cotton Blchd etc.	1.73	1.83
6535	Woven Synthetic Fabric	1.50	1.59
7242	Radio Broadcast Receiver	1.20	1.28
7249	Telecomm Equipment Nes	0.90	0.95
7293	Transistors, Valves etc.	1.82	1.93
7299	Other Electrical Machinery	1.16	1.23
8411[1]	Textile Clothes not Knit	1.74	1.84
8412	Textile Clothing Acsry, Non Knit	1.62	1.72
8414	Clothing Acsry Knit	1.81	1.92
8510	Footwear	1.73	1.83
8930	Articles of Plastic Nes	1.17	1.24
8942	Toys, Indoor Games	1.80	1.91

Source: Total import figures are from *Direction of Trade,* IMF; GNP figures are from *IFS;* and other figures are from *Commodity Trade Statistics,* UN.

[1] 1963–65 to 1969–71
[2] 1964–65 to 1969–71

also succeeded in increasing their share of the import market for many of these commodities. The annexed tables and charts cover eleven major commodities[2] entering the U.S. market and show the shares of that market captured by the three countries being studied, plus Japan and selected other major supplying countries during the past decade.

Plywood is an example of a commodity where the new industrial export-

[2] The coverage is limited to those commodities for which total imports exceeded $100 million in 1971.

ing countries of Asia- in this case Korea and Taiwan, have taken away much of the old exporter's, i.e. Japan's market. The combined shares of Korea and Taiwan have risen from 13 per cent in 1962 to nearly 60 per cent in 1971, while Japan's share has dropped from 53 per cent to 21 per cent. The same pattern is found in toys, where Hong Kong and Taiwan have taken over much of Japan's share;transistors and clothing where all three have moved in on Japan. In the case of knitted goods, plastics, and other manufactures the three new exporters have increased their shares of the U.S. market substantially but Japan's share has declined to only a limited degree. Japan has managed to hold a dominant position in radio receivers and other electrical machinery and has even increased its share of telecommunications equipment.

In the Japanese market there has been increasing competition among the suppliers of food imports and raw materials. Taiwan has taken over the dominant position from Korea in the rapidly-expanding market for frozen fish. Ecuador, in recent years, has supplanted Taiwan as the main supplier of bananas. Cuba and Ryuku have taken away the sugar market from Taiwan. On the other hand Hong Kong, Korea and Taiwan have become the major suppliers of knit accessories.

The market for unthrown silk shows a more complex pattern. Japan was the dominant supplier of the U.S. in the early 1960's using silk from domestic sources. Korea and Italy were taking over that market by the mid-1960's but U.S. demand was switching to synthetic fibers and by 1970 U.S. imports of unthrown silk had practically stopped. Japan on the other hand became a net importer in the mid-1960's and its total imports by 1971 reached $80 million. Mainland China supplied 45 per cent of that market and Korea 38 per cent.

The main conclusions that one can draw from this analysis are that the new exporters have been very successful at penetrating and taking over the export markets and part of the domestic markets of the old exporters. They have found their best markets in the developed countries and in the area of manufactured goods.

The old guideline for import-substitution in developing countries was to look over the country's list of major imports to see what might be produced domestically. The new guidelines for the export-oriented developing countries should be to look at what the more developed countries are exporting to each other in the way of manufactured goods to find items for which the demand is income elastic, the technology is relatively labor intensive and capable of being mastered by the developing country.

David C. Cole

Appendix 1.

U.S. Imports and Major Market Shares

Unit: Thousand U.S. Dollars & Percent

	Total	from Japan	from Taiwan	from Korea	from Hong Kong
		Plywood (SITC 6312)			
1962	100,638	53.3%	10.0%	2.5%	
1963	108,900	51.0%	10.0%	5.1%	
1964	123,238	41.2%	15.6%	7.6%	
1965	124,909	40.5%	15.1%	11.7%	
1966	150,340	37.0%	14.4%	16.8%	
1967	142.397	33.3%	13.6%	21.1%	
1968	217,956	33.0%	15.7%	24.5%	
1969	250,548	27.7%	15.9%	29.0%	
1970	209,304	24.0%	17.5%	35.4%	
1971	262.035	20.5%	21.5%	37.0%	
		Toys, Indoors Games (SITC 8942)			
1963	73,597	68.8%	0.1%		12.7%
1964	88,196	62.2%	0.3%		17.0%
1965	96,178	54.3%	0.5%		21.8%
1966	106,341	50.9%	0.6%		23.1%
1967	125,244	45.2%	1.1%		24.8%
1968	169,766	38.7%	2.2%		26.0%
1969	205.801	35.6%	2.9%		28.3%
1970	248.201	33.8%	5.2%		31.7%
1971	253,325	28.9%	8.5%		34.7%
		Transistors, Valves, etc. (SITC 7923)			
1962	26,355	42.2%	—	—	
1963	31,065	44.1%	—	—	
1964	34,354	38.5%	—	—	0.5%
1965	63,246	39.1%	—	—	5.4%
1966	101,983	34.4%	0.3%	—	14.3%
1967	101,271	29.3%	2.8%	—	18.7%
1968	140,607	19.7%	5.2%	0.8%	18.0%
1969	174,460	18.8%	5.4%	4.8%	14.6%
1970	223,596	13.8%	5.0%	9.0%	18.3%
1971	259,160	12.7%	6.5%	10.5%	16.2%
				12.0%	12.5%

Appendix 1. *(Continued)*

Unit: Thousand U.S. Dollars & Percent

	Total	from Japan	from Taiwan	from Korea	from Hong Kong
Clothing or Textile (SITC 8411)					
1962	160,567	35.3%	3.7%	0.3%	27.7%
1963	159,482	34.4%	3.4%	2.2%	27.4%
1964	187,997	35.2%	4.0%	1.6%	29.6%
1965	214,194	35.3%	3.8%	3.8%	27.4%
1966	238,805	36.0%	3.7%	3.0%	27.0%
1967	262,620	33.8%	4.6%	3.3%	28.7%
1968	345,330	31.9%	5.3%	5.8%	29.1%
1969	467,305	29.4%	6.4%	7.4%	27.1%
1970	566,785	26.6%	7.9%	10.1%	26.7%
1971	629,938	21.8%	10.0%	12.9%	28.2%
Footwear (SITC 8510)					
1962	133,995	43.0%	—	—	0.3%
1963	129,269	37.2%	0.2%	0.5%	1.7%
1964	141,436	35.6%	0.4%	0.5%	—
1965	159,932	32.5%	0.9%	2.3%	—
1966	189,906	25.7%	2.0%	2.5%	—
1967	263,220	23.4%	2.9%	2.6%	—
1968	388,135	20.6%	4.0%	2.5%	—
1969	488,172	17.3%	4.4%	1.6%	—
1970	629,402	14.6%	6.3%	2.0%	—
1971	757,914	12.5%	8.7%	3.5%	—
Clothing Accessory Knit (SITC 8414)					
1962	115,901	17.0%	0.9%	—	11.5%
1963	147,491	12.4%	0.4%	0.2%	10.2%
1964	166,458	12.1%	0.6%	0.1%	13.8%
1965	221,530	14.9%	1.3%	1.1%	23.0%
1966	255,750	19.8%	2.0%	2.4%	22.1%
1967	270,832	15.2%	4.5%	6.8%	24.1%
1968	365,799	11.4%	7.9%	10.9%	25.2%
1969	449,593	13.4%	11.8%	12.7%	23.9%
1970	489,590	12.8%	19.2%	11.4%	20.8%
1971	682,420	13.2%	26.4%	13.5%	20.8%

156 *David C. Cole*

Appendix 1. *(Continued)*

Unit: Thousand U.S. Dollars & Percent

	Total	from Japan	from Taiwan	from Korea	from Hong Kong
Telecommunication Equipment (SITC 7249)					
1962	—	—	—		—
1963	65,485	21.3%	—		0.4%
1964	73,246	32.2%	—		0.8%
1965	105,265	38.1%	1.2%		4.1%
1966	178,770	39.7%	3.3%		5.2%
1967	167,913	33.8%	3.7%		7.6%
1968	213,700	34.0%	4.7%		5.8%
1969	295,767	42.2%	4.2%		3.3%
1970	308,620	39.6%	6.6%		2.2%
1971	405,428	42.4%	6.6%		2.2%
Radio Broadcast Receivers (SITC 7242)					
1962	129,630	71.2%	—	—	0.3%
1963	120,252	74.5%	0.4%	—	3.1%
1964	111,915	75.7%	1.0%	0.2%	6.4%
1965	148,953	74.2%	1.7%	0.8%	9.1%
1966	191,103	70.7%	2.5%	0.6%	12.6%
1967	242,865	68.0%	4.3%	0.5%	8.8%
1968	320,753	67.6%	5.0%	0.6%	10.1%
1969	412,554	68.2%	6.0%	1.2%	12.8%
1970	479,225	68.6%	6.9%	0.8%	12.3%
1971	498,208	65.5%	6.8%	0.8%	14.3%
Other Electrical Machinery (SITC 7299)					
1962	76,974	9.0%	—	—	0.4%
1963	64,474	11.2%	—	—	1.2%
1964	41,153	26.7%	—	—	3.2%
1965	56,856	32.0%	—	—	4.2%
1966	85,713	36.5%	0.2%	—	9.4%
1967	111,993	32.8%	1.4%	—	11.3%
1968	131,797	30.5%	3.5%	1.4%	13.7%
1969	154,141	27.6%	5.8%	2.6%	14.2%
1970	159,018	25.4%	4.9%	1.2%	15.6%
1971	165,680	27.7%	6.2%	1.3%	12.7%

Appendix 1. *(Continued)*

Unit: Thousand U.S. Dollars & Percent

	Total	from Japan	from Taiwan	from Korea	from Hong Kong
		Articles of Plastic Nes. (SITC 8930)			
1962	6,885	23.0%	—	—	8.6%
1963	21,073	47.6%	1.3%	—	7.6%
1964	57,611	53.1%	4.7%	2.0%	7.3%
1965	71,051	49.2%	5.8%	0.4%	12.6%
1966	80,871	39.5%	6.0%	0.2%	15.4%
1967	94,639	38.2%	8.4%	0.3%	16.4%
1968	144,851	32.9%	8.0%	0.5%	25.3%
1969	201,462	27.1%	8.5%	0.6%	32.7%
1970	236,161	24.0%	8.2%	0.8%	32.9%
1971	213,251	27.7%	11.5%	0.8%	18.1%
		Other Manufactured Goods (SITC 899)			
1962	99,245	26.9%	0.2%	—	29.7%
1963	101,611	25.5%	0.2%	0.2%	32.2%
1964	121,115	22.8%	0.4%	0.4%	37.4%
1965	147,156	21.7%	0.7%	1.7%	38.5%
1966	155,601	21.3%	0.6%	7.4%	31.9%
1967	199,102	19.7%	1.4%	10.8%	40.0%
1968	217,213	21.5%	2.0%	14.8%	34.3%
1969	249,860	19.4%	1.9%	21.4%	32.2%
1970	323,857	14.6%	2.1%	26.8%	35.6%
1971	273,652	16.8%	4.3%	17.8%	36.8%

Source: United Nations, *Commodity Trade Statistics.*

Appendix 2.

Japan Imports and Major Market Shares

Unit: Thousand U.S. Dollars & Percent

	Total	from Korea	from Taiwan	from U.S.A.
	Fish, Fresh, Chilled or Frozen (SITC 0311)			
1962	4,628	91.8%	—	—
1963	6,464	59.5%	—	—
1964	12,932	40.7%	—	18.2%
1965	15,394	45.4%	1.4%	4.4%
1966	20,516	36.0%	4.9%	5.9%
1967	21,643	32.5%	6.0%	7.1%
1968	30,238	24.4%	13.7%	6.3%
1969	34,093	19.6%	18.1%	16.3%
1970	60,634	22.8%	30.7%	8.4%
1971	82,144	21.2%	34.1%	7.4%

	Total	from Taiwan	from Ecuador
	Bananas (SITC 0513)		
1962	12,534	60.5%	38.6%
1963	37,160	21.4%	78.3%
1964	55,173	58.5%	40.4%
1965	60,645	90.0%	8.0%
1966	65,124	82.0%	16.0%
1967	70,965	88.0%	16.0%
1968	101,068	55.0%	38.0%
1969	116,527	49.0%	36.0%
1970	144,140	25.0%	56.0%
1971	139,848	31.0%	43.0%

	Total	from Taiwan	from Cuba	from Ryuku	from Australia
	Raw Beet and Cane Sugar (SITC 0611)				
1962	102,900	29.8%	31.7%	11.4%	17.3%
1963	215,804	35.6%	10.4%	10.6%	22.9%
1964	241,622	25.3%	22.0%	13.9%	21.2%
1965	149,781	16.8%	18.7%	28.3%	20.2%
1966	123,554	15.6%	16.2%	34.3%	24.4%
1967	120,417	3.3%	20.2%	33.4%	24.8%

Appendix 2.

(Continued)

Unit: Thousand U.S. Dollars & Percent

	Total	from Taiwan	from Cuba	from Rukyu	from Australia
1968	145,240	6.3%	20.2%	32.9%	18.8%
1969	196,940	5.0%	32.5%	23.7%	21.0%
1970	282,742	3.8%	37.6%	17.0%	18.3%
1971	317,417	5.9%	39.2%	16.8%	16.8%

	Total	from Korea	from Mainland China
Raw Silk, Not Thrown (SITC 2613)			
1962	104	—	—
1963	652	—	47.2%
1964	811	—	34.9%
1965	4,380	—	78.7%
1966	17,483	10.1%	60.5%
1967	30,007	27.7%	54.9%
1968	23,663	34.2%	45.6%
1969	28,999	36.9%	47.2%
1970	72,245	48.6%	34.7%
1971	109,043	35.5%	48.5%

	Total	from Taiwan	from Korea	from Hong Kong
Clothing Accessory, Knit (SITC 8414)				
1963	4,871	—	—	3.9%
1964	3,968	—	—	6.0%
1965	2,748	—	—	9.7%
1966	3,558	—	16.4%	4.8%
1967	7,651	8.0%	9.3%	22.7%
1968	13,720	8.4%	12.1%	29.9%
1969	23,185	9.3%	16.0%	26.5%
1970	55,927	21.7%	16.8%	24.7%
1971	81,627	n.a.	17.5%	22.8%

Source: United Nations, *Commodity Trade Statistics.*

IV

POLICY TOWARDS TRADE
AND INVESTMENT

An Econometric Simulation Model of the Korean Economy and Analysis of Trade Policy Alternatives

Charles R. Frank, Jr. and Kwang Suk Kim[*]

In this paper we use an econometric model to test a number of important hypotheses concerning the effects of commercial policy variables on macro-economic behavior. A number of other relationships are carefully investigated such as the interest rate elasticity of savings and foreign capital imports. The basic model is used then to determine the effects of commercial policy variables on the growth of the South Korean economy by simulation techniques.

I. THE BASIC MODEL

In matrix form, the basic model can be expressed as follows:

$$(1) \qquad B \cdot \psi_t + \Delta\psi_{t-\tau} + \Gamma_1\phi_{1t} + \Gamma_2\phi_{2t} + \Gamma_3\phi_{3t} + e_t = 0$$

*The authors are respectively policy planning staff member at the Department of State, U.S.A. and senior fellow at the Korea Development Institute. This article will appear as a chapter in the book *Foreign Exchange Regimes and Economic Development: South Korea* by C.R. Frank Jr., K. Kim and L. Westphal, which will be published in 1975 by the NBER. It forms part of a major project undertaken by the NBER with the financial support of the USAID.

where B is a square matrix, ψ_t is a column vector of endogenous variables, $\psi_{t-\tau}$ is a column vector of lagged endogenous variables, ϕ_{1t}, ϕ_{2t}, and ϕ_{3t} are each vectors of exogenous variables, e_t is a column vector of error terms, and Γ_1, Γ_2, Γ_3 and Δ are matrices. The exogenous variables ϕ_{1t} are called *basic* commercial policy variables; ϕ_{2t} are *derived* commercial policy variables, and ϕ_{3t} are other exogenous variables.

The endogenous variables of the system are described in Table 1. All of the endogenous variables are measured in terms of constant 1965 won. The exogenous variables are shown in Table 2. All exogenous variables except for rates and ratios, population, and dummy variables are in terms of 1965 constant won. Tables 3 and 4 show the matrix structure of the basic model expressed in (1). To facilitate discussion of the model the endogenous variables (and therefore equations of the model) are separated into six groups. Group 1 contains two equations, one of which determined non-agricultural output and an identity which involves the determination of total GNP. Group 2 contains three equations relating to direct and indirect tax revenues and government savings. Group 3 contains four equations relating to grain consumption, grain imports and grain inventories. Group 4 involves equations for household savings, corporate savings, fixed investment, foreign loans, and domestic consumption. Group 5 contains five equations relating to exports, imports, and short-term capital movements. Group 6 contains two identities, one concerning the balance of payments and the other concerning savings and investment.

II. THE DATA

The data used to estimate the basic model and its variations are for the most part compiled by the Bank of Korea and published in their annual series, *Economic Statistics Yearbook*. The data for all variables were compiled for the period 1955 to 1970 or 16 years. In some cases data were available back to 1953. Thus all equations, except those containing lagged variables, could be run on 16 annual observations or more.

All of the endogenous variables and most of the exogenous variables are in terms of constant 1965 won. Since many of the variables used in the model (e.g. imports of goods by type, capital imports of various kinds, and tax variables) are not given by the Bank of Korea in constant 1965 won, we deflated the Bank constant price or dollar data in a variety of ways. Exchange rate variables were adjusted by a purchasing-power-parity

Table 1

Endogenous Variables of the Model

$\psi_{1,t} = YNA_t$: Non-agricultural Value Added

$\psi_{2,t} = Y_t$: Gross National Product

$\psi_{3,t} = DTR_t$: Direct Tax Revenues

$\psi_{4,t} = INT_t$: Indirect Tax Revenues, excluding customs duties

$\psi_{5,t} = SG_t$: Government Savings

$\psi_{6,t} = GC_t$: Grain Consumption

$\psi_{7,t} = IVG_t$: Investment in Grain Inventories

$\psi_{8,t} = MG_t$: Imports of Grain

$\psi_{9,t} = ILG_t$: Level of Grain Inventories

$\psi_{10,t} = SC_t$: Corporate Savings

$\psi_{11,t} = YDP_t$: Disposable Income of Households

$\psi_{12,t} = SH_t$: Household Savings

$\psi_{13,t} = INA_t$: Non-agricultural Gross Fixed Investment

$\psi_{14,t} = I_t$: Total Gross Fixed Investment

$\psi_{15,t} = CK_t$: Foreign Commercial Loans

$\psi_{16,t} = DC_t$: Consumption Expenditures

$\psi_{17,t} = MC_t$: Imports of Consumption Goods

$\psi_{18,t} = MK_t$: Imports of Capital Goods

$\psi_{19,t} = XGM_t$: Manufactured Exports

$\psi_{20,t} = X_t$: Total Export of Goods

$\psi_{21,t} = MI_t$: Imports of Intermediate Goods

$\psi_{22,t} = M_t$: Total Import of Goods

$\psi_{23,t} = SK_t$: Short-term Capital Movements and Changes in Foreign
Reserves

$\psi_{24,t} = IV_t$: Inventory Investment

Table 2

Exogenous Variables of the Model

A. Basic Commercial Policy Variables

    $\phi_{1,1,t} = ORD_t$: Official Exchange Rate on Purchasing-Power-Parity Basis

    $\phi_{1,2,t} = XPX_t$: Export Premium per Dollar of Exports

    $\phi_{1,3,t} = SOX_t$: Subsidies per Dollar of Exports

    $\phi_{1,4,t} = TAM_t$: Tariffs and Foreign Exchange Tax per Dollar of Imports

B. Derived Commercial Policy Variables

    $\phi_{2,1,t} = XPM_t$: Export premia per Dollar of Imports

    $\phi_{2,2,t} = SUBM_t$: Tariffs and Tariff Equivalents per Dollar of Imports

$\phi_{2,\ 3,t} = SUBX_t$: Subsidies and Subsidy Equivalents per Dollar of Exports

$\phi_{2,\ 4,t} = SXDT_t$: Total Subsidies on Exports in the Form of Internal Tax Relief

$\phi_{2,\ 5,t} = TAR_t$: Total Tariffs and Foreign Exchange Taxes

$\varphi_{2,\ 6,t} = MARDEV_t$: Average Rate of Devaluation averaged over current and the two previous years.

C. Other Exogenous Variables

$\phi_{3,\ 1,t} = YA_t$: Agricultural Value Added

$\phi_{3,\ 2,t} = G_t$: Current Government Expenditures

$\phi_{3,\ 3,t} = IA_t$: Investment in Agriculture

$\phi_{3,\ 4,t} = PK_t$: Government Capital Improvements

$\phi_{3,\ 5,t} = NFI_t$: Net Factor Incomes from Abroad

$\phi_{3,\ 6,t} = MST_t$: Net Service Imports (including factor payments), and Net Transfer Payments Abroad

$\phi_{3,\ 7,t} = RPG_t$: Wholesale Price of Grains Relative to Overall Wholesale Price Level

$\phi_{3,\ 8,t} = POP_t$: Population

$\phi_{3,\ 9,t} = GP_t$: Grain Production

$\phi_{3,10,t} = RD_t$: Rate of Interest on Domestic Savings Deposits

$\phi_{3,11,t} = LR_t$: Rate of Interest on Domestic Commercial Bank Loans

$\phi_{3,12,t} = RF_t$: Rate of Interest on Foreign Commercial Loans

$\phi_{3,13,t} = RINF_t$: Current Rate of Inflation (GNP Deflator)

$\phi_{3,14,t} = RINF_{t-1}$: Lagged Rate of Inflation (GNP Deflator)

$\phi_{3,15,t} = CKDM_t$: Dummy Variable Used in Foreign Commercial Loan (CK) Equation

$\phi_{3,16,t} = MNC_t$: Imports of Non-classified Goods

$\phi_{3,17,t} = NTOSH_t$: Transfers from Government and Corporate Sectors to Households

$\phi_{3,18,t} = XGP_t$: Exports of Primary Products

$\phi_{3,19,t} = RT$: Current Account Transfers from Abroad

$\phi_{3,20,t} = I$: Constant Term

---

index. Adjustments were made to other Bank data; for example, domestic savings was adjusted to exclude changes in grain inventories and include transfers from abroad. A detailed description of the data sources and adjustments to the data is given in the appendix to this chapter.

Table 3

B-Matrix for Endogenous Variables

	1 YNA	2 Y	3 DTR	4 INT	5 SG	6 GC	7 IVG	8 MG	9 ILG	10 SC	11 YDP	12 SH	13 INA	14 I	15 CK	16 DC	17 MC	18 MK	19 XGM	20 X	21 MI	22 M	23 SK	24 IV	
1 YNA	1																								Group 1
2 Y	−1	1																							
3 DTR	β		1																						Group 2
4 INT			−1	1																					
5 SG			−1	−1	1																				
6 GC	β					1																			Group 3
7 IVG						1	1	−1																	
8 MG							−1	1																	
9 ILG								β	1																
10 SC	β					1				1															Group 4
11 YDP	−1		1	1						1	1	1													
12 SH	β						β			β	β	1													
13 INA							β			β	β	−1	1												
14 I													β	1											
15 CK						1				1				β	1										
16 DC	−1						1			1			β			1									
17 MC	β													β	β		1								Group 5
18 MK														β	β			1							
19 XGM	β																		1						
20 X																	−1	−1	β	1					
21 MI	β																		β	1	1				
22 M								−1									−1	−1				1			
23 SK					−1					−1			−1			1				1	1	−1	1	−1	Group 6
24 IV											−1									1	1		−1	1	

Table 4

Basic Matrices of the Macro-mode

	Δ-Matrix — Lagged Endogenous Variables					Γ₁-Matrix — Basic Commercial Policy Variables				Γ₂-Matrix — Derived Commercial Policy Variables						
	YNA_{-1}	YNA_{-2}	$INA_{-1}*ILG_{-1}$			ORD	XPM	SOX	TAM	XPX	SUBM	SUBX	SXDT	TAR	MARDEV	
	1	2	3	4	5	1	2	3	4	1	2	3	4	5	6	
1 YNA	-1		δ													Group 1
2 Y													1	-1		Group 2
3 DTR																
4 INT																
5 SG																
6 GC																
7 IVG					1											Group 3
8 MG																
9 ILG																
10 SC																
11 YDP																
12 SH																
13 INA		δ	δ													
14 I																Group 4
15 CK																
16 DC																
17 MC						γ_1					γ_2				γ_2	
18 MK						γ_1						γ_2				Group 5
19 XGM						γ_1										
20 X																
21 MI						γ_1				γ_2	γ_2					
22 M																
23 SK																
24 IV																Group 6

Table 4

Basic Matrices of the Macro-model (continued)

Γ_3-Matrix

	1 YA	2 G	3 IA	4 PK	5 NFI	6 MST	7 RPG	8 POP	9 GP	10 RD	11 LR	12 RF	13 RINF	14 RINF-1	15 CKDM	16 MNC	17 NTOSH	18 XGP	19 Con-stant	Error Terms e	
1 YNA																			γ_3	e_1	Group 1
2 Y	-1																				
3 DTR																			γ_3	e_3	Group 2
4 INT																			γ_3	e_4	
5 SG			1																		
6 GC							γ_3	γ_3											γ_3	e_6	Group 3
7 IVG																					
8 MG									1												
9 ILG									γ_3										γ_3	e_9	Group 4
10 SC										γ_3									γ_3	e_{10}	
11 YDP																	1				
12 SH										γ_3									γ_3	e_{12}	
13 INA				γ_3								γ_3	γ_3						γ_3	e_{13}	
14 I				-1																	
15 CK											γ_3	γ_3		γ_3	γ_3				γ_3	e_{15}	
16 DC					-1																
17 MC																			γ_3	e_{17}	Group 5
18 MK																			γ_3	e_{18}	
19 XGM																			γ_3	e_{19}	
20 X																		-1			
21 MI																			γ_3	e_{21}	
22 M																-1					
23 SK	1					-1															
24 IV						-1															Group 6

III. BASIC HYPOTHESES AND TESTS

Hypotheses tested in fitting the basic model and its variations include the following general types:
1) Exchange rate variables affect savings and investment behavior directly as well as exports, imports, and capital flows,
2) Various types of tariff and tariff equivalents and export subsidies have differential effects on imports and exports,
3) Private savings are sensitive to both nominal interest rate changes and expected rates of inflation, and
4) Foreign loans are sensitive to nominal interest rates, expected rates of inflation and expected rates of devaluation.

Hypotheses of these types are tested using the conventional tests of significance. The results are described below. In addition, we tested the general hypothesis that the basic structure of the economy changed after the 1964 devaluation and liberalization. For all equations for which there were enough degrees of freedom, we ran regressions over the sample period 1964 to 1970 as well as over the whole period for which data were available to determine if the structure was changed. We also tested all our equations using eleven observations from 1960 to 1970 and from 1957 to 1970 when this was possible. The rationale for the 1960–1970 period is that 1960 is the year of the overthrow of the Rhee regime and the first year in which basic economic reforms were attempted. The 1957 to 1970 period is used since the post-Korean War years 1953 to 1956 were so significantly affected by reconstruction that data from these years bias the results. In choosing what we call our "best results" we chose the longest sample period for which the results seemed to be stable. If the regression coefficients changed markedly, however, when a shorter sample period was used, we chose the results from the shorter sample period.

All of the equations of the model were estimated initially using ordinary least squares or the Cochrane-Orcutt technique if there seemed to be significant autocorrelation of the error terms. Various types of simultaneous estimation were then used to determine whether the simultaneous nature of the model seriously biased the estimated coefficients.

IV. FURTHER DESCRIPTION AND ESTIMATION RESULTS

IV.1 *Group 1: Determination of GNP.*

The first two equations of the model concern output in agriculture and non-agriculture. Output in non-agriculture sectors is YNA assumed to be related to non-agricultural investment INA in previous years.[1] In the estimated relationship, there was strong evidence for decreasing returns to investment. That is, the higher the level of investment, the greater seems to be the net incremental capital-output ratio.[2] The best results among several functional forms tried seem to be the following equation for non-agricultural output:

(2) $YNA = -281.8254 + 0.9413 \ YNA_{-1} + 80.0668 \ \log_e(INA_{-1})$
          $(-2.96) \qquad (10.02) \qquad\qquad (2.64)$

Estimation Technique: Ordinary Least Squares
Sample: 1957 to 1971[3]
$R^2 = 0.9960$
$d = 2.2310$

The t-statistics are given in parentheses under each of the coefficients of variables in the equations. R^2 is the coefficient of determination and d is the Durbin-Watson statistic. The strength of decreasing returns in non-agriculture can be indicated by comparing incremental capital-output ratios when non-agricultural investment runs about 50 billion won in constant 1965 prices, as was the case in the late fifties and early sixties, as opposed to investment of about 400 billion won in constant 1965 prices,

---

[1] The implicit production function which we use is

$$YNA_t = f(INA_{t-1}, INA_{t-2}, \ldots, INA_{t-T})$$

where INA_t is the investment in non-agriucltural sectors in period t. We also assume that depreciation takes place at a rate γ with respect to earlier years investment and that investment enters the function f in a logarithmic form, i.e.,

$$YNA_t = \alpha + \beta \, [\log_e (INA_{t-1}) + \gamma \log_e (INA_{t-2}) + \ldots + \gamma^{T-1} \log_e (INA_{t-T})]$$

Defined recursively, this becomes (approximately for very large T)

$$YNA_t = (\alpha - \gamma\alpha) + \gamma \, YNA_{t-1} + \beta \log_e (INA_{t-1})$$

The estimate of the coefficient γ is the estimated depreciation rate.

[2] The suggestion that we test for an increasing incremental capital-output ratio was made by Albert Fishlow.

[3] The sample period was extended to 1971 since preliminary data for 1971 were available for YNA.

as was the case in 1970. The capital-output ratio is approximately 1.6 when investment is 50 billion won and about 2.0 when investment is 400 billion won.[4]

The second equation in Group 1 is an identity relating total output Y to agricultural output YA and non-agricultural output YNA.

(3) $Y = YNA + YA.$

IV.2 *Group 2: Government Taxation and Savings Equations.*

The regression equations for government direct and indirect tax revenues were very well behaved. They exhibited very high coefficients of determination and were generally stable, regardless of the sample period used.

The dependent variable in the direct tax regression was potential taxation. That is, direct tax exemptions for exporters $SXDT$ were added to actual direct tax revenues DTR to get potential direct taxes. The results were as follows:

(4) $DTR + SXDT = -63.6088 + 0.1104Y$
                            $(-7.14)\qquad (16.42)$

> Estimation Technique: Cochrane-Orcutt Iterative Technique
> Sample: 1953 to 1970
> $R^2 = 0.9946$
> $d = 0.9741$
> $\rho = 0.8808$[5]

For indirect taxes INT, excluding tariffs and foreign exchange taxes, the results were:

(5) $INT = -16.2991 + 0.1193YNA$
             $(-3.63)\qquad (15.86)$

> Estimation Technique: Cochrane-Orcutt Iterative Technique
> Sample: 1953 to 1970
> $R^2 = 0.9787$
> $d = 1.4114$
> $\rho = 0.4968$

The regression results indicate a very high degree of elasticity of both direct and indirect tax revenues over the entire period 1953 to 1970. The

---

[4] This is the incremental capital-output ratio on a net basis, i.e., allowing for estimmated depreciation.

[5] ρ is the coefficient of autocorrelation as estimated in the terminal iteration of the Cochrane-Orcutt technique.

average elasticity for direct tax revenues was 2.53 and for indirect tax revenues 1.40. Since direct tax exemptions grew rapidly, particularly in the last half of the sixties, potential tax revenues (excluding exemptions) were even more elastic. The average for direct taxes was 2.79.[6]

Government expenditure G is assumed to be exogenous in our model, and government savings SG is specified as an identity.

$$(6) \qquad SG = DTR + INT + TAR - G.$$

where TAR is tariffs and foreign exchange taxes.

IV.3 *Group 3: The Grain Sector.*

Grain consumption was assumed to be dependent on income Y, the relative price of grains RPG, total population POP, and the split between rural and urban population. Since urban population has been growing quite steadily and so has total population, any measure of the relative rural-urban population is highly correlated with total population and the usual problems associated with multicollinearity arise. The coefficients on the two correlated variables are extremely sensitive to the sample used and the estimation technique used. We finally concluded that the best results could be obtained by using the population variable only. The results are:

$$(7) \qquad GC = 6.5619 + 0.02696Y - 31.3328RPG + 7.8016POP$$
$$ (0.20) \quad (1.58) \qquad (-2.21) \qquad (5.18)$$

Estimation Technique: Ordinary Least Squares
Sample: 1955 to 1970
$R^2 = 0.9582$
$d = 1.7957$

The income variable Y and the population variable POP are also quite collinear, and this probably accounts for the lack of significance of the coefficient of the Y variable. Nevertheless, we felt on *a priori* grounds that the income variable should be retained.

The implicit average income elasticity for grain consumption in the period 1955 to 1970 is 0.1031 and the price elasticity is -0.0422. As one would expect, grain consumption is relatively price and income inelastic. Population growth is the major factor in determining growth in consump-

---

[6] These elasticities are estimated from the regression equations by multiplying the coefficient of Y by the ratio of the means of DTR and Y or INT and YNA as the case may be.

tion.

Korean domestic savings figures are very much affected by changes in grain inventories. The harvest comes in late in the year and most of the production is held in inventories at the end of the year. Fluctuations in the level of grain inventories are more a function of grain production than anything else. Grain imports also affect the levels of grain inventories, but, for the most part, changes in inventory do not represent conscious savings decisions but are more a function of the weather which affects the size of the harvest.

Since changes in grain inventories are such an important component of savings, we estimated the level of grain inventories ILG as a function of grain production GP and grain imports MG. The best results are:

(8) $$ILG = -77.9743 + 0.5782MG + 0.7196GP$$
$$(-7.25) \qquad (7.52) \qquad (12.07)$$

Estimation Technique: Ordinary Least Squares
Sample: 1955 to 1970
$R^2 = 0.9607$
$d = 1.9038.$

Once the level of grain inventories is determined by the stochastic equation (8.8), investment in grain inventories IVG is determined by the identity

(9) $$IVG = ILG - ILG_{-1}.$$

Imports of grain are determined also as grain consumption GC plus inventory change IVG less production GP. Production of grain is assumed to be exogenous.

(10) $$MG = IVG + GC - GP.$$

IV.4 *Group 4: Savings and Investment Behavior.*

Savings is broken down into household savings and corporate savings. Household savings SH is expected to be a function of the expected real rate of interest on local savings deposits and disposable income of households YDP. The basic specification is:

(11) $$SH = a_0 + a_1 YDP + a_2 RRD^*.$$

Of course, the expected real rate of interest RRD is not an observable variable. We assume, however, that the expected real rate of interest is a function of the current *nominal* rate of interest RD less the expected rate of inflation. The expected rate of inflation RRD* is assumed to be a function of current and past rates of inflation *RINF*.[7]

(12) $$RRD^* = RD - b_0 RINF - b_{-1} RINF_{-1}.$$

If (12) is substituted back into (11),we obtain the following result:

(13) $$SH = a_0 + a_1 YDP + a_2 RD - b_0 a_2 RINF - b_1 a_2 RINF_{-1}.$$

This is the equation which was estimated with the following result:

(14) $$SH = -71.5504 + 0.08578 YDP + 193.0218 RD - 44.7071\ RINF$$
$$\quad\ (-4.47) \qquad (4.23) \qquad\quad (2.94) \qquad\qquad (-2.48)$$
$$-35.0608 RINF_{-1}$$
$$\ (-2.87)$$

Estimation Technique: Cochrane-Orcutt Iterative Technique
Sample: 1955 to 1970
$R^2 = 0.9550$
$d = 3.0033$
$\rho = 0.7070.$

The results were only somewhat different for other sample periods, but all sample periods reveal a high degree of significance for the real interest rate. The average interest rate elasticity over the sample period is 1.82, a very high interest rate elasticity.

Corporate savings *SC,* which forms the bulk of private savings in South Korea, was assumed to be a function of non-agricultural value added, the expected real rate of interest on savings deposits,[8] the average rate of protection on imports and the average rate of subsidy on exports. The ration-

---

[7] The current rate of inflation and the rate of inflation lagged once were sufficient to explain the expected rate of inflation. The rate of inflation lagged more than once had very low explanatory power.

[8] Several readers of the draft manuscript commented that they did not understand how corporate savings could be affected positively by the interest rate. One reader, for example, commented that "given that corporations save only to invest in productive capacity, marginal efficiency of investment is the relevant variable." This is a common fallacy and represents a failure to understand the concept of reservation demand. Self-financed investment by a tightly controlled corporation, typical in Korea, represents a decision not to distribute profits for the purpose of increased consumption and a decision not to seek out-side financing, but rather to retain profits for financing investment. As concerns the substitution effect, a higher interest rate makes self-financing more attractive than outside financing for both working and fixed capital and saving a better alternative to consumption. Of course, it is well-known that the income effect works in the opposite direction so that the coefficient of the interest rate has no *a priori* sign and must be determined empirically.

176   *Charles R. Frank, Jr. & Kwang Suk Kim*

ale for including rates of protection or subsidy was that high levels of protection and subsidy should increase profits and lead to higher savings. The level of tariffs and tariff equivalents and subsidies per dollar of export did not seem to affect savings in any consistent or significant fashion. Furthermore, rates of inflation did not seem to possess much explanatory power and frequently carried the wrong sign in the regression. The best results were obtained using only two variables, non-agricultural value added YNA and the rate of interest on savings deposits RD.

(15) $$SC = -0.5689 + 0.0730YNA + 115.2640RD$$
$$(-0.16) \quad (10.51) \quad (4.13)$$

Regression Technique: Ordinary Least Squares
Sample: 1960 to 1970
$R^2 = 0.9827$
$d = 1.6131$

Both non-agricultural value added and the rate of interest were highly significant for all sample periods and various specifications. For corporate savings, the average interest rate elasticity is 0.34 over the sample period. Household savings seem to be substantially more interest rate elastic, but the significance of deposit rates for corporate savings is nonetheless substantial (a t-ratio of 4.13). The rate of inflation was not a significant explanatory variable. Thus it seems that in Korea, corporate savings depend on the nominal rate of interest rather than on the expected real rate of interest (in contrast to household savings). The reason may be that although inflation reduces real interest costs, it also may be associated with increased profit rates which have a positive effect on corporate savings and investment. The two effects tend to cancel each other so that corporate savings show little sensitivity to the rate of inflation.

Disposable income of households YDP is determined by the identity:

(16) $$YDP = Y - SC - INT - TAR - DTR + NTOSH.$$

That is, disposable income of households is total income less retained earnings, less taxes, and plus net transfers from the government and corporate sectors to households.

Investment in South Korea is financed by four main sources, private savings channeled through the commercial banking system in the form of deposits, government savings channeled through both the commercial bank and a series of development finance institutions,[9] retained earnings, and borrowing from abroad.

---

[9] For example, the Medium Industry Bank and the Korea Development Bank.

The demand for loans from both commercial banks and development finance institutions far exceeds the available supply of loanable funds even at the relatively high interest rates which marginal borrowers must pay.[10] Loans are rationed since legal interest rate ceilings cannot clear the market. The result is that much investment is financed through the unorganized money market and borrowing from abroad. Since interest rates are controlled and credit rationing takes place, we decided to include as an independent variable for the non-agricultural investment equation, the total level of savings largely available to government or channeled through the banking system. This includes government savings, SG, public capital imports PK, corporate savings SC and household savings SH. It does not include other sources of savings such as foreign commercial loans, reductions in foreign exchange reserves, and inventory disinvestment. The other explanatory variables tried were current and lagged income growth, the real local commercial bank loan rate, the real rate of interest on foreign loans, average tariffs and tariff equivalents per dollar of imports, export subsidies per dollar of export, and effective exchange rates.

Of all these explanatory variables, current and lagged income growth and available savings $(SG + PK + SC + SH)$ seemed to give the only good results. Import tariffs and export subsidies did not seem to have a direct impact on investment demand. The loan rates, foreign and domestic, were not good explanatory variables, although the domestic loan rate was nearly significant at the 5 percent level for some regressions. The lack of strong significance of the domestic loan rate is probably due to the fact that there are a wide variety of loan rates by different types of banks and for different purposes. With such a variety of subsidized rates and the prevalence of credit rationing, it is expected that official loan rates would not have substantial explanatory value. The equation which we felt best for purposes of simulation, however, did include the domestic loan rate and was as follows:

(17) $INA = -19.0111 + 0.5802(YNA\text{-}YNA_{-1}) + 0.7525(YNA_{-1} - YNA_{-2})$
$(-1.39)\quad (2.97)\phantom{+ 0.5802(YNA-YNA_{-1}) }(3.39)$
$+ 0.7263(SG + PK + SC + SH) - 36.8952RLR$
$(4.44)(-1.08)$

Estimation Technique: Cochrane-Orcutt Iterative Technique
Sample = 1957 to 1970
$R^2 = 0.9948$

---

[10] Loan rates of commercial banks were more than 24 percent over the last half of the sixties which correponds to a real interest rate of more than 10 percent.

$d = 1.7044$

$p = 0.5643$

where RLR is the expected real rate of interest for domestic loans. The expected real rate of interest is the nominal rate less the expected rate of inflation which is assumed to be approximated by last year's rate of inflation:

(18) $$RLR = LR - RINF._{-1}$$

Since a large component of non-agricultural investment is available savings, the problem of simultaneity (discussed later) is particularly acute for this equation and requires further investigation.

Total investment I equals non-agricultural investment INA plus investment in agriculture IA.

(19) $$I = INA + IA.$$

The next equation in Group 4 is a demand equation for foreign loans. Although, in principle, foreign loans over three years require approval from the Economic Planning Board, the Board has encouraged investors to borrow abroad. Beginning about 1970, however, concern over the rising level of debt service payments led the IMF to insist on restriction of the flow of foreign capital, and the restrictions imposed seemed to be effective.

The demand for foreign loans is assumed to be a function of the level of total fixed investment I, the expected real rate of interest on domestic loans RLR, and the expected real rate of interest on foreign loans RRF. That is,

(20) $$CK = \alpha_0 + \alpha_1 I + \alpha_2 RLR + \alpha_3 RRF + \alpha_4 CKDM,$$

where $CKDM$ is a dummy variable equal to unity for 1970 and zero for all other years. The expected rate of interest on foreign loans involves not only the expected rate of inflation but the expected rate of devaluation. We assume that the expected rate of devaluation is approximated by the average of the current and two previous years' rate of devaluation. Thus

(21) $$RRF = RF - RINF_{-1} + (RDEV + RDEV_{-1} + RDEV_{-2})/3$$

Equation (19) was estimated as follows:

(22) $$CK = -23.7637 + 0.2634I + 148.5346RLR$$
$$(-7.06) \quad (7.86) \quad (2.87)$$
$$-77.5319RRF - 27.8443CKDM$$
$$(-2.02) \quad (-3.06)$$

Estimation Technique: Ordinary Least Squares
Sample: 1959 to 1970

$R^2 = 0.9847$

$d = 2.5668$

The demand for foreign loans is sensitive to both the domestic and foreign loan interest rate. The average elasticities are 0.326 and -0.477. The significance of the dummy variable indicates that the restrictions on foreign borrowing had a singnificant effect in 1970.

The final equation in Group 4 is an indentity for domestic consumption expenditure.

(23) $DC = Y - SC - SH - SG - IVG + RT + NFI.$

Consumption equals income less savings, both private and government, less inventory investment in grains, and plus net transfers from abroad and net factor incomes from abroad.

IV.5 Group 5: Import and Export Equations.

Group 5 contains three import equations, an export equation and two identities. Imports of consumption goods are assumed to depend on various components of the effective exchange rate for imports and the level of domestic consumption. Initially, the effective exchange rate for imports was broken up into three components: (1) the official rate, (2) tariffs and tariff equivalents, and (3) the total value of export premia per dollar of import. The coefficients for parts 2 and 3 were not significant and were unstable with respect to the sample used for all of the import equations. Thus parts 2 and 3 were combined into a single variable called $SUBM$. For imports of consumption goods MC, the two parts $SUBM$ and ORD were combined since there was no significant difference between their coefficients. The best results are:

(24) $MC = -8.1035 + 0.0596DC - 0.1055 (SUBM + ORD)$
                     (-2.15) (11.75) (-5.43)

Estimation Technique: Ordinary Least Squares
Sample: 1955 to 1970
$R^2 = 0.9163$
$d = 1.2058$

where DC is domestic consumption. This equation results in an average elasticity of -2.10 for the effective exchange rate of imports, $SUBM + ORD$[11]

---

[11] These elasticities were determined with respect to percentage changes in the total effective exchange rate, i.e., $ORD + SUBM$.

For capital goods imports, a somewhat different model must be used. Most capital goods enter duty free and by special channels such as foreign aid loans or loans from abroad. The official exchange rate is the most relevant exchange rate to use. Since most foreign loans are tied to capital goods imports we would expect the level of foreign borrowing to be an important determinant of capital goods imports. The level of investment is also a determinant of the magnitude of capital goods imports. The best regression results for MK, imports of capital goods, are obtained with foreign commercial loans CK, investment I, and the official exchange rate ORD as explanatory variables.

(25) $MK = 3.881 + 0.3610CK + 0.3311I - 0.0853ORD$
           (0.61)   (2.22)   (6.58)   (-2.44)

> Estimation Technique: Ordinary Least Squares
> Sample: 1955 to 1970
> $R^2 = 0.9876$
> $d = 1.6974$

The elasticity of capital goods imports with respect to ORD is -0.36.

For imports of intermediate goods, we used the official exchange rate ORD and total tariffs, tariff equivalents, and export premia per dollar of import $SUBM$ as the commercial policy variables. Other explanatory variables are gross national product Y and exports X. Manufactured exports XGM is used as a separate explanatory variable since we believe that in general exports of manufactures are more intensive in their use of imports than other elements of expenditure on gross national product. The resulting equation is:

(26) $MI = 9.9287 + 0.1772Y + 0.3610XGM + 0.3714SUBM - 0.2197ORD$
         (0.42)   (3.53)   (1.67)   (-2.53)   (-2.68)

> Estimation Technique: Cochrane-Orcutt Iterative Technique
> Sample: 1955 to 1970
> $R^2 = 0.9893$
> $d = 1.5915$
> $\rho = 0.2554$

The average elasticity is -0.46 for the official exchange rate ORD and -0.80 for $SUBM$. One would expect a higher elasticity for $SUBM$ if tariffs and tariff equivalents are levied selectively on commodity items with higher than average elasticity.

The export equation was the most difficult to estimate. The estimation procedures involved exports of manufactured goods (XGM) as the dependent variable, and non-agricultural output (YNA), the official exchange rate on a purchasing-power-parity basis (ORD), and all other export incentives (i.e., a combination of multiple exchange rate premia and subsidies denoted by $SUBX$) as explanatory variables. If the whole period 1955 to 1970 is used, the results are very poor. Using the period 1957 to 1970, we obtain the following result:

(27) $XGM = -241.4847 + 0.3323\,YNA + 0.2629\,ORD + 0.147\,SUBX$
          (-3.92) (11.29) (1.70) (1.27)

> Estimation Technique: Cochrane-Orcutt Iterative Technique
> $R^2 = 0.9900$
> $d = 0.3742$
> $\rho = 0.8701$

The coefficient of YNA is highly significant, indicating that general capacity in non-agriculture was the most significant factor explaining exports. That is, the general capacity of the economy to produce was probably an important determinant of exports. The elasticity of manufactured exports with respect to changes in the exchange rate (ORD) is 2.14 and with respect to export subsidies is 0.95. The coefficients of the official exchange rate ORD and the subsidy level for exports $SUBX$, however, are not significant.

This result can be greatly modified, however, if the time period is changed from 1957–1970 to 1963–1970. The coefficient of ORD becomes 1.713 and the t-ratio is over 13.8; the coefficient of $SUBX$ becomes 1.305 with a t-ratio of 10.9.[12] With such a short time period, however, the degrees of freedom are limited. The exchange rate variable ORD and the subsidy variable $SUBX$ are almost constant and show fairly limited variation in the period 1963 to 1970, further making the results suspect. Finally, the implied elasticities for the exchange rate and subsidy variables for the period 1963–1970 are enormous, equal to 6.16 for ORD and 4.69 for $SUBX$. Any period beginning prior to 1963, however, gives insignificant results for the coefficients of ORD and $SUBX$.

It seems reasonable to infer that the responsiveness of exports changed sharply after about 1963, but the period is too short to allow for accurate

---

[12] The full equation, obtained by the Cochrane-Orcutt technique is:
$XGM = -651.5 + 0.3357\,YNA + 1.713\,ORD + 1.305\,SUBX$
          (-17.0) (61.7) (13.8) (10.9)
($R^2 = 0.9997$ and Durbin-Watson $= 2.3205$). If ordinary least-squares are used, the coefficients of ORD and $SUBX$ become significant whenever the period is 1964–1970. Before 1963 or 1964, however, the data do not reveal any significant relationship.

estimation of parameters. We may infer that prior to 1963, the lack of sensitivity to exchange rate policy occurred because exports, particularly manufactured exports, were insignificant, and the system of multiple exchange rates used in that period was very inefficient. After 1963, both government officials and private entrepreneurs were more export-oriented.

The system of multiple exchange rates gave way to a system which relied more heavily on high official exchange rates combined with export subsidies, particularly in the form of tax and tariff relief. Exports became very much more sensitive to exchange rate policies. The effective exchange rate on exports was maintained at a high level after the exchange rate reforms of 1964, despite rapid inflation, by a combination of official devaluations and growing export subsidies.

Another factor which may have been responsible for the increased responsiveness of exports after 1963, was the reduction of the risk and uncertainty associated with exporting since the price-level-deflated effective exhcange rate for exports was so stable from 1964 on. The reduction in uncertainty reduced the variance in expected export earnings and made it more reasonable for individual entrepreneurs to concentrate efforts on exports.

The last two equations of Group 5 are identities giving the value of total imports and exports:

(28) $$M = MG + MC + MK + MI + MNC$$

(29) $$X = XGM + XGP.$$

IV.6 *Demand and Supply Balance.*

The final group of equations contains two identities. The first is the balance of payments identity relating movements of short term capital and changes in monetary assets SK to the demand and supply of foreign exchange.

(30) $$SK = M + MST - X - CK - PK$$

where MST is net service imports plus net transfer payments abroad. The second identity makes inventory change the equilibrating item for aggregate demand and supply or between savings and investment

(31) $$IV = SG + SC + SH + M + MST - X - I.$$

V. SIMULTANEOUS ESTIMATION

So far we have only discussed results in terms of single equation estimation techniques. We have not attempted a simultaneous estimation approach. There is some heuristic justification for this. A glance at the B-matrix in Table 3 reveals a structure which is very nearly triangular.[13] The system is triangular except for one block of equations, the *IVG, MG,* and *ILG* equations. (See the block with solid lines in the B-matrix of Table 3.) It is well-known that if a structure is triangular (i.e. recursive) and the errors across equations are uncorrelated, ordinary least squares estimation is a consistent estimation technique. A slight generalization of this theorem is relatively easy to prove: if the system is block-triangular and the errors across blocks are uncorrelated, each block may be treated as a simultaneous system and consistent estimation of each block results in consistent estimation for the system as a whole.

With this in mind, we attempted to estimate the block of equations, *IVG, MG,* and *ILG,* as a simultaneous system. This system can be written as follows:

$$(32) \qquad IVG = ILG - ILG_{-1}$$

$$(33) \qquad MG = IVG + GC - GP$$

$$(34) \qquad ILG = \beta MG + \gamma_1 GP + \gamma_0 + e$$

where *e* is an error term. If we substitute (32) into (33) into (34) and solve for *ILG,* we obtain the following result:

$$(35) \quad ILG = \frac{\beta}{(1-\beta)}(GC - ILG_{-1}) + \frac{(\gamma_1 - \beta)}{(1-\beta)} GP + \frac{\gamma_0}{(1-\beta)} + \frac{1}{(1-\beta)} e.$$

This equation can be estimated by regressing *ILG* on the combination variable $(GC - ILG_{-1})$ and on *GP.* The result is

$$(36) \qquad ILG = -139.51 + 0.654 (GC - ILG_{-1}) + 0.625 GP$$

Estimation Technique: Ordinary Least Squares
Sample: 1955 to 1970
$R^2 = 0.8460$
$d = 1.52$

The original structural coefficients, β, γ_0 and γ_1 can be estimated then by

---

[13] We made no attempt to specify the structure so that the system was triangular. After the model was specified on *a priori* grounds, we then attempted to triangularize the matrix.

indirect least squares by solving the following equations:

(37) $$\frac{\gamma_0}{(1 - \beta)} = -139.51$$

(38) $$\frac{\beta}{(1 - \beta)} = 0.654$$

(39) $$\frac{(\gamma_1 - \beta)}{(1 - \beta)} = 0.625.$$

The solution gives the following estimate of the structural equation (34):

(40) $$ILG = -79.17 + 0.395MG + 0.773GP.$$

Comparing this result with the ordinary least squares result in equation (8), we see that the constant term changes relatively little, the coefficient of MG is reduced and the coefficient of GP increases.

If all the equations are regarded together as one large system, estimation is impossible because of too few observations. For example, consider the problem with a two-stage least squares approach. There are 35 exogenous and lagged endogenous variables. There are a maximum, however, of 18 observations, from 1953 to 1970. Thus it is impossible to regress any of the endogenous variables on all the exogenous and lagged endogenous variables. Some technique has to be found to reduce the number of instrumental variables (exogenous and lagged endogenous variables).

A method for choosing instruments has been proposed by Fisher (1965). Some exogenous variables of the system of equations may add little causal information to the equation and hence be of little value to reduce the bias in estimation. Thus Fisher suggests the use of a causal ordering system for the set of all predetermined variables.

The ordering system which we use is similar to that of Fisher and works as follows:

1) The predetermined variables in equation i are called zero order causal variables for equation i.

2) For each endogenous variable in an equation (other than the dependent variable), we may determine the set of predetermined variables in the equation explaining that endogenous variable. Each set of such predetermined variables are first-order causal variables.

3) For each equation i explaining an endogenous variable in equation i, there are a set of endogenous variables. The predetermined variables in the equations explaining this set of endogenous variables are second-

order causal variables. The predetermined variables in the equation for a lagged endogenous variable contained in equation i are also called second-order causal variables.

The causal ordering described here may be defined more precisely in a recursive fashion.

It is very difficult to choose a set of predetermined variables as instruments. If one chooses too few instruments, the simultaneous equations bias to the estimates is likely to be a problem. If one chooses too many instruments, the endogenous variables, when regressed on the instruments are nearly predicted perfectly, a problem of lack of degrees of freedom. We decided to run two sets of two-stage least squares estimates, one with

Table 5

Instrumental Variables on the Basis of Causal Orderings

Stochastic Equation	Zero- and First-Order Instruments	Second-Order Instruments	Additional Instruments Due to Autocorrelation
YNA	YNA_{-1}, INA_{-1}	$INA_{-2},\quad PK$	—
DTR	$SXDT, YA$	YNA_{-1}, INA_{-1}	$(DTR + SXDT)_{-1} Y_{-1}$
INT	YNA_{-1}, INA_{-1}	—	INT_{-1}
GC	RPG, POP, YA	YNA_{-1}, INA_{-1}	—
ILG	GP	ILG_{-1}, RPG, POP	—
SC	RD, YNA_{-1}, INA_{-1}	—	—
SH	$RD, RINF, RINF_{-1}, NTOSH, TAR$	$YA, RPG, POP, SXDT$	$RINF_{-2}, RD_{-1}, SH_{-1}, YDP_{-1}$
INA	$PK, TAR, G, RD, RINF, RINF_{-1}, YNA_{-1}, YNA_{-2}, INA_{-1}$	$YNA_{-2}, INA_{-2}, SXDT, NTOSH$	$PK_{-1}, (SG+SC+SH)_{-1}, YNA_{-3}, RLR_{-1}$
CK	$RLR, RRF, CKDM, IA$	YNA_{-1}, YNA_{-2}, PK	—
MC	$(SUBM + ORD), RT, NFI$	$YA, RD, RINF, RINF_{-1}, TAR, G, ILG_{-1}$	—
MK	$ORD, RLF, RRF, CKDM, IA$	YNA_{-1}, YNA_{-2}, PK	—
MI	$SUBM, ORD, YA, SUBX$	YNA_{-1}, INA_{-1}	$SUBM_{-1}, ORD_{-1}, MI_{-1}, Y_{-1}, XGM_{-1}$
XGM	$SUBX, ORD, YNA_{-1}, INA_{-1}$	—	$SUBX_{-1}, ORD_{-1}, XGM_{-1}$

Table 6

Two-Stage Least Squares Estimates with Fisher's First-Order Instrumental Variables

	R^2	d	Estimation Technique
$DTR = -61.5843 + 0.1092Y - SXDT$ $\quad\quad (-6.56)\quad\quad (15.26)$	.9944	0.9381	*TSCORC*
$INT = -17.2787 + 0.1202YNA$ $\quad\quad (-3.76)\quad\quad (15.84)$	.9792	1.4411	*TSCORC*
$GC = 111.8904 + 0.0964Y - 40.4563$ $\quad\quad (1.30)\quad\quad (1.81)\quad\quad (-1.78)$ $\quad\quad RPG + 2.2082POP$ $\quad\quad\quad\quad (0.50)$	.9006	0.8621	*TS*
$SC = -0.5678 + 0.0725YNA +$ $\quad\quad (-0.16)\quad\quad (10.41)$ $\quad\quad 116.5768RD$ $\quad\quad (4.16)$	.9827	1.6273	*TS*
$SH = -69.6454 + 0.08412YDP +$ $\quad\quad (-4.43)\quad\quad (4.16)$ $\quad\quad 192.2094RD - 45.1081RINF$ $\quad\quad (2.92)\quad\quad (-2.48)$ $\quad\quad - 34.9772RINF_{-1}$ $\quad\quad (-2.85)$	.9549	3.0123	*TSCORC*
$INA = -19.0076 + 0.5802(YNA - YNA_{-1})$ $\quad\quad (-1.39)\quad\quad (2.97)$ $\quad\quad +0.7525 (YNA_{-1} - YNA_{-2})$ $\quad\quad +0.7263(SG + SC + SH)$ $\quad\quad\quad\quad (4.44)$ $\quad\quad - 36.8973RLR$ $\quad\quad (-1.08)$	.9948	1.7044	*TSCORC*
$CK = -24.9579 + 0.2889I + 115.0503RLR$ $\quad\quad (-6.23)\quad\quad (5.31)\quad\quad (1.50)$ $\quad\quad -52.8461RRF - 32.4248CKDM$ $\quad\quad (-0.93)\quad\quad (-2.69)$	.9834	2.7436	*TS*
$MC = -7.3710 + 0.0548DC - 0.09356$ $\quad\quad (-1.84)\quad (7.44)\quad\quad (-4.02)$ $\quad\quad (SUBM + ORD)$	.9101	1.0454	*TS*
$MK = 0.7415 + 0.2091CK + 0.3637I$ $\quad\quad (0.11)\quad\quad (1.00)\quad\quad (5.60)$ $\quad\quad - 0.0740ORD$ $\quad\quad (-1.94)$	.9861	1.6003	*TS*
$MI = 18.0854 + 0.1564Y + 0.4503XGM$ $\quad\quad (0.74)\quad\quad (2.98)\quad\quad (1.99)$			

$$-0.3586SUBM - 0.1975ORD \qquad .9890 \quad 1.6074 \quad TSCORC$$
$$(-2.39) \qquad\quad (-2.39)$$

$$XGM = -242.4649 + 0.3332YNA + 0.2642ORD$$
$$(-3.94) \quad\;\; (11.26) \qquad\;\; (1.71)$$
$$+0.1480SUBX \qquad\qquad\qquad .9900 \quad 1.3756 \quad TSCORC$$
$$(1.27)$$

Note: *TSCORC* stands for two-stage least squares with Cochrane-Orcutt iterations.
TS stands for ordinary two-stage least squares.

Table   7

Two-Stage Least Squares Estimation with Fisher's Second-Order Instrumental Variables

	R^2	d	Estimation Technique
$DTR = -66.2773 + 0.1119Y - SXDT$ $(-6.46) \qquad (15.24)$	.9944	0.9745	*TSCORC*
$GC = 17.5453 + 0.03193Y - 33.3742$ $(0.47) \quad (1.67) \qquad (-2.27)$ $RPG + 7.3280POP$ (4.28)	.9577	1.7572	*TS*
$ILG = -92.5178 + 0.6702MG + 0.7853GP$ $(-6.30) \qquad (5.04) \qquad (10.15)$	.9477	1.6311	*TS*
$SH = -72.2550 + 0.08657YDP + 192.7797RD$ $(-4.49) \qquad (4.26) \qquad\;\; (2.93)$ $-44.6751RINF + 35.0964RINF_{-1}$ $(-2.50) \qquad\quad (-2.87)$	.9550	2.9992	*TSCORC*
$CK = -23.6744 + 0.2615I + 151.0420\ RLR$ $(-7.02) \qquad (7.73) \qquad (2.89)$ $-79.3805RRF - 27.5013CKDM$ $(-2.05) \qquad\quad (-3.01)$	.9847	2.5466	*TS*
$MC = -8.3930 + 0.0597DC - 0.1049$ $(-2.25) \quad (11.67) \quad (-5.41)$ $(SUBM + ORD)$	.9162	1.2160	*TS*
$MK = 1.5311 + 0.2117CK + 0.3717I$ $(0.23) \quad (1.15) \qquad (6.63)$ $-0.0846ORD$ (-2.33)	.9866	1.6893	*TS*
$MI = 10.3928 + 0.1760Y + 0.3672XGM$ $(0.44) \quad (3.50) \qquad (1.69)$ $-0.3700SUBM - 0.2188ORD$ $(-2.51) \qquad\quad (-2.66)$	.9891	1.5930	*TS*

Note: *TSCORC* is two-stage least squares with Cochrane-Orcutt iterations and *TS* is ordinary two-stage least squares.

the Fisher instruments of zero- and first-order causal variables, and another with a larger set of instruments up to the second order of causality.

In addition to the Fisher instruments, Fair (1970) suggests that when the errors in an equation are serially correlated a consistent estimation procedure requires the addition of all lagged variables in the equation as instruments.

Table 5 lists the instruments which are used for each equation. Tables 6 and 7 give the results using the two different sets of Fisher instrument, the first set using zero- and first-order causal variables and the second set using variables through the second order of causality. Note that for the YNA equation, there are no other endogenous variables in the equation. Thus two-stage least squares and ordinary least squares are equivalent. Note also in Table 5 that for the INT, SC, and XGM equations, there are no second-order causal variables.

Thus the two-stage least squares estimates are identical whether or not second-order causal variables are included. When only the Fisher first-order causal variables are included, the ILG equation does not have enough instruments so that the equation is under-identified. It is only possible to estimate with two-stage least squares when second-order instruments are included. Finally, when instruments through the second order of causality are used, it is not possible to estimate the INA equation. There are too many instruments and no degrees of freedom.

The results using two-stage least squares with first-order instruments are almost identical to the ordinary least squares results except for the GC, CK, MK, and MI equations. When second-order instruments are used, only the coefficient of the CK variable in the MK equation is substantially different from the ordinary least-squares result. Furthermore, all the equations listed in Table 7 still have substantial degrees of freedom except for the CK equation. We must conclude that the problem of simultaneity is not great for our Korean econometric model.

VI.   COMMERCIAL POLICY VARIABLES AND SIMULATION OF POLICY ALTERNATIVES

The basic commercial policy variables to be considered are:
1) the official exchange rate, 2) the export premium per dollar of exports which arises because of a multiple exchange rate system favoring export

earnings, 3) other subsidies and subsidy equivalents per dollar of exports, and 4) tariffs and foreign exchange taxes per dollar of imports. All basic commercial policy variables are computed on a purchasing-power-parity basis.

The basic commercial policy variables are combined to form a number of derived commercial policy variables. The effective exchange rate on imports is a combination of the official exchange rate, tariffs and foreign exchange taxes per dollar of imports, and total export premia per dollar of imports. That is, the cost of imports is raised above the official rate not only because of tariffs and foreign exchange taxes but because of the fact that some imports are financed by purchases of export dollars under the multiple exchange rate system. The effective exchange rate on exports is a combination of the official exchange rate, the export dollar premium, and the total of other subsidies per dollar of export. The overall effective exchange rate is defined as the weighted average effective exchange rate on exports and imports (where the weights are exports and imports.) Finally, the rate of devaluation is defined as the percentage increase in the overall effective exchange rate averaged over the current year and the two previous years.

A major effect of the commercial policy variables is the influence of the effective exchange rate for exports on export performance and of the effective exchange rate for imports on import demand. The export performance, of course, affects the availability of foreign exchange required to finance purchases of imported capital goods for investment purposes and imported raw materials and intermediate goods for current production purposes. The demand for imports affects the amount of foreign exchange required to finance a given level of production or investment.

The rate at which devaluation of the overall effective exchange rate takes place affects the real private cost of servicing foreign loans. The more rapid the rate of devaluation, the greater is the local cost of financing foreign loans and the lower is the demand for foreign commercial capital imports. A reduction in the level of foreign capital imports reduces the availability of foreign exchange to finance imports for current production purposes as well as for investment *and* reduces total savings and investment because of the reduction in foreign savings.

The *way* in which various effective exchange rates are maintained also affects macro-economic relationships. To the extent that exports are encouraged by tax subsidies, either direct or indirect, the government budget is affected. An increase in export subsidies of this sort, at given levels of government expenditure, reduces government savings and hence total investment. Export encouragement by a multiple exchange rate system, however, does not have the same adverse effect on government revenues.

Similarly, tariffs and foreign exchange taxes affect government revenues. If the aggregate elasticity of demand for imports is less than unity, an increase in the average tariff rate increases government revenues and savings at a given level of government expenditures. Purchases of export certificates which carry import entitlement, while they result in an addition to local currency cost of imports beyond the official exchange rate, do not result in government revenue in the same way as tariffs.

The *net* effect of all these relationships and interactions is difficult to determine on an *a priori* basis. The interactions are too complex. For example, an increase in import tariffs reduces the demand for imports and hence conserves on foreign exchange but may reduce government revenues if the aggregate elasticity of import demand is greater than unity.[14] The conservation of foreign exchange makes more rapid growth possible with a limited amount of foreign exchange, but the reduction in government revenues reduces government savings and investment, which has a deleterious effect on growth. Similarly, an increase in the rate of devaluation increases export earnings and reduces import demand thus enabling more rapid growth if foreign exchange is scarce, but it also reduces the inflow of foreign commercial capital which tends to reduce growth. The net effect of various policies depends on a complex set of interrelations among the parameters of the aggregate behavioral functions. In this chapter, we will perform some experiments on a simulation model using different policy strategies to attempt to determine the efficacy of various exchange rate policies in promoting growth. Our results will be analyzed to determine the important parameters and relationships.

VII.   THE SIMULATION MODEL

The basis of the simulation model is the econometric model estimated in the previous chapter. In more general form, the model may be written as follows:

(41) $B \cdot \psi_t + \Gamma_1 \phi_{1t} + \Gamma_2 \phi_{2t} + \Gamma_3 \phi_{3t} + \Delta \psi_{t-\tau} + e_t = 0$

---

[14] We must assume also that the supply of imported goods is infinitely elastic.

where ψ_t is a vector of endogenous variables, ϕ_{1t} is a vector of basic commercial policy variables, ϕ_{2t} is a vector of derived commercial policy variables, ϕ_{3t} is a vector of all other exogenous variables in the model, $\psi_{t-\tau}$ is a vector of predetermined endogenous variables and e_t is a vector of error terms. B, Γ_1, Γ_2, Γ_3, and Δ are matrices of parameters of the model and are estimated in the previous chapter. The variables in the system and the structure of the matrices are given in Tables 1 though 5.

In addition to the basic econometric model given by (41), the simulation model has a number of equations giving the derived commercial policy variables as functions of the basic commercial policy variables and a number of inequality constraints which the system must satisfy. The derived commercial policy variables are determined as follows: The first derived commercial policy variable, export premia per dollar of *imports,* is export premia per dollar of *exports* multiplied by total exports and divided by total imports.

$$(42) \qquad \phi_{2,1,t} = XPM_t = (XPX_t \cdot X_t)/M_t.$$

Total tariffs and tariff equivalents per dollar of imports, i.e., the difference between the official exchange rate and the effective rate on imports, is the second derived commercial policy variable and is the sum of tariffs and foreign exchange taxes per dollar of imports and export premia per dollar of imports.

$$(43) \qquad \phi_{2,2,t} = SUBM_t = TAM_t + XPM_t.$$

Similarly, total subsidies and subsidy equivalents per dollar of exports is the sum of export subsidies on exports and export premia per dollar of exports.

$$(44) \qquad \phi_{2,3,t} = SUBX_t = SOX_t + XPX_t.$$

Subsidies on exports in the form of internal tax relief is expressed as a fraction of total export subsidies times a factor required to express these total subsidies in terms of 1965 prices.[15]

$$(45) \qquad \phi_{2,4,t} = SXDT_t = \alpha_1 SOX_t \cdot X_t \cdot \alpha_{2t}$$

Total tariffs and foreign exchange taxes are equal to the effective tariff rate (i.e., total tariffs and foreign exchange taxes per dollar of imports) times total imports multiplied by the factor α_{2t} required to express these revenues in terms of 1965 prices.

$$(46) \qquad \phi_{2,5,t} = TAR_t = TAM_t \cdot M_t \cdot \alpha_{2t}.$$

---

[15] In terms of the original data, $\alpha_{2t} = RY_t \cdot WPI_t/(OR_{1965} \cdot WPITP_t \cdot CY_t)$

The rate of devaluation is the percentage rate at which the overall effective exchange rate devalues. The overall effective exchange rate is a weighted average of the effective exchange rate on imports and exports. The effective exchange rates on exports and imports are

(47) $$RX_t = ORD_t + SUBX_t,$$

and

(48) $$RM_t = ORD_t + SUBM_t,$$

respectively. The overall or average effective exchange rate is

(49) $$R_t = (RX_t \cdot X_t + RM_t \cdot M_t)/(X_t + M_t).$$

The rate of devaluation, then, is

(50) $$RDEV_t = (R_t - R_{t-1})/R_{t-1}.$$

The moving average rate of devaluation is the last derived commercial policy variable.

(51) $$\phi_{2,6,t} = MARDEV_t = (RDEV_t + RDEV_{t-1} + RDEV_{t-2})/3.$$

The model is also subject to a number of inequality constraints. The first set of these constraints refers to the level of foreign exchange reserves at the end of year t denoted by $LFXR$. The level of foreign exchange reserves is determined recursively from period to period.

(52) $$LFXR_{t+1} = LFXR_t + \varDelta LFXR_t$$

where the change in reserves in year t is denoted by $\varDelta LFXR_t$.[16] The level of foreign exchange reserves must be greater than some minimum fraction of imports and less than some maximum fraction of total imports.

(53) $$LFXR_{t+1} \geqq \alpha_3 M_t.$$

(54) $$LFXR_{t+1} \leqq \alpha_4 M_t.$$

The purpose of these constraints is to require reserves which are "adequate" but no "excessive" where the policy parameters α_3 and α_4 define adequacy and excessiveness in terms of a fraction of imports.

Similarly, inventory levels are constrained to be greater than a minimum fraction of total income and less than some maximum fraction of total income.

---

[16] In terms of our original data, the change in reserves is
$$\varDelta LFXR_t = -SK_t + DCKS_t \cdot (RMG_t + RMOS_t)/DMGS_t$$
See Tables 8.8 and 8.9 for definitions of the variables.

(55) $$LIV_{t+1} \geq \alpha_5 Y_t$$

(56) $$LIV_{t+1} \leq \alpha_6 Y_t$$

where the level of inventories at the end of year t is determined recursively as follows:

(57) $$LIV_{t+1} = LIV_t + IV_t$$

where IV_t is the level of investment in inventories in year t (excluding grain inventories). Unless inventory levels are restricted to be greater than some fraction of total income, investment will not be constrained by availability of savings, i.e., investment could be financed by unlimited drawing down of inventories. The upper limit on inventories is to ensure that production is limited by total effective demand.

VIII. METHOD OF SIMULATION

The simulation of the model expressed in equations (41) through (57) were performed over the period 1960 to 1970 with several variations of the values of the basic commercial policy variables. These are:

$\phi_{1,1,t} = ORD_t$: Official exchange rate on a purchasing-power-parity basis

$\phi_{1,2,t} = XPX_t$: Export premia per dollar of exports

$\phi_{1,3,t} = SOX_t$: Subsidies per dollar of exports

$\phi_{1,4,t} = TAM_t$: Tariffs and foreign exchange taxes per dollar of imports.

The parameters α_1, α_3, α_4, α_5, and α_6 are aslo basic policy parameters. These were set at what we regarded as "reasonable" values, given historical experience. The proportion of export subsidies in the form of internal tax relief (α_1) was, in fact, set equal to its historical value for each year from 1960 to 1970. In the final simulations, values of α_3 through α_6 were set as follows:

$\alpha_3 = 0.17$ lower limit on foreign exchange as a proportion of imports

$\alpha_4 = 0.35$ upper limit on foreign exchange as a proportion of imports

$\alpha_5 = 0.05$ lower limit on inventories (excluding grains) as a proportion of output

$\alpha_6 = 0.14$ upper limit on inventories (excluding grains) as a proportion of output.

Historically, over the period 1960 to 1970, foreign exchange reserves ranged from 17 to 67 percent of total imports while inventories ranged from 10 to 14 percent of total GNP. If the historical upper limit on foreign exchange reserves is maintained in the simulations, considerable reserves are accumulated for some of the simulation runs. In order that excess reserves can be translated into extra growth, an upper limit of 35 percent, or four months' import is postulated as a reasonable upper limit. Similarly we use a lower limit of 5 percent on inventories as a percent of output to allow a tighter regime which enables more of a running down of inventories to finance investment.

In addition to the variations in these values and parameters, we have two policy adjustment variables, EC_t and $IG_t \cdot EC_t$ is an excess capacity variable which comes into play whenever foreign exchange reserves or inventories are inadequate. We assume that the government will attempt to adjust to a balance of payments crisis (inadequate reserves) or an inflationary gap (pressure on inventories indicating that desired investment exceeds savings) by pursuing deflationary monetary and fiscal policies which generate excess capacity in the economy. IG_t is a variable denoting a change in total investment induced by government policy actions, including inflationary or deflationary monetary policy and direct government investment. We assume that in addition to excess capacity, the government is able to cut down on investment when a balance of payments problem arises or an inflationary gap emerges. Conversely, when there are excess reserves or high levels of inventory, the government pursues policies to increase total investment.

The model is non-linear because of the relationships (42), (46), (49), and (50). Rather than using a general non-linear solution technique such as Gauss-Seidel, a special solution technique was devised for this particular model which takes advantage of the rather simple nature of the non-linearities. The non-linear solution technique is described in the Appendix to this chapter.

At each period of time in the simulations, the constraints (53) through (56) are checked. If foreign exchange reserves are less than the required minimum level relative to imports or inventories are below the minimum level relative to income (constraints (53) and (55) violated), the excess capacity variable EC_t is increased and the level of investment is reduced by lowering IG_t.[17] If there are excess reserves or excess inventories (constra-

---

[17] Income and investment are reduced by a ratio of one to three.

ints (54) and (56) violated), investment is increased by increasing IG_t. These policy adjustments are continued in an iterative fashion until the constraints which are violated are satisfied. Initially the policy values EC_t and IG_t are set equal to zero in each period; so if none of the constraints are violated there is no excess capacity and no government induced changes in investment.

IX. SIMULATION EXPERIMENTS

Using the model described above, two sets of simulation experiments were performed to determine the behavior of the macro-economic aggregates over the period 1960 to 1970. The first set of experiments involved variations in the "pure" effective exchange rate, a completely unified exchange rate with no subsidies on exports and no tariffs or tariff equivalents on imports. With a "pure" effective exchange rate, there are no distortions of international prices and the exchange rate regime is completely liberal. These experiments are designed first of all to determine how much can be gained by complete liberalization and secondly to estimate various "equilibrium" exchange rates.

The second set of experiments involved variations, positive and negative, in the basic commercial policy variables in comparison with their historical values. The official exchange rate (ORD) was varied between 80 and 120 percent of its historical value. The exchange rate premium per dollar of export (XPX) varied between 0 and 200 percent of its historical value to determine the effect of the multiple exchange rate system. Subsidies per dollar of exports (SOX) were varied between 0 and more than 500 percent of its historical value and tariffs and foreign exchange tax per dollar of imports (TAM) were varied between 0 and more than 300 percent of its historical value.

In all of the experiments, we assume that some "optimal" solution exists in the sense that there exists some combination of basic commercial policy variables which maximizes a "well-behaved" utility function difined with respect to the endogenous macro-variables. We did not, however, attempt to define such a utility function and use optimization techniques to determine the maximum value of the utility function. Rather we looked at two separate "performance indicators" for each simulation run: 1) the discounted value of total GNP over the time horizon 1960 to 1970, and 2) the discounted value of consumption. Neither is really an appropriate measure of utility. The discounted value of consumption may be high because savings and investment are low in the last few years so that future growth beyond 1970 is sacrificed for consumption over the period of 1960 to 1970. The discounted value of GNP may be high because consumption is low so that future growth beyond 1970 is bought at the price of low consumption during the period 1960 to 1970. One growth path, however, may dominate another in the sense that both consumption and total income are higher. This is, in fact, the situation most frequently encountered in our simulation runs so that there is no practical conflict between maximization of income and consumption.

The use of optimization techniques presents problems other than that of an appropriate definition of a utility function. The model is complex and non-linear, involving 40 equations and inequalities in each time period. Thus there are more than 400 constraints over the horizon 1960 to 1970 which would involve formidable computational difficulties for a non-linear optimization model. The simulation approach enables us to determine "near optimal" solutions. Furthermore, we are able to examine the time path of the macro-aggregates for selected sets of policy choices which would not be possible if we used an optimization model.

X. EQUILIBRIUM EXCHANGE RATES

The first set of experiments involved an attempt to determine the exchange rate which, if subsidies, taxes, and tariffs on foreign trade were eliminated, would result in a growth path of the economy which approximated the actual path of the economy over the period 1960 to 1970. Variations above and below this "equilibrium" rate were also made to determine the behavior of the discounted value of output and consumption over the period 1960 to 1970.

The first step in the procedure was to set the official exchange rate so that the purchasing-power-parity effective exchange rate (without tariffs and subsidies) was equal to the historical pruchasing-power-parity effective rate (including taxes, tariffs, and subsidies). The result of this experiment is a growth performance which is somewhat inferior in terms of GNP, but superior in terms of consumption (see Figure 1). The reason for the poorer performance as regards GNP is that government revenues from tariffs

Fig.   1

*Income and Consumption Over Time: Pure Effective Exchange Rate Equal
to Historical Exchange Rate Including Taxes and Subsidies*

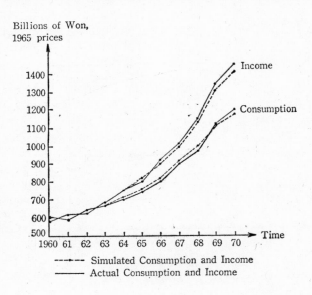

Billions of Won,
1965 prices

- - - - - Simulated Consumption and Income
———— Actual Consumption and Income

and foreign exchange taxes are reduced and less government savings occur.
The economy runs into inflationary pressures, especially in 1968 and 1969.
Investment tends to exceed available savings, both domestic and foreign.
Inventories are run down, resulting in a violation of the inventory (i.e.
savings-investment) constraint in the model. Deflationary government
fiscal and monetary policy reduces investment and generates excess capacity, thus slowing the growth of the economy. Consumption on the other
hand is greater. The basic reason for this result is that with less government
revenues, disposable income and hence consumption is greater.

The next step was to vary the "pure" effective exchange rate above and
below the actual historical value of the effective exchange rate. The results
in terms of the total discounted values of GNP and consumption are
shown in Figure 2. If the "pure" rate is reduced to 99.5 percent of the historical effective rate, the results are slightly better, both as regards output
and consumption, but the results are not significantly different. If the
"pure" rate is reduced much below 99.5 percent, the results are worse, both in terms of output and in terms of consumption. For example, if the pure

Fig. 2.

Behavior of Discounted Values of Income and Consumption with Variations in the Pure Effective Exchange Rate

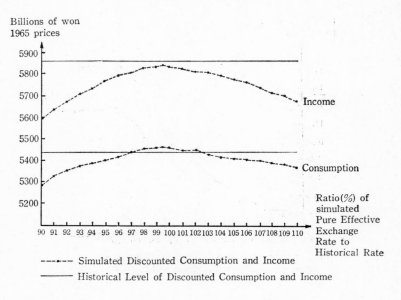

Billions of won
1965 prices

------ Simulated Discounted Consumption and Income

——— Historical Level of Discounted Consumption and Income

effective exchange rate is reduced to only 90 percent of the historical values, the total discounted value of income drops by more than four percent and of consumption by about two percent. The reason for the poorer performance is that the economy runs into a foreign exchange constraint in the middle of the decade. Investment must be reduced and excess capacity appears. Similarly, if the pure effective exchange rate is raised above 99.5 percent of the historical levels, consumption and income growth are constrained. The cause is a lack of savings. Savings are insufficient because of the decline in foreign savings $(M-X)$ as imports tend to decline more than exports when the pure effective exchange rate is reduced.

Part of the conventional economic wisdom concerning Korea asserts that the 1965 exchange rate for South Korea is an equilibrium exchange rate and that if the purchasing-power-parity vlaue of that exchange rate were maintained,there would have been no need to have increased the level of export subsidies to maintain balance of payments equilibirum. This hypothesis was tested in the following way: The 1965 effective purchasing-power-partity exchange rate was converted to a pure exchange rate by

Fig. 3

Behavior of Discounted Values of Income and Consumption with Pure Effective Exchange Rate Valued Relative to 1965 Effective Exchange Rate

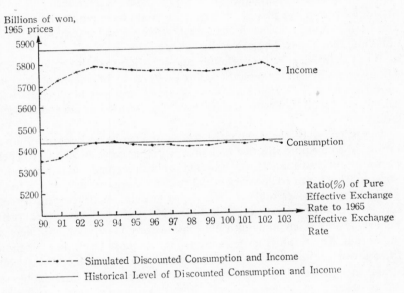

Billions of won,
1965 prices

----•---- Simulated Discounted Consumption and Income

————— Historical Level of Discounted Consumption and Income

eliminating export subsidies, import tariffs and foreign exchange taxes. The pure exchange rate was varied between 90 and 110 percent of the 1965 effective exchange rate for the years 1964 to 1970.

The results of this experiment indicated that when the pure exchange rate is set at 102 percent of the 1965 effective exchange rate, both the discounted value of total output and consumption achieve their maximum and the path of the economy follows most closely the historical path of the economy. The discounted value of consumption is about the same as the historical value, but the discounted value of income is about 1.2 percent below the historical value. This result stems from a lack of savings due to the reduction in government tariff revenues and hence government savings. When the pure exchange rate is set at 100 percent of the 1965 effective exchange rate, the growth of income and consumption is somewhat less than that achieved with the 102 percent level (see Figure 3). These results tend to support the view that roughly the 1964 exchange rate was an "equilibrium" exchange rate. The 1965 rate is an equilibrium rate in the sense that all tariffs and export subsidies could have been eliminated and the official exchange rate devalued to approximately the 1965 rate on a purchasing-power-parity basis and the economy would have followed most closely the same path in terms of all of the economic aggregates. Of course, maintenance of the 1965 rate on a purchasing-power-parity basis over the period 1964 to 1970 would have required a continuous devaluation in line with changes in domestic and international price inflation, that is, a gliding peg exchange rate.

When the pure effective exchange rate is reduced much below the 1965 effective rate during the period 1964 to 1970, say to 90 percent of the 1965 effective rate, the foreign exchange constraint becomes binding, particularly in 1965. This results in considerably less growth in income and consumption.

The behavior of the discounted values of income and consumption is erratic when the pure effective exchange rate is set between 93 and 102 percent of the effective rate. Local maxima for both income and consumption occur at 93, 97, and 102 percent. At 93 percent, there are some excess foreign exchange reserves in 1967. This helps growth. At 97 percent, excess foreign exchange reserves occur in both 1966 and 1967. The government policy variables then come into play, stimulating investment and increasing output. The result is more rapid growth in those years, but the more rapid growth results in an inflationary gap and a savings-investment constraint in 1968 and 1969. At 102 percent, the excess foreign exchange reserves occur even earlier, in 1964, but the savings-investment constraint becomes operative earlier and more persistently from 1966 thorugh 1970. The erratic behavior, then, is caused by the interaction of the savings-investment and foreign exchange constraints.

XI. VARIATIONS IN COMMERCIAL POLICY VARIABLES

The next set of experiments involved an attempt to determine an optimal of commercial policy variables. This required simulations in which the four basic commercial policy variables were varied over a considerable range from their historical values. The official exchange rate (ORD) was set at 80,100 and 120 percent of its historical values over the period 1964 to 1970. Export premia per dollar of export arising from the working of the multiple exchange rate system (XPX) were varied between zero and more than three times its historical values in varying steps. Other subsidies per dollar of export (*SOX*) were varied from zero to more than five times its historical values in varying steps. Finally, tariffs and foreign exchange taxes per dollar of imports (*TAM*) were varied between zero and three times the historical values.[18] In all, more than 1,000 experiments were run. The results give a fairly good indication of the responsiveness of the Korean economy to changes in commercial policy. Only a few of the more interesting results are presented here.

The variations in *XPX,* export premia per dollar of exports, did not make much of a difference, so none of these results are reported here.[19] First, we discuss variations in export subsidies per dollar of exports (*SOX*) and tariffs and foreign exchange taxes per dollar of imports (*TAM*), holding the official exchange rate constant at its historical values. Table 8 gives the figures for the discounted value of output over the period 1960 to 1970

Table 8

Discounted Value of Total Output with Official Exchange Rate at Its Historical Values and Variations in Tariffs and Foreign Exchange Taxes per Dollar of Import (TAM) and Subsidies per Dollar of Export (SOX)

SOX as percent of historical value	*TAM* as percent of historical value 80	120	160	200	240
0	5830	5891	5920	5985	NF
40	5852	5886	5928	5999	NF
80	5850	5882	5938	6015	NF
120	5840	5887	5952	6026*	NF
160	5839	5897	5953	6013	NF
200	5838	5880	5928	5988	NF
240	5820	5853	5894	5937	NF
280	5795	5813	5869	5868	NF
320	5752	5776	5807	5820	NF

Note: NF means not feasible.

*Maximum value of the discounted value of output for the period 1960 to 1970.

---

[18] It should be kept in mind that export subsidies and tariffs were a relatively small percent of the effective exchange rate (e.g. 13 percent and 9 percent, respectively, in 1965); so that a doubling or tripling is equivalent to a much smaller change in the effective exchange rate.

[19] Export premia were very small during the period covered by the simulations.

and Table 9 gives the discounted value of consumption over the same period for this set of experiments. The figures marked with asterisks in Tables 8 and 9 give the maximum values of discounted output and consumption, respectively. The optimal value of discounted output exceeds the historical level, 5860, by four percent; the optimal value of discounted consumption exceeds the historical level, 5421, by about one percent. The italicized numbers in Tables 3 and 9 represent combinations of values for *TAM* and *SOX* which result in *both* greater consumption *and* greater output over the period 1960 to 1970 than the historical values. Both the maximum value of output and the maximum value of consumption lie within the region for which both output and consumption exceed historical values. Thus one could maximize the discounted value of output without lowering the discounted value of consumption below its historical value. Alternatively, one could maximize the discounted value of consumption without lowering the discounted value of output below its historical value.

Table 9

Discounted Value of Consumption with Official Exchange Rate at its Historical Values and Variations in TAM and SOX

SOX as percent of historical value	TAM as percent of historical value				
	80	120	160	200	240
0	5396	5407	5398	5408	NF
40	5416	5411	5411	5424	NF
80	5423	5417	5424	5442	NF
120	5425	5428	5441	5458	NF
160	5433	5443	5452	5462*	NF
200	5442	5443	5447	5458	NF
240	5440	5437	5438	5439	NF
280	5435	5423	5433	5410	NF
320	5418	5410	5407	5393	NF

Note: NF means not feasible.
*Maximum value of discounted value of consumption for the period 1960 to 1970.

The maximum discounted values of output and consumption occur at very nearly the same combinations of the values of *SOX* and *TAM* (with the official exchange rate being held at its historical value). The level of tariffs and foreign exchange taxes per dollar of imports (TAM) is double the historical level and the level of export subsidies is somewhat greater than the historical level (20 percent in the case of maximum output and 60 percent in the case of maximum consumption). The increased value of TAM results in increased government revenues. Since the level of government expenditures is assumed to be exogenous, the effect is to increase government savings. The increase in the value of SOX tends to reduce government revenues, but since export subsidies are increased by a smaller percentage than tariffs, since exports are less than total imports, and since only part of export subsidies have a direct budgetary impact, the net effect is a substantial increase in government savings which increases total investment and accelerates growth. The increase in SOX and TAM both generate extra foreign exchange accumulation through increased exports and reduced imports. The accumulation of foreign exchange also makes possible increased investment and growth. The time path of output and consumption is shown in Figure 4 for the case in which the discounted value of output is maximized. By 1970, the simulated value of output exceeds the historical value by 95 billion won (constant prices) or almost 7 percent. Furthermore in the simulation, historical values of output and consumption are almost equalled or exceeded for every year in the period 1960 to 1970. Thus the increase in SOX and TAM results in a dynamically more efficient growth path.

The doubling of TAM does not involve very high levels of tariffs and foreign exchange taxes. In 1970, for example, tariffs (there were virtually no foreign exchange taxes) were only about 7 percent of imports so that a doubling of the level implies a tariff rate of about 14 percent. If the level of tariffs and foreign exchange taxes is raised much above this, however, the simulation run becomes unfeasible. This occurs because some of the smaller import items become negative. This is an inevitable result whenever import demand functions are specified to be linear. Even if the specification were made more realistic, however, the imposition of higher tariffs would probably eventually lead to less growth. This is because very high tariff levels would probably result in a very elastic demand for imports. As tariffs are raised, import demand eventually decreases by a larger percentage; government tariff revenues decline; government savings are lower: and investment and growth are less.

If export subsidies are raised beyond 20 percent more than historical levels, the growth in output also declines. This occurs because of the reduction in government revenue and savings. This in turn reduces investment. In the simulation run with export subsidies higher than 120 percent

Fig. 4

Time Paths of Consumption and Output with SOX Equal 120 *Percent*
of Historical Values and TAM Equal 200 *Percent of Historical Values*

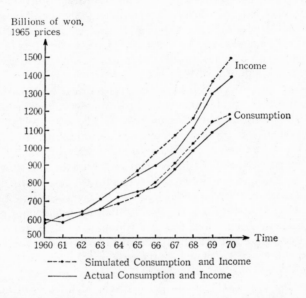

--•-- Simulated Consumption and Income
——— Actual Consumption and Income

of historical values and tariffs double historical values, the savings-investment constraint is violated in 1966 and 1967. Investment has to be reduced
because of deficient savings, and growth is correspondingly less. Savings
are deficient because of the reduction in government revenues and savings.

If export subsidies are reduced below 120 percent of historical levels,
growth is also less since fewer foreign reserves are accumulated which can
be utilized through government policies to increase imports needed for
investment. The increase in investment financed from accumulated reserves is less than it is for the optimal growth path.

Tables 10 and 11 show discounted values of output and consumption,
respectively, for simulations in whcih the official exchange rate is held 20
percent below its historical value and *SOX* and *TAM* are varied. Again
the italicized figures represent combinations of *SOX* and *TAM* which would have resulted in equal or better than historical values for both output
and consumption. In this case, the maximum discounted value of output
and the maximum discounted value of consumption require widely divergent
policies. Output is maximized whenever export subsidies are increased 50

Table 10

*Discounted Value of Output with Official Exchange Rate at **80**
Percent of Its Historical Value and Variations in TAM and SOX*

SOX as percent of historical value	TAM as percent of historical value					
	200	250	300	350	400	450
0	NF	NF	NF	NF	NF	NF
50	NF	NF	5832	5964	6046	NF
100	NF	5731	5879	6003	6055	NF
150	5612	5776	5911	6029	6065*	NF
200	5663	5819	5951	6041	NF	NF
250	5710	5863	5985	6042	NF	NF
300	5754	5901	6018	6019	NF	NF
350	5796	5922	6010	6007	NF	NF
400	5810	5943	5977	6019	NF	NF
450	5812	5961	5963	6034**	NF	NF
500	5827	5921	5962	6032	NF	NF
550	5846	5900	5931	5985	NF	NF
600	5831	5849	5883	5931	NF	NF
650	5781	5808	5806	5918	NF	NF

Note: NF means not feasible.
*Maximum discounted value of output.
**Maximum discounted value of ouptut subject to constraint that discounted value of consumption exceeds historical value.

percent and tariffs 300 percent above their historical values. The discounted value of consumption, however, is far less than its historical value. The discounted value of consumption is maximized whenever export subsidies are increased 350 percent and import duties are 150 percent above historical values. In the former case emphasis is placed on tariffs and in the latter case emphasis is placed on export subsidies. In both cases, there is additional growth because of accumulations of foreign exchange reserves which allows increased investment. Increased export subsidies, however, lead to relatively more consumption because of the reduction in direct tax revenues as a subsidization measure and the resultant increase in disposable income.

Since the two objectives of output maximization and consumption ma-

Table 11

*Discounted Value of Consumption with Official Exchange
Rate at **80** Percent of Its Historical Value and Variations in TAM
and SOX*

SOX as percent of historical value	TAM as percent of historical value					
	200	250	300	350	400	450
0	NF	NF	NF	NF	NF	NF
50	NF	NF	5274	5312	5319	NF
100	NF	5253	5306	5340	5332	NF
150	5217	5286	5331	5362	5346	NF
200	5255	5319	5363	5378	NF	NF
250	5293	5355	5393	5390	NF	NF
300	5330	5388	5423	5389	NF	NF
350	5366	5412	5431	5397	NF	NF
400	5387	5438	5426	5417	NF	NF
450	5403	5464*	5433	5430	NF	NF
500	5427	5455	5447	5456	NF	NF
550	5455	5458	5447	5447	NF	NF
600	5462	5443	5436	5435	NF	NF
650	5446	5436	5408	5388	NF	NF

Note: NF means not feasible.
*Maximum discounted value of consumption.

ximization are divergent, one is led to investigate the maximum discounted value of output subject to the constraint that the discounted value of consumption be at least as great as its historical value. This occurs whenever tariffs are 250 percent and export subsidies 350 percent above historical values. Perhaps an even better solution occurs whenever export subsidies are increased to 400 percent above historical values with tariffs remaining 250 percent above historical values. There is a large jump in consumption and only a small loss in output. The values of output and consumption are roughly similar to those achieved in the prior case in which the official exchange rate is equal to its historical value. The difference is that with the official exchange rate below its historical value, tariffs and subsidies have to be increased to very high levels to increase foreign exchange availability. The high tariffs generate the revenue required to offset the loss in revenue due to export subsidies.

Table 12 gives the discounted values of consumption and output when the official exchange rate is set at 20 percent greater than its historical value. In this case the maximum values of output and consumption occur with the same values of *SOX* and *TAM*. Furthermore, the maximum values are below historical values and far below the maximum values achievable when the official exchange rate is set equal to its historical values or 20 percent below historical values (see Tables 8 through 11). In the experiments with a high level of the official exchange rate, foreign exchange is no problem. Growth is inhibited by a lack of savings. The maximum for both output and consumption occurs when export subsidies are set at a zero level and tariffs are only 30 percent of historical values. I export subsidies are raised or tariffs are reduced, government revenue and savings decline, further exacerbating the savings-investment constraint. If tariffs are raised, some of the minor imports become negative. Even if non-linear import demand functions were specified, an increase in tariffs would probably lead to an elastic demand and less revenue which would also exacerbate the savings-investment constraint. We are led to the conclusion that higher values of the official exchange rate would have led to less growth in output and consumption.

XII. CONCLUDING REMARKS

The experiments performed on the simulation model suggest that commercial policy has been an important factor in South Korea's growth performance. The results indicate, however, that the manner in which South Korea has attempted to promote exports, through subsidies of various sorts, and a relatively low level of tariffs has meant sacrifices in government revenues which have resulted in less than optimal growth performance. This conclusion is based on the assumption that increased government revenues would have resulted in increased government savings and that these savings would have been channeled into directly productive investments. The South Korean government has maintained a good performance in keeping the growth of current expenditures low and in channeling government funds into productive investments. Whether they could have achieved the same degree of success with further increases in revenues is not certain.

Table 12

Discounted Values of Consumption and Output with Official Exchange Rate at **120** *Percent of Its Historical Value and Variations in TAM and SOX*

SOX as percent of historical value	Output				
	TAM as percent of historical value				
	0	10	20	30	40
0	5171	5713	5738	5745*	NF
10	5690	5717	5726	5740	NF
20	5697	5707	5713	5729	NF
30	5684	5693	5714	5712	NF
40	5671	5694	5702	5688	NF

SOX as percent of historical value	Consumption				
	TAM as percent of historical value				
	0	10	20	30	40
0	5373	5366	5376*	5376*	NF
10	5358	5370	5370	5374	NF
20	5365	5366	5365	5370	NF
30	5358	5359	5367	5361	NF
40	5352	5362	5361	5348	NF

Note: NF means not feasilbe.
* Maximum values.

The experiments also tend to support the view that the 1965 exchange rate was an equilibrium rate in the sense that all subsidies and tariffs could have been eliminated and the same historical growth performance achieved. This definition of equilibrium exchange rate is somewhat different from the usual definition in terms of the rate which would equilibrate demand and supply of foreign exchange. The more traditional definition, however, is not a very useful or operational one. Government monetary and fiscal policies help determine the demand and supply of foreign exchange so that there may be one or more equilibrium exchange rate for each possible set of government policies. A more interesting concept is the optimal combination of exchange rate and government fiscal and monetary policies. Our experiments indicate that the optimal "pure" exchange rate is one slightly higher than the actual exchange rate (about 102 percent of the historical rate) combined with more expansionary monetary and fiscal policy.

If subsidies and taxes on exports and imports are combined with exchange rate policy, the optimal exchange rate is about equal to the historical rate. The optimal rate should be combined, however, with higher import duties (or fewer exemptions) and roughly similar export subsidies.

Appendix 1

Data Used in Econometric Model

Most of the data used for the regressions in this chapter are compiled by the Bank of Korea and published in their *Economic Statistics Yearbook*. A description of the raw data and their sources is contained in Table 13.

Table 13

Description of Raw Data and Sources

A. Data in billions of constant 1965 won
   1. *RY:* Gross National Product; BOK, *ESY* 1971, pp. 10–11.[1]
   2. *RYNA:* Value-Added in Non-Agricultural Sectors; BOK, *ESY* 1971, pp. 14–15.
   3. *RI:* Gross Domestic Fixed Capital Formation; BOK, *ESY* 1971, pp. 10–11.
   4. *RIA:* Investment in Agriculture; BOK, *ESY* 1971, pp. 28–29.
   5. *RNFI:* Net Factor Income from Abroad; *ESY* 1971, pp. 10–11.
   6. *RGRC:* Grain Consumption; BOK National Accounts Division.
   7. *RIVG:* Grain Inventory Investment; *Ibid.*
   8. *RILG:* Grain Inventory Level; *Ibid.*
   9. *RMG:* Imports of Goods, including freight and insurance; BOK, *ESY* 1971, pp. 44–45.
   10. *RXG:* Exports of Goods, including freight and insurance; *Ibid.*
   11. *RMOS:* Imports of Services, other than freight and insurance; *Ibid.*
   12. *RXOS:* Exports of Services, other than freight and insurance; *Ibid.*
   13. *RT:* Net Transfer Receipts from Abroad on Current Account; *Ibid.*
B. Data in billions of current won
   1. *CY:* Gross National Product; BOK, *ESY* 1971, pp. 8–9.
   2. *CYDP:* Personal Disposable Income; BOK, *ESY* 1971, pp. 36–37.
   3. *CSH:* Savings by Households and Private Non-Profit Institutions; BOK, *ESY* 1971, pp. 22–23.
   4. *CSC:* Gross Savings (including capital consumption allowances) by Corporations and Unincorporated Enterprises; *Ibid.*

---

[1] BOK, *ESY* 1971 is Bank of Korea, *Economic Statistics Yearbook* 1971. If series is not continuous to 1953 in 1971 yearbook, the series was traced back as far as possible in earlier yearbooks. 1970 revised figures were obtained from August 1971 issue of the Bank of Korea, *Monthly Economic Statistics*, August 1971.

Table 13

Description of Raw Data and Sources (continued)

---

4. *CGS:* Gross Savings by Government, including government enterprises; *Ibid.*
5. *CSTD:* Statistical Discrepancy between Savings and Gross Domestic Capital Formation; *Ibid.*
6. *CDTR:* Direct Tax Revenues; BOK, *ESY* **1971**, pp. 38–39.
7. *CITR:* Indirect Taxes; *Ibid.*
8. *CGT:* Government Transfers to the Private Sector; *Ibid.*

C. Data in current millions of dollars
   1. *DMGS:* Imports of Goods and Services; BOK, *ESY* **1971**, pp. 266–67.
   2. *DMG:* Imports of Goods, including freight and insurance; *Ibid.*
   3. *DCKL:* Long-term Private Capital Imports; *Ibid.*
   4. *DCKS:* Short-term Capital Imports; *Ibid.*
   5. *DMA:* Net Reduction in Foreign Assets of Monetary Institutions; *Ibid.*
   6. *DXG:* Total Exports of Goods; MOF, *FTOK* (annual through 1971).[2]
   7. *DMGR:* Imports of Grain (SITC 04); *Ibid.*
   8. *DMC:* Imports of Consumption Goods (SITC 0 (excl. 04), 1, 732.1, 8); *Ibid.*
   9. *DMK:* Imports of Capital Goods (SITC 7 (excl. 732.1)); MOF, *Ibid.*
   10. *DMI:* Imports of Intermediate Goods (SITC 2, 3, 4, 5, 6); *Ibid.*
   11. *DXGM:* Exports of Manufactured Goods; *Ibid.*

D. Exchange rate and export premia in won per dollar[3]
   1. *OR:* Exchange rate.
   2. *RXS:* Export Premium per Dollar of Export.

E. Tariffs, tariff equivalents, export subsidies, and export premia in billion won, current prices[4]
   1. *TM:* Tariffs and Tariff Equivalents
   2. *PX:* Total Export Premiums
   3. *SX:* Total Export Subsidies
   4. *SXTAXD:* Export Subsidies in Form of Direct Tax Relief
   5. *SXTAXI:* Export Subsidies in Form of Indirect Tax Exemption

---

[2] MOF, *FTOK* (annual through 1971) is Ministry of Finance, Republic of Korea, *Foreign Trade of Korea,* published annually through 1971. Page numbers differ by year.

[3] Data sources for these items are mainly primary sources, including files of the Bank of Korea, Ministry of Finance, and the United States AID Mission in Seoul. See Tables 5.8 and 5.9 in Chapter V for further description of the data.

[4] Data sources for these items are mainly primary sources, including files of the Bank of Korea, Ministry of Finance, and the United States AID Mission in Seoul. See Tables 5.1 and 5.2 in Chapter V for further description of the data.

Table 13

Description of Raw Data and Sources (continued)

F. Price Indices

    1. *WPI:* Wholesale Price Index; BOK, *ESY* **1971**, pp. 314–15.

    2. *WPIG:* Wholesale Price Index for Grains; *Ibid.*

    3. *WPIOG:* Wholesale Price Index for Commodities Other than Grains; *Ibid.*

    4. *WPITP:* Wholesale Price Index for Major Trading Partners; International Monetary Fund, *International Financial Statistics*[5]

G. Other Data

    1. *PR:* Farm Population in millions of persons; BOK, *ESY* 1971, p. 6.

    2. *PU:* Non-farm Population in millions of persons; *Ibid.*

    3. *NRD:* Nominal Interest Rate on Time Deposits One Year and Over; BOK, *ESY* 1971, 0. 135 and *ESY* 1960.

    4. *NRF:* Interest Rate on Business Loans in the United States; United States Department of Commerce, *Survey of Current Business.*

    5. *NLR:* Commercial Bank Lending Rate; BOK, *ESY*, 1957–1971.

Table 14 gives the transformations to the raw data which are required to obtain the values of the endogenous and exogenous variables for the model. Much of the raw data are current price data and must be deflated to obtain values in terms of constant won. Direct and indirect tax revenues, private savings, government savings, government transfers to private sector, and subsidies in the form of direct and indirect tax exemptions are all deflated by a *GNP* deflator (i.e., multiplied by *RY/CY* as in Table 14). Imports of goods of various types are deflated by the overall import price deflator used in determining real *GNP* (i.e., multiplied by *RMG/DMG*). Capital imports are deflated by the price deflator for imports of goods and services (i.e., multiplied by *(RMG + ROMS)/DMGS*). Non-classified imports *MNC*, consumption *DC*, inventory investment *IV*, government expenditure *G*, public capital imports *PK*, and net transfers of other sectors to households *NTOSH* are all defined in terms of the other variables so that the deflation procedures do not alter any of the identities of the model. The basic commercial policy variables are deflated by a purchasing-power-parity index which is the ratio of the Korean wholesale price index to the wholesale price index of major trading partners.

Tables 15A through 15G give the actual values of the raw data used and Tables 16A through 16D give the values of the derived endogenous and exogenous variables.

---

[5] Wholesale price indices for the United States and Japan were averaged, using weights derived from their respective shares in total trade.

Table 14

Transformations of Raw Data[1]

A. Endogenous Variables
1. $YNA = RYNA$
2. $Y = RY$
3. $DTR = (RY/CY)*CDTR$
4. $INT = (RY/CY)*(CITR - TM$
5. $SG = (RY/CY)*CGS$
6. $GC = RGRC$
7. $IVG = RIVG$
8. $MG = (RMG/DMG)*DMGR$
9. $ILG = RILG$
10. $SC = (RY/CY)*CSC$
11. $YDP = (RY/CY)*CYDP$
12. $SH = (RY/CY)*(CSH + CSTD) - RIVG$
13. $INA = RI - RIA$
14. $I = RI$
15. $CK = ((RMG + RMOS)/DMGS)*DCKL$
16. $DC = Y - SC - SH - IVG - SG + RNFI$
17. $MC = (RMG/DMG)*DMC$
18. $MK = (RMG/DMG)*DMK$
19. $XGM = (RXG/DXG)*DXGM$
20. $X = RXG$
21. $MI = (RMG/DMG)*DMI$
22. $M = RMG$
23. $SK = ((RMG + RMOS)/DMGS)*(DMA + DCKS)$
24. $IV = SG + SC + SH - I + M + RMOS - RXOS - RT - X$

B. Basic Commercial Policy Variables
1. $ORD = OR*(WPITP/WPI)$
2. $XPX = RXS*(WPITP/WPI)$
3. $SOX = ((SX*1000)/DXG)*(WPITP/WPI)$
4. $TAM = ((RM*1000)/DMG)*(WPITP/WPI)$

C. Derived Commercial Policy Variables
1. $XPM = ((PX*1000/DMG)*(WPITP/WPI)$
2. $SUBM = XPM + TAM$
3. $SUBX = SOX + XPX$
4. $SXDT = (RY/CY)*SXTAXD$
5. $TAR = (RY/CY)*TM$
6. $MARDEV + (RDEV + RDEV_{-1} + RDEV_{-2})/3$
   where
   $RDEV = (R - R_{-1})/R_{-1}$ and

---

[1] Multiplication is denoted by asterisk.

Table 14

Transformations of Raw Data (Continued)

$$R = ORD + (SUBM*RMG + SUBX*RXG)/(RMG + RXG)$$

D. Other Exogenous Variables

1. $YA = RY - RYNA$
2. $G = INT + TAR + DTR - SG$
3. $IA = RIA$
4. $PK = M + RMOS - RXOS - RT - X - CK - SK$
5. $MFI = RNFI$
6. $MST = RMOS - RXOS - RT$
7. $RPG = WPIG/WPIOG$
8. $POP = PR + PU$
9. $GP = RGRC + RIVG - (RMG/DMG)*DMGR$
10. $RD = NRD$
11. $LR = NLR$
12. $RF = NRF$
13. $RINF = (GNPD - GNPD_{-1})/GNPD_{-1}$
    where
    $GNDP = CY/RY$
14. $MNC = M - MC - MK - MI - MG$
15. $NTOSH = Y - INT - TAR - DTR - SC - YDP$
16. $XGP = (RXG/DXG)*(DXG - DXGM)$

Table 15A

Raw Data In Billions of 1965 Constant Won

Year	RY	RYNA	RI	RIA	RNFI	RGRC	RIVG
1953	421.93	218.60	35.38	4.04	9.42	—	36.13
1954	447.36	228.30	41.66	3.45	7.56	—	3.53
1955	474.54	250.50	48.98	4.53	7.75	162.87	0.95
1956	480.47	268.20	52.77	5.07	7.38	161.04	−11.32
1957	522.73	292.20	61.31	6.48	7.59	156.64	16.90
1958	551.69	305.40	57.79	5.35	7.59	180.61	9.45
1959	575.84	332.20	59.29	5.99	7.75	186.66	−3.73
1960	589.07	345.10	61.71	6.97	7.38	176.40	2.04
1961	613.61	345.10	65.26	8.35	5.79	192.47	6.81
1962	634.97	382.60	84.05	6.72	6.48	194.39	−15.25
1963	693.03	422.50	105.95	10.28	6.79	186.53	22.93
1964	750.31	436.00	93.33	10.66	6.53	218.38	20.85
1965	805.85	494.20	117.64	13.67	7.65	229.01	−0.15
1966	913.82	567.90	190.63	23.16	13.08	235.12	8.40
1967	995.16	668.30	232.09	19.24	21.53	238.91	−12.40
1968	1127.32	796.50	325.63	23.82	22.24	239.97	−12.47
1969	1306.19	935.80	407.76	24.26	23.04	246.20	30.08
1970	1422.33	1055.00	416.76	25.06	10.17	253.51	14.34

Year	RILG	RMG	RXG	RMOS	RXOS	RT
1953	36.13	91.67	10.64	1.83	13.30	49.92
1954	39.66	64.57	6.82	2.12	9.50	34.92
1955	40.61	86.95	4.91	2.57	13.83	39.84
1956	29.29	100.88	6.98	3.69	10.19	74.63
1957	46.19	117.12	7.09	6.61	13.80	83.07
1958	55.64	99.87	5.65	7.25	18.87	75.50
1959	51.91	80.02	6.29	7.85	21.20	54.59
1960	53.95	90.40	9.69	10.24	21.39	61.31
1961	60.76	82.30	11.89	9.00	26.75	46.93
1962	45.51	112.90	15.45	7.43	27.87	63.74
1963	68.44	143.56	23.78	9.98	22.80	66.65
1964	89.29	104.83	32.51	9.93	23.49	50.96
1965	89.14	120.15	47.80	9.44	29.12	53.95
1966	97.54	192.87	69.09	13.54	51.59	58.29
1967	85.14	263.59	87.82	17.73	82.81	59.76
1968	72.67	374.93	133.65	35.56	99.97	63.01
1969	102.75	468.83	183.02	47.40	122.38	64.65
1970	117.09	513.69	252.93	64.85	117.72	45.23

Table 15B
Raw Data In Billions of Won
Current Prices

Year	CY	CYDP	CSH*	CSC	CGS*
1953	48.18	44.14	3.44	2.24	1.11
1954	66.88	60.23	2.97	3.31	0.35
1955	116.06	106.33	3.87	5.00	1.32
1956	152.44	140.25	−3.08	6.57	8.50
1957	197.78	179.63	9.55	8.85	8.18
1958	207.19	183.78	7.85	10.20	7.65
1959	221.00	190.85	3.11	12.35	7.18
1960	246.69	212.69	−2.65	13.11	11.91
1961	296.82	260.16	2.51	17.25	14.10
1962	348.58	295.71	−10.48	25.25	21.62
1963	487.96	421.98	6.15	35.60	24.57
1964	696.79	617.14	11.06	46.44	34.75
1965	805.85	696.87	2.30	62.66	49.74
1966	1032.04	886.32	42.05	76.66	62.19
1967	1242.35	1043.24	11.73	97.59	88.25
1968	1575.65	1286.04	15.26	121.93	133.97
1969	2047.11	1701.32	114.41	149.44	159.51
1970	2545.92	2081.66	84.19	182.85	206.43

Year	CSTD**	CDTR	CITR	CGT
1953	—	0.99	1.70	0.41
1954	—	1.27	3.29	0.50
1955	—	1.90	5.22	0.50
1956	—	2.32	6.74	0.61
1957	—	4.37	10.42	1.93
1958	—	4.89	12.64	3.08
1959	—	6.02	16.19	2.17
1960	1.92	6.46	18.73	1.51
1961	2.18	8.44	19.98	0.64
1962	2.58	9.09	28.65	3.23
1963	3.62	12.18	30.94	0.0
1964	3.14	16.63	33.92	−1.89
1965	5.06	22.14	47.13	0.35
1966	14.16	38.03	72.31	5.27
1967	22.71	53.46	98.66	3.69
1968	28.36	81.00	147.71	23.22
1969	33.11	115.01	196.90	31.75
1970	45.58	145.01	250.37	7.84

*Includes current account transfers from abroad
**Before 1960, savings were estimated as a residual since then separate estimation of savings has resulted in a statistical discrepancy between savings and gross domestic capital formation

Table 15C
Raw Data in Millions of Dollars
1965 *Dollar Prices*

Year	DMGS	DMG	DCKL	DCKS	DMA	DXG
1953	—	345.40	—	—	—	40.10
1954	—	243.30	—	—	—	25.70
1955	337.30	327.60	0.0	−0.90	15.30	18.50
1956	394.00	380.10	0.0	−3.20	−18.70	26.30
1957	466.20	441.30	0.0	−2.90	4.10	27.60
1958	403.60	376.30	0.0	7.00	−45.30	21.30
1959	331.10	301.50	0.80	−0.60	−15.10	23.70
1960	379.20	340.60	2.60	0.60	−14.50	36.50
1961	344.00	310.10	0.20	−2.00	−30.30	44.80
1962	453.40	425.40	2.80	−6.70	56.50	58.20
1963	578.50	540.90	42.60	18.40	55.80	89.60
1964	432.40	395.00	10.30	−3.30	2.70	122.50
1965	488.30	452.70	19.10	−2.50	−16.20	180.10
1966	777.70	726.70	177.20	6.40	−119.20	260.30
1967	1060.00	971.90	233.40	45.20	−118.20	345.40
1968	1546.60	1412.60	383.10	13.20	−3.00	503.60
1969	1945.00	1766.40	372.10	56.50	−95.00	689.60
1970	2149.60	1940.00	292.10	122.40	29.20	922.80

Year	DMGR	DMC	DMK	DMI	DXGM
1953	—	—	—	—	0.90
1954	—	—	—	—	1.20
1955	6.36	25.42	57.02	189.81	1.40
1956	31.19	32.54	42.81	238.16	1.50
1957	84.33	40.98	41.94	235.57	3.10
1958	51.05	30.56	36.25	234.21	2.40
1959	17.53	16.08	41.81	209.75	3.00
1960	20.56	17.00	40.07	217.15	5.50
1961	30.21	15.65	42.39	195.80	8.50
1962	33.55	20.10	68.56	291.56	10.60
1963	107.23	24.14	113.17	314.54	39.60
1964	60.78	13.27	69.17	259.87	58.50
1965	54.44	16.28	73.23	319.66	107.00
1966	61.30	25.17	168.35	461.60	153.80
1967	76.57	40.48	305.27	573.79	215.40
1968	129.35	93.93	517.58	721.57	338.40
1969	250.33	129.84	571.64	870.90	481.60
1970	244.78	140.55	572.46	1025.44	651.50

Table 15D
Exchange Rate and Export Premia
Won Per Dollar

Year	OR	RXS
1953	6.50	0.0
1954	18.00	8.50
1955	30.00	48.10
1956	50.00	52.90
1957	50.00	58.90
1958	50.00	64.00
1959	50.00	84.70
1960	62.50	83.90
1961	127.50	14.60
1962	130.00	0.0
1963	130.00	39.80
1964	214.30	39.70
1965	265.40	0.0
1966	271.30	0.0
1967	270.70	0.0
1968	276.60	0.0
1969	288.20	0.0
1970	310.70	0.0

Table 15E
Tariffs and Tariff Equivalents, Export Subsidies
Billlons of Won Current Prices

Year	TM	PX	SX	SXTAXD	SXTAXI
1953	0.30	0.0	0.0	0.0	0.0
1954	0.84	0.22	0.0	0.0	0.0
1955	1.15	0.89	0.0	0.0	0.0
1956	1.50	1.39	0.0	0.0	0.0
1957	2.38	1.57	0.0	0.0	0.0
1958	4.39	1.36	0.02	0.0	0.0
1959	8.29	2.01	0.03	0.0	0.0
1960	10.20	3.06	0.04	0.0	0.0
1961	5.56	0.65	0.35	0.0	0.0
1962	6.93	0.0	1.18	0.31	0.26
1963	6.17	3.57	1.70	0.53	0.57
1964	8.51	4.86	3.26	0.99	1.20
1965	12.85	0.0	6.86	2.84	2.69
1966	18.00	0.0	12.93	5.02	5.33
1967	25.41	0.0	20.88	7.72	8.22
1968	37.88	0.0	37.78	11.13	19.26
1969	44.72	0.0	49.45	17.21	22.55
1970	50.92	0.0	76.48	26.50	34.70

Table 15F
Price Indices

Year	WPI	WPIG	WPIOG	WPITP
1953	—	—	—	93.10
1954	—	—	—	94.70
1955	27.80	25.70	28.10	92.40
1956	36.60	41.40	34.30	96.70
1957	42.50	47.20	40.10	100.40
1958	39.90	38.70	39.60	97.20
1959	40.80	33.90	42.60	97.70
1960	45.20	40.60	46.10	97.90
1961	51.20	50.30	51.40	98.30
1962	56.00	53.30	56.50	97.60
1963	67.50	84.50	64.20	98.30
1964	90.90	106.70	87.80	98.50
1965	100.00	100.00	100.00	100.00
1966	108.80	105.00	109.40	102.80
1967	115.80	117.00	115.70	104.00
1968	125.20	130.00	124.50	105.60
1969	133.70	152.70	130.80	108.80
1970	145.90	168.60	142.50	112.80

Table 15G
Other Data

Year	PR	PU	NRD	NRF	NLR
1953	—	—	0.0480	0.0369	0.1830
1954	—	—	0.0900	0.0361	0.1830
1955	13.33	8.09	0.1200	0.0370	0.1830
1956	13.45	8.85	0.1200	0.0420	0.1830
1957	13.59	9.36	0.1200	0.0462	0.1830
1958	13.75	9.86	0.1200	0.0434	0.1830
1959	14.13	10.17	0.1120	0.0500	0.1750
1960	14.56	10.43	0.1000	0.0516	0.1750
1961	14.51	11.19	0.1210	0.0497	0.1750
1962	15.10	11.34	0.1500	0.0500	0.1640
1963	15.27	11.92	0.1500	0.0501	0.1570
1964	15.55	12.41	0.1500	0.0499	0.1590
1965	15.81	12.94	0.1790	0.0506	0.1850
1966	15.78	13.59	0.2640	0.0600	0.2600
1967	16.08	13.99	0.2640	0.0599	0.2600
1968	15.91	14.84	0.2610	0.0668	0.2580
1969	15.59	15.82	0.2390	0.0821	0.2400
1970	15.35	15.96	0.2280	0.0848	0.2400

Table 16A
Endogenous Variables

Year	YNA	Y	DTR	INT	SG	GC
1953	218.60	421.93	8.67	12.26	9.72	—
1954	228.30	447.36	8.50	16.39	2.34	—
1955	250.50	474.54	7.77	16.64	5.40	162.87
1956	268.20	480.47	7.31	16.52	26.79	161.04
1957	292.20	522.73	11.55	21.25	21.62	156.64
1958	305.40	551.69	13.02	21.97	20.37	180.61
1959	332.20	575.84	15.69	20.58	18.71	186.66
1960	345.10	589.07	15.43	20.37	28.44	176.40
1961	345.10	613.61	17.45	29.81	29.15	192.47
1962	382.60	634.97	16.56	39.56	39.38	194.39
1963	422.50	693.03	17.30	34.41	34.90	186.53
1964	436.00	750.31	17.91	27.36	37.42	218.38
1965	494.20	805.85	22.14	34.28	49.74	229.01
1966	567.90	913.82	33.67	48.09	55.07	235.12
1967	668.30	995.16	42.82	58.68	70.69	238.91
1968	796.50	1127.32	57.95	78.58	95.85	239.97
1969	935.80	1306.19	73.38	97.10	101.78	246.20
1970	1055.00	1422.33	81.01	111.43	115.33	253.51

Year	IVG	MG	ILG	SC	YDP	SH
1953	36.13	—	36.13	19.62	386.55	−6.00
1954	3.53	—	39.66	22.14	402.88	16.34
1955	0.95	1.69	40.61	20.44	434.76	14.87
1956	−11.32	8.28	29.29	20.71	442.05	1.61
1957	16.90	22.38	46.19	23.39	474.76	8.34
1958	9.45	13.55	55.64	27.16	489.36	11.45
1959	−3.73	4.65	51.91	32.18	497.28	11.83
1960	2.04	5.46	53.95	31.31	507.88	−3.78
1961	6.81	8.02	60.76	35.66	537.82	2.89
1962	−15.25	8.90	45.51	46.00	538.66	0.86
1963	22.93	28.46	68.44	50.56	599.32	−9.05
1964	20.85	16.13	89.29	50.01	664.54	−5.56
1965	−0.15	14.45	89.14	62.66	696.87	7.51
1966	8.40	16.27	97.54	67.88	784.79	41.37
1967	−12.40	20.77	85.14	78.17	835.67	39.99
1968	−12.47	34.33	72.67	87.24	920.11	43.68
1969	30.08	66.44	102.75	95.35	1085.55	64.05
1970	14.34	64.81	117.09	102.15	1162.96	58.16

Table 16A (continued)

Year	INA	I	CK	DC	MC	MK
1953	31.24	35.28	—	421.81	—	—
1954	38.21	41.66	—	445.49	—	—
1955	44.45	48.98	0.0	480.47	6.75	15.13
1956	47.70	52.77	0.0	524.69	8.64	11.36
1957	54.83	61.31	0.0	543.14	10.88	11.13
1958	52.44	57.79	0.0	566.35	8.11	9.62
1959	53.30	59.29	0.21	579.19	4.27	11.10
1960	54.74	61.71	0.69	599.76	4.51	10.64
1961	56.91	65.26	0.05	591.83	4.15	11.25
1962	77.33	84.05	0.74	634.20	5.33	18.20
1963	95.67	105.95	11.31	667.14	6.41	30.04
1964	82.67	93.33	2.73	705.08	3.52	18.36
1965	103.97	117.64	5.07	747.69	4.32	19.44
1966	167.47	190.63	47.03	812.47	6.68	44.68
1967	212.85	232.09	61.94	900.00	10.98	82.79
1968	301.81	325.63	101.68	998.27	24.93	137.38
1969	383.50	407.76	98.76	1102.62	34.46	151.72
1970	391.70	416.76	78.62	1187.75	37.22	151.58

Year	XGM	X	MI	M	SK	IV
1953	0.24	10.64	—	91.67	—	—
1954	0.32	6.82	—	64.57	—	—
1955	0.37	4.91	50.38	86.95	3.82	22.67
1956	0.40	6.98	63.21	100.88	−5.81	9.11
1957	0.82	7.09	62.52	117.12	0.32	11.81
1958	0.64	5.65	62.16	99.87	−10.17	8.29
1959	0.80	6.29	55.67	80.02	−4.17	9.22
1960	1.46	9.69	57.63	90.40	−3.69	2.50
1961	2.26	11.89	51.96	82.30	−8.57	8.16
1962	2.81	15.45	77.38	112.90	13.22	15.46
1963	10.51	23.78	83.48	143.56	19.69	10.76
1964	15.53	32.51	68.97	104.83	−0.16	−3.66
1965	28.40	47.80	84.84	120.15	−4.96	0.99
1966	40.82	69.09	122.51	192.87	−29.74	1.13
1967	54.77	87.82	155.62	263.59	−19.37	7.69
1968	89.81	133.66	191.52	374.93	2.71	14.99
1969	127.82	183.02	231.15	468.83	−10.22	−0.40
1970	178.57	252.93	271.52	513.69	40.80	21.54

Table 16B

Basic Commercial Policy Variables

Year	ORD	XPX	SOX	TAM
1953	—	—	—	—
1954	—	—	—	—
1955	99.71	159.87	0.0	11.67
1956	132.10	139.77	0.0	10.43
1957	118.12	139.14	0.0	12.74
1958	121.80	155.91	2.29	28.42
1959	119.73	202.82	3.03	65.84
1960	135.37	181.72	2.37	64.86
1961	244.79	28.03	15.00	34.42
1962	226.57	0.0	35.34	28.39
1963	189.32	57.96	27.63	18.07
1964	232.22	43.02	28.84	23.35
1965	265.40	0.0	38.09	28.39
1966	256.34	0.0	46.93	23.40
1967	243.12	0.0	54.29	23.48
1968	233.30	0.0	63.28	22.62
1969	234.53	0.0	58.35	20.60
1970	240.21	0.0	64.08	20.29

Table 16C

Derived Commercial Policy Variables

Year	XPM	SUBM	SUBX	SXDT	TAR	MARDEV
1953	—	—	—	0.0	2.63	—
1954	—	—	—	0.0	5.62	—
1955	9.03	20.70	159.87	0.0	4.70	—
1956	9.67	20.10	139.77	0.0	4.73	—
1957	8.42	21.16	139.14	0.0	6.29	—
1958	8.83	37.25	158.20	0.0	11.69	—
1959	15.94	81.79	205.85	0.0	21.60	0.106
1960	19.47	84.34	184.10	0.0	24.36	0.165
1961	4.05	38.47	43.03	0.0	11.49	0.200
1962	0.0	28.39	35.34	0.56	12.62	0.076
1963	9.60	27.67	85.59	0.75	9.53	0.006
1964	13.34	36.69	71.86	1.07	9.16	0.004
1965	0.0	28.39	38.09	2.84	12.85	0.060
1966	0.0	23.40	46.93	4.45	15.94	0.088
1967	0.0	23.48	54.29	6.19	20.35	−0.002
1968	0.0	22.62	63.28	7.96	27.10	−0.035
1969	0.0	20.60	58.35	10.98	28.53	−0.024
1970	0.0	20.29	64.08	14.80	28.45	0.001

Table 16D

Other Exogenous Variables

Year	YA	G	IA	PK	NFI	MST
1953	203.40	13.84	4.04	—	9.42	−61.39
1954	219.10	28.16	3.45	—	7.56	−42.30
1955	224.10	23.71	4.53	27.12	7.75	−51.10
1956	212.20	1.77	5.07	18.58	7.38	−81.13
1957	230.60	17.47	6.48	19.45	7.59	−90.26
1958	246.30	26.31	5.35	17.27	7.59	−87.12
1959	243.70	39.16	5.99	9.74	7.75	−67.94
1960	244.00	31.71	6.97	11.25	7.38	−72.46
1961	268.50	29.60	8.35	14.25	5.77	−64.68
1962	252.40	29.36	6.72	−0.69	6.48	−84.18
1963	270.60	26.35	10.28	9.31	6.79	−79.47
1964	314.30	17.01	10.66	5.23	6.53	−64.52
1965	311.60	19.53	13.67	−1.39	7.65	−73.63
1966	345.90	42.63	23.16	10.35	13.08	−96.34
1967	326.90	51.16	19.24	8.36	21.53	−124.84
1968	330.80	67.78	23.82	9.46	22.24	−127.42
1969	370.40	97.24	24.26	57.64	23.04	−137.63
1970	367.40	105.56	25.06	43.24	10.17	−98.10

Year	RPG	POP	GP	RD	LR	RF
1953	—	—	—	0.0480	0.1830	0.0369
1954	—	—	—	0.0900	0.1830	0.0361
1955	0.91	21.42	162.13	0.1200	0.1830	0.0370
1956	1.20	22.30	141.44	0.1200	0.1830	0.0420
1957	1.18	22.95	151.16	0.1200	0.1830	0.0462
1958	0.98	23.61	176.51	0.1200	0.1830	0.0434
1959	0.80	24.30	178.28	0.1120	0.1750	0.0500
1960	0.88	24.99	172.98	0.1000	0.1750	0.0516
1961	0.98	25.70	191.26	0.1210	0.1750	0.0497
1962	0.94	26.44	170.24	0.1500	0.1640	0.0500
1963	1.32	27.19	181.00	0.1500	0.1570	0.0501
1964	1.22	27.96	223.10	0.1500	0.1590	0.0499
1965	1.00	28.75	214.41	0.1790	0.1850	0.0506
1966	0.96	29.37	227.25	0.2640	0.2600	0.0600
1967	1.01	30.07	205.74	0.2640	0.2600	0.0599
1968	1.04	30.75	193.17	0.2610	0.2580	0.0668
1969	1.17	31.41	209.84	0.2390	0.2400	0.0821
1970	1.18	31.31	203.04	0.2280	0.2400	0.0848

Table 16D (continued)

Year	RINF	MNC	NTOSH	XGP	RT
1953	—	—	−7.79	10.40	49.92
1954	0.309	—	−8.16	6.50	34.92
1955	0.636	13.00	−9.77	4.54	39.84
1956	0.297	9.40	−10.84	6.58	74.63
1957	0.193	10.21	−14.51	6.27	83.07
1958	−0.007	6.43	−11.50	5.01	75.50
1959	0.022	4.33	−11.49	5.49	54.59
1960	0.091	12.16	−10.27	8.23	61.31
1961	0.155	6.91	−18.63	9.63	46.93
1962	0.135	3.09	−18.43	12.64	63.74
1963	0.283	−4.83	−18.09	13.27	66.65
1964	0.319	−2.15	−18.67	16.98	50.96
1965	0.077	−2.90	−22.95	19.40	53.93
1966	0.129	2.73	−36.55	28.27	58.29
1967	0.105	−6.57	−40.53	33.05	59.76
1968	0.120	−13.23	−43.66	43.85	63.01
1969	0.121	−14.95	−73.73	55.20	64.65
1970	0.142	−11.45	−63.67	74.36	45.23

Appendix 2

Solution of Non-Linear Simulation Model

The simulation model given by (9.1) through (9.17) is non-linear because of equations (9.2), (9.6), (9.9) and (9.10). The way in which the non-linear solution is obtained involves first the solution for YNA_t (see equation (8.2)).

(A.1) $YNA_t = 281.8254 + 0.9413\,YNA_{t-1} + 80.0668\,log_e\,(INA_{t-1}) + \hat{e}_{1,t}$
$\qquad - EC_t$

All the variables on the right hand side are predetermined; $\hat{e}_{1,t}$ is the estimated residual from the regression equation (8.2) and EC_t is excess capacity, a policy adjustment variable. The value of the derived commercial policy variable $SUBX_t$ can be determined from (9.4) since it is the sum of two basic commercial policy variable. SOX_t and XPX_t. Then exports of manufactured goods can be determined from (see equation (8.27))

(A.2) $XGM_t = - 241.4847 + 0.3323\,YNA_t + 0.2629\,ORD_t$
$\qquad + 0.1471\,SUBX_t + \hat{e}_{19,t}$

where ORD_t is also a basic commercial policy variable and $\hat{e}_{19,t}$ is the estimated residual from regression equation (8.27). Equation (8.29) may be used next to determine the value of total exports X_t as the sum of XGM_t and primary product exports XGP_t which exogenous to the model. Equation (9.2) may be used then to obtain a first estimate of XPM_t as follows:

(A.3) $XPM_t = (XPX_t \cdot X_t)/M_t^0$

where M_t^0 is the actual historical value of imports in year t. This enables us to obtain initial first estimates of all the remaining derived commercial policy variables $\phi_2^0 t$, from equations (9.3) through (9.11).

After initial estimates of the derived commercial policy variables have been determined, initial estimates of the endogenous variables of the linear econometric model (9.1) may be obtained recursively by inverting the B-matrix.

(A.4) $\psi_t = -\mathbf{B}^{-1}\Gamma_1\phi_{1t} - \mathbf{B}^{-1}\Gamma_2\phi_{2t}^0 - \mathbf{B}^{-1}\Gamma_3\phi_{3t} - \mathbf{B}^{-1}\Delta\psi_{t-\tau} - \mathbf{B}^{-1}e_t$

where $\hat{e}_t$ are the estimated residuals from the regression equations used to estimate the linear system. Note that although the exogenous variables, ϕ_{1t}, ϕ_{2t}, and ϕ_{3t} and the predetermined variables $\psi_{t-\tau}$ will change from simulation to simulation, we continue to use the estimated error terms $\hat{e}_t$ derived from the regressions on the original data. The justification for this is the assumption that the error terms are assumed to be uncorrelated with the exogenous variables, and we would like to determine the path of the economy under different assumptions concerning the values of the commercial policy variables.

The solution of (A.4) results in a new estimate of total imports:

(A.5) $$M_t^1 = MC_t^0 + MK_t^0 + MI_t^0 + MG_t^0 + MNC_t$$

which may differ from the original estimate M_t^0. If this new estimate is substituted in (A.3) for the original estimate M_t^0 and the remaining derived commercial policy variables are determined from equations (9.3) through (9.11), we obtain a second estimate of the derived commercial policy variables $\phi_{2,t}^1$. Similarly, a second estimate of the endogenous variables ψ_t is determined by solving (A.4) recursively with $\phi_{2,t}^1$ substituted for $\phi_{2,t}^0$. This process is repeated as often as is necessary until the successive estimated values of total imports differ by an arbitrarily small amount.

REFERENCES

Adelman, Irma, ed. *Practical Approaches to Development Planning: Korea's Second Five-Year Plan.* Baltimore: Johns Hopkins Press, 1969.

Bank of Korea. *Economic Statistics Yearbook.* Seoul: 1960 through 1973. (In both English and Korean).

Bank of Korea. *Effect of Export on GNP by Input-Output Method, 1963–1968.* Seoul: March 1969.

Bank of Korea. *Monthly Statistical Review.* Seoul: Research Department, for selected months in 1960 through 1973.

Bank of Korea. *National Income Statistics Yearbook.* Seoul: 1953 through 1972. (Only major statistics are provided with English translations).

Bhagwati, Jagdish N., and Cheh, John. "The Share of Manufacturing Exports in Total Exports of LDC's: A Cross Section Analysis." In *Essays in Honor of Raul Prebisch,* D. Manio, ed., New York: Academic Press, 1972.

Bhagwati, Jagdish, and Krueger, Anne O. *Exchange Control Liberalization and Economic Development: Analytical Framework.* New York: National Bureau of Economic Research, May 1970. Mimeographed.

Bhagwati, Jagdish, and Krueger, Anne O. "Exchange Control, Liberalization, and Economic Development." *American Economic Review* 63 (1973): 419–27.

Bhagwati, Jagdish and Krueger, Anne O. *Foreign Trade Regimes and Economic Development: Theory and Experience.* New York: National Bureau of Economic Research, forthcoming.

Fair, Ray C. "The Estimation of Simultaneous Equation Models with Lagged Endogenous Variables and First Order Serially Correlated Errors." *Econometrica* 38 (1970): 507–16.

Fisher, Franklin M. "The Choice of Instrumental Variables in the Estimation of Economy-Wide Econometric Models." *International Economic* Review 6 (1965): 245–74.

Kim, Mahn Je. *Macro Planning Model for the Third Five-Year Plan.* Seoul: Economic Planning Board, April 15, 1970.

Korea, (Republic). *An Outline of Foreign Exchange System and Policy in Korea.* Seoul: Ministry of Finance, 1967. (In Korean).

Korea, (Republic). *Statistical Yearbook of Foreign Trade.* Seoul: Ministry of Finance 1964 through 1972. (In both English and Korean).

Lee, Eric Y. *The Effects of Exchange Rate Devaluation on the Dynamics of Inflation in Korea.* A paper prepared for USAID/Korea. Seoul: 1973. Mimeographed.

McKinnon, Ronald I., "The Financial Feasibility of Increasing Private Saving in Korea." Seoul: Korea Development Institute, July 26, 1973 (mimeo).

Nam, Choi Myong, and Kim, Kwang Suk. *A Study of Korea's Export Function.* A paper prepared for USAID/Korea. Seoul: November 6, 1968.

An Economic Study of the Masan Free Trade Zone

*Boum Jong Choe**

I. INTRODUCTION

A free trade zone is a specifically designated area where unrestricted trade in goods and factors is permitted with the rest of the world. Traditionally, free trade zones operated primarily as trade intermediaries without much processing or manufacturing activity of their own. The free trade zones recently established by several developing countries are, however, quite different in nature. They are basically large bonded processing zones with foreign capital investments. This is a clear feature of such prototypes as Jurong Town in Singapore and the Kaohsiung Export Processing Zone in Taiwan. Korea followed suit by establishing the Masan Free Export Zone (MAFEZ henceforth) in 1970. Another one near Iri is under construction.[1]

There has been little consensus as to whether free trade zones are potentially or actually beneficial to economic development. Discussions of this topic have been largely based on piecemeal evidence and have tended to be complicated by nationalistic bias. The only economic study that I am aware of is the one by Lee, who measured the economic costs and benefits

---

*Visiting fellow at the Korea Development Institute and assistant professor of economics at Seoul National University.

[1] Masan is located on the southeastern coast of Korea and Iri on the midwestern coast.

of the Kaohsiung Export Processing Zone and came up with an estimated benefit-cost ratio of 3.59.

The purpose of this study is to assess the economic costs and benefits of the MAFEZ. Standard cost-benefit analysis is adopted in this study. Included in the cost and benefit items are the more obvious ones, which is also the case with Lee. Unlike Lee, however, I attempt to use shadow wage rates and a shadow price of foreign exchange in evaluating net benefits. Data on costs are obtained from the budget documents of the responsible Ministries. Estimates are based on the planned full operation level of the firms admitted into the MAFEZ. The record of their actual operation is also consulted.

The next section is devoted to a descriptive summary of the MAFEZ. Section III discusses the problem of identifying and measuring costs and benefits. Section IV presents the result of measuring the benefit-cost ratio. The last section considers different ways of increasing benefits and reducing costs and draws some conclusions.

II. A SURVEY OF THE MAFEZ

(1) Construction of the MAFEZ

The MAFEZ is an enclosed industrial park comprising, when fully constructed, a total area of 527,015 pyungs (1 acre = 1,224 pyungs). For the sake of construction planning, the total area was subdivided into three parts as shown in Table 1 below.

Investors in the MAFEZ can either build their own factories on a leased factory site or simply install equipment in leased (or purchased) standard factory space constructed by the MAFEZ. Six three-story standard factory buildings are planned for subdivision I, but none for the other subdivisions. The rentable area of a standard factory building is computed from the engineering specifications.[2] The rentable area figures for self-constructed factories are based on the ratios of rentable to total areas that appear in Bechtel's report.[3]

---

[2] See "Occupancy Guide to Standard Factory Buildings in Korea's MAFEZ", Office of the MAFEZ Administration.

[3] See Bechtel International Corporation, p. 71. The ratios of rentable to total areas are 66% for subdivision I and 73% for subdivisions II and III combined.

Table   1

Subdivision of the MAFEZ [1]

Sub-division	Total Area (pyung)	Rentable Area (pyung)		Number of Firms Granted Occupancy[2]	Construction Status
		Sites for Factories Constructed by User	Standard Factory Space Built by MAFEZ		
I	204,078	109,485	19,440	95	completed
II	237,765	173,568	0	0	completion date uncertain
III	85,172	62,175	0	17	completed
Total	527,015	345,228	19,440	112	

[1] The total area figures appear in a brochure for foreign investors put out by the Office of the MAFEZ Administration. These are slightly higher than that planned by the Bechtel International Corporation, pp. 71–72.

[2] As of May 31, 1974. The figures are derived from the "Monthly Survey of Investments in the MAFEZ (May, 1974)", Office of the MAFEZ Administration.

Table 2 below presents summary statistics on the development costs of the MAFEZ. The Ministry of Construction took charge of zone development and port construction while the Office of the MAFEZ Administration was responsible for building the structures on it. The cost estimates of Table 2 are derived from annual budgets of these two organizations. For the years through 1973, we may safely take these budget figures to represent actual incurred costs. The figures for the remaining years are cost estimates based on Bechtel's report (p. 135).

The estimated total development cost of the MAFEZ amounts to 12,177 million won which may be compared with Bechtel's estimate of 11,681 million won (not including port construction).

Total zone construction cost of about 6.2 billion won can be divided into two parts: planned expenditures through 1972 of about 2.4 billion won are mostly related to subdivisions I and III, and the estimated development cost of subdivision II is roughly 3.8 billion won. This reflects the much more difficult reclamation work required in area II, a problem which may even preclude construction of this part of the Zone.

MAFEZ's own port, including a 20,000 ton vessel wharf, is expected to cost about 3.1 billion won. Some doubts have been raised as to whether

Table 2
Development Costs of the MAFEZ

Unit: In Thousand Won

Expenditure Items	Total	Planned Expenditures in 1971	Planned Expenditures in 1972	Planned Expenditures in 1973	Estimated Future Expenditures
1. Zone Construction	6,202,000	1,904,000	477,000	645,000	3,176,000
a. Land acquisition	1,163,000	448,000	410,000	50,000	255,000
b. Land reclamation	2,093,000	503,000		151,000	1,439,000
c. Roads, Wharves and Bridges	2,308,600	663,000	67,000	406,600	1,172,000
d. Drainage	267,000	82,000			185,000
e. Water Supply	320,000	170,000		25,000	125,000
f. Survey & Design	50,400	38,000		12,400	
2. Port Construction & Dredging	3,131,000	281,000	180,441	708,000	1,901,559
a. Port construction	2,371,000	81,000	180,441	470,000	1,639,559
b. Dredging	760,000	200,000		238,000	322,000
3. Structures	2,843,507	1,113,984	1,108,504	621,019	
a. Standard Factories	1,834,434	678,889	559,122	596,423	
b. Public Service Facilities	402,609	245,979	156,630		
c. Apartments	314,736	89,736	225,000		
d. Auxiliary Facilities	148,729	39,071	90,773	18,885	
e. Misc. Expenditures	142,999	60,309	76,979	5,711	
Total	12,176,507	3,298,984	1,765,945	1,974,019	5,137,559

Sources: (1) Items 1 & 2 from the Budget Document (1973) of the Ministry of Construction, pp. 46, 83–86.
(2) Item 3 from the Budget Document (1973) of the office of the MAFEZ Administration.

the MAFEZ really deserves its own port at this much cost. Pusan, the nation's biggest port, is only 38 miles away by a modern highway. Port construction still remains in the preparatory stage.

Expenditures on facilities, standard factory buildings and miscellaneous items are relatively small, totaling only 2.8 billion. These expenditures are related mostly to subdivisions I and III.

(2) Operation of the MAFEZ

The following is a brief summary on how the MAFEZ is run. This summary is based on the laws, regulations, and policies set by the Korean government.

Eligible Enterprises

Business firms eligible for occupancy in the MAFEZ should produce only for export, be capable of realizing net foreign exchange earnings[4] of not less than 20 per cent of the export value, employ superior technology, and require intensive use of labor. These standards, however, have been applied quite flexibly.

Foreign investment should be at least U.S. $150,000 for a self-constructed factory and U.S. $50,000 for a standard factory. The firms can be either a company owned totally by foreigners or a joint venture between Koreans and foreigners. In the latter case, the policy at the beginning was that foreigners should own at least 50 per cent of the equity. This policy, however, was reversed in May, 1973 and now foreigners can own a maximum of 50 per cent of the equity.

The firms can produce and export almost any kind of product. Some items, mostly textile products, are restricted but the list is by no means extensive.

Rentals

A plant site for a self-constructed factory is presently available at a monthly rental of 60.391 won per pyung. Although standard factory space can be either sold or rented, no firm has yet availed itself of the purchase option. The present rental rates, including the site utilization charge, is as follows:

---

[4] Net foreign exchange earning here is defined as the export value minus the value of imported raw materials and intermediate inputs, excluding indirect import requirements.

Floor	Monthly Rental per Pyung (won)
1st	650.15
2nd	579.48
3rd	553.60

The lease contract is for a maximum of ten years and the rental fee re-mains fixed for five years. The contract is renewable after the ten year period.

Major Incentives of the MAFEZ

Admission into the MAFEZ is a simple procedure. Import of raw ma-terials, parts, semi-finished goods, and equipment necessary for export production requires only an initial approval and is thereafter exempt from domestic tariffs or duties. A simplified customs inspection procedure is applied to both imports and exports.

Companies are exempt from the individual business income, corporate income, property and property acquisition taxes during the first five years, and receive a 50 per cent reduction for the next three years.

They are also exempt from the business activity tax and the income tax on salaries and wages of foreign employees. The income tax on dividends and surplus distributions to foreign investors is not payed for the first five years and reduced by 50 per cent for the subsequent three years. It should be noted that some of these tax incentives are also offered to domestic exporters and foreign-invested firms.

Overseas remittance of profits and dividends by foreign investors is guaranteed from the first year of business operation. Remittance overseas of proceeds from the sale of stocks and shares owned by foreign investors is guaranteed up to 20 per cent of the capital subscription every year from the third year of buisness operation.

The MAFEZ firms, if incorporated in Korea (as all of them have been to date), are entitled to the same export subsidies as domestic exporters. In addition to tax concessions, they also receive loans at a substantially reduced interest rate.

Adaptable low-cost labor, all with at least primary education, is expect-ed to be continually available from the surrounding towns. Moreover, as is the case with other foreign-invested firms, workers are not allowed to organize labor unions or to take any collective action.

Sufficient industrial water can be supplied at the low price of 16 won per cubic meter. Electric power supply will be adequate for the foreseeable future and a 30 per cent discount on the domestic rate is offered.

(3) Foreign Investments in the MAFEZ

As of May 31, 1974, 112 enterprises had been admitted to the MAFEZ as shown in Table 1. Of this number, 41 occupied standard factories and the remaining 71 constructed their own. As of the same date, 83 of the enterprises were in operation.[5] The planned total investment of these firms amounts to U.S. $89 million and they are expected to export U.S. $410 million and employ 43 thousand man-years of labor when they reach their planned full operation level.

The number of enterprises totally owned by foreigners is 82 (Japan, 76; U.S., 4; Europe, 2) while the remaining 30 are joint-venture firms generally involving Korean and Japanese investors. Of the planned total investment, U.S. $83 million is accounted for by foreign investments, predominantly from Japan.

The major business of the MAFEZ firms is processing and assembling light manufactured goods: e.g., electronic products, simple machinery, optical instruments, textile products, and food processing. Machinery and metal items are produced by the largest number of firms (40), followed by electronic and electric products (26 firms); chemical products (15 firms); handicrafts and toys (11 firms); optical instruments (8 firms); textile products (6 firms); miscellaneous (5 firms); and food processing (1 firm). Electronic and electric products consist mostly of transistor radios, integrated circuits, cables and coils. Machinery and metals involve bolts and nuts, screws, bearings, nails, etc. Items in other categories include synthetic rubber shoes, camera lenses and eye-glasses, bicycles, artificial leather goods, umbrellas, men's suits, fishing reels, and so forth. Practically none of these requires advanced technology and most of them are now also produced domestically for export.

The size distribution of investments is given in Table 5 below. It is clearly shown here that investments less than one million dollars dominate the scene. This level, in comparison with foreign investments elsewhere in Korea, is of small scale. This characteristic is more pronounced in the standard factory investments than those in the self-constructed fac-

---

[5] Data presented in this section are derived from the "Monthly Survey of Investments in the MAFEZ (May, 1974)," Office of the MAFEZ Administration.

Table 5

Size Distribution of Investments

(Number of Investments)

Range (In Thousand U.S. Dollars)	100 and under	100 — 300	300 — 600	600 — 1,000	1,000 — 2,000	2,000 — 4,000	more than 4,000
Standard Factory	11	16	4	5	5	0	0
Self-constructed Factory	0	14	17	18	14	5	3
Total Number	11	30	21	23	19	5	3

tories. It merely indicates that the MAFEZ, especially its standard factories, is suitable for medium or small-scale industries that process or assemble labor-intensive goods.

III. ECONOMIC COSTS AND BENEFITS FROM A FREE TRADE ZONE

Establishment of a free trade zone of the type described above has a diversified impact on the domestic economy. Since it may be considered to be a way of attracting foreign capital, theories on international capital mobility should have some relevance to analyzing the effects. On practical grounds, however, it is believed that the problem can be simplified by assuming that a free trade zone can not affect the domestic shadow prices of factors. One justification for this assumption is the standard one that free trade zones are in fact small relative to the domestic economy. Furthermore, if the domestic supply of labor is abundant as is presumably the case in many developing countries, productivity of the marginal worker will be affected only negligibly, if at all, by a free trade zone even if its labor absorption is substantial.[6] Essentially, the assumption of fixed shadow

---

[6] One would, of course, expect that the shift of domestic capital to a free trade zone could partially offset the possible increase in the marginal productivity of labor due to labor absorption. We, however, assume that it takes up only a negligible part of total domestic capital availability so that the issue can be ignored.

prices of factors allows us to exclude from our evaluation all the benefits and costs that could be induced by changes in relative factor scarcity.

The following is an enumeration of cost and benefit items that are considered relevant for the MAFEZ. Problems of measuring each item are also discussed.

(1) Costs

Zone Construction and Development

The cost of constructing and developing the Zone, obviously an important item, has been borne by government expenditure as shown in Table 2. An important problem in measuring this cost is choosing the appropriate shadow multiplier for fiscal expenditure.

If the level of taxation is suboptimal so that the marginal utility of public goods is greater than the marginal utility of income in the private sector, then the shadow multiplier for fiscal expenditure is greater than one. This implies that projects financed by fiscal expenditure should be expected to perform better than those financed by the private sector, unless the projects costs are evaluated at the shadow multiplier for fiscal expenditure. Due to the difficulties in measuring this shadow multiplier, we will assume that it is equal to one and then see whether the resulting benefit-cost ratio comes out significantly greater than unity.

Management and Maintenance Cost

The Office of the MAFEZ Administration is responsible for management and maintenance of the Zone and no doubt the cost, reflected in the budget of the Office, should be included. The preceding argument on the shadow multiplier for fiscal expenditure also applies in this case.

Private-sector Capital Investment

We will treat private domestic capital investment, all in the form of joint-ventures with foreigners, as a project cost and returns to the investment as a project benefit.

Subsidy through Loans to Exporters

Korean exporters, including the MAFEZ firms, are eligible for loans at a special low rate of interest.[7] The difference between this subsidy rate and

---

[7] The interest rate on loans for exports was raised from six per cent a year to nine per cent in January, 1974, while that on commercial bills remained at 15.5 per cent.

the shadow rate of interest should be counted as an additional project cost per won of loans outstanding. We will use 14 per cent for the shadow rate of interest.

Cost of Environmental Pollution

At the beginning, the MAFEZ attracted mostly light processing industries producing minimal environmental pollution. During the later phase, however, machinery and metal industries rushed in, making pollution by heavy metals (lead, mercury, etc.) a more serious problem. Although the cost of pollution could be important for the MAFEZ, our inability to measure the cost precludes its inclusion.

(2) Benefits

Labor Employment Benefit

When labor is abundant relative to the availability of capital, a free trade zone can be an effective way of generating new employment opportunities. This is clear from the fact that the capital-labor ratio of the project must be much smaller than others because the relevant capital outlay need include only the domestic provision of overhead capital.

Benefits from additional labor employment arise from possible gap between the wage rate transferred workers will actually get and the shadow wage rate. Given the actual wage rate, the size of the employment benefit and, hence, the resulting benefit-cost ratio hinges critically on what we think the relevant shadow wage rate is.

By the shadow wage rate, we measure the reduction in domestic output due to the labor reallocation. Current domestic output may be reduced by the decrease in domestic labor input. Future domestic output may be reduced by increased present consumption that comes primarily from two sources. One is the cost of relocating the labor force (e.g., transportation, urban overhead). The other is the presumption that transferred workers get a higher income and increase their absolute level of consumption. It is these additional claims on scarce investible resources that reduce future output.

Putting these considerations together, Little and Mirrless propose the shadow wage formula,

$$W^* = m + c + \left(1 - \frac{1}{S}\right)(W - m), \quad \ldots\ldots\ldots\ldots\ldots(1)$$

where W^* is the shadow wage rate, m the marginal productivity of labor,

W the actual wage rate, S the shadow multiplier for savings, and c the social cost of relocating labor. Warr, however, indicated that this formula implicitly assumes extreme values for saving propensities and, therefore, always produce an upper bound on the shadow wage rate. Warr instead proposes an alternative shadow wage formula

$$W^* = \frac{W[(S-1)(\beta - \gamma)] + m[S(1-\alpha) + \alpha]}{S(1-\gamma) + \gamma} \quad \ldots\ldots\ldots\ldots(2)$$

where notation is the same as above except that α, β, γ are the average propensities to consume out of m, W, and income generated by the project respectively. When $\alpha = \beta = 1$ and $\gamma = 0$, the Warr formula reduces to the Little-Mirrless formula, assuming that $c = 0$.

Even if both formulae produce reasonable approximations to the true shadow wage rate, there remains the difficult problem of measuring the variables and parameters in these formulae. At this point we should be more specific about the kinds of labor involved in our case.

An attempt in this direction is made in Table 6 below. It clearly shows that the bulk of labor absorption by the MAFEZ consists of unskilled labor, particularly female unskilled labor, presumably drawn from the surrounding rural areas. The proportion of semi-skilled and unskilled workers (apprentices) is 83 per cent of total employment while that of female semi-

Table 6
MAFEZ Employees by Labor Category

Labor Category	Number of Workers Employed		Percentage (Male & Female)
	Male	Female	
Clerical & Others	1,250	849	8.7%
Engineers	295	1	1.2%
Technicians	302	0	1.3%
Skilled-Workers	474	838	5.4%
Semi-Skilled Workers	914	5,799	27.9%
Apprentices	2,295	11,056	55.5%
Total	5,530	18,543	100.0%

Note: Figures shown here cover all Korean employees as of May 31, 1974. The Office of the MAFEZ Administration provided the data. The labor classification presented here is the standard one adopted by the Office of Labor Affairs.

skilled and unskilled workers is 70 per cent. The percentage may be even higher because the clerical and others category includes some unskilled workers. Shadow wage rates will be estimated separately for each labor category by formulas (1) and (2) with particular attention given to those for semi-skilled and unskilled labor.[8]

Let us start with the problem of estimating the marginal productivity of labor by labor category. As far as unskilled labor is concerned, the usual approach is to assume that this part of the labor force has been withdrawn from the agricultural sector.[9] Adhering to this assumption, Hong estimated the marginal productivity of agricultural labor as value-added per man-year times the share of labor in value-added. He obtained 57,100 won a year for 1971 or 4,758 won a month.[10] Without a better alternative, we take this figure for the marginal productivity of unskilled labor.

Lee estimated a Bruno production function from the Korean manufacturing time-series data and his results indicate that the marginal productivity of an average worker is about 90 per cent of the wage rate. The first column of Table 7 shows the average monthly wage rate by type of worker in Korean manufacturing. Based on Lee's result, we assume that the marginal productivity of engineers is 90 per cent of their average wage rate, while those of technicians and skilled workers are 85 and 80 respectively. This is rather arbitrary but it is not expected to affect our result very much because these types of workers account for only 8 per cent of total employment.

Table 7 also shows that the marginal productivity of agricultural labor

---

[8] Since not much difference can be found between semi-skilled and unskilled labor except that it requires more than a year's experience to become semi-skilled, we will sometimes refer to both as unskilled.

[9] We conducted an independent survey of the MAFEZ employees in June, 1973 to find out about their previous employment and residence. In a sample of 60 male and 171 female employees, 29 male and 34 female employees replied that they had previous employment experience. Of the total, 120 were from Masan itself, 40 from the vicinity of Masan, and 38 from Kyungnam Province of which Masan is a part. This strongly indicates that geographical proximity is an important factor in determining the movement of labor. However, the proportion of those from the rural agricultural sector may not be as low as these figures indicate because a substantial number of those from Masan could have been replaced by migration from the agricultural sector. This justifies our use of agricultural marginal productivity as part of the shadow price of labor.

[10] He included housekeeping non-economically active population in the agricultural sector in the agricultural labor force. The imputed wage payment to self-employed farmers was incorporated in the share of labor in value-added which comes out to about 42 per cent. See Hong, pp. 29–30.

Table 7

Shadow Wage Rates

Unit: Won per Month

Labor Category	Going Wage Rate in Domestic Manufacturing Sector(A)	MPL/A (percentage)	MPL	Going Wage Rate in the MAFEZ	SWR by Formula (1) (B)	SWR by Formula (2) (C)
Clerical & Others	30,827	70	21,578	33,532	27,840	24,854
Engineers	49,032	90	44,129	56,276	50,429	46,347
Technicians	34,162	85	29,038	39,903	34,729	31,325
Skilled Workers	20,447	80	16,358	24,628	20,690	18,181
Semi-Skilled Workers	12,029	60	7,217	14,075	10,809	9,010
Apprentices	9,482	50	4,758	11,574	8,328	6,592

Note: The Office of the MAFEZ Administration investigated the wage rates of the MAFEZ employees by sex and by labor category as of January, 1973. To get the going wage rate figures in the MAFEZ, we took the average of their estimates weighted by the sex composition shown in Table 6. The Office, at the same time, investigated the average wage rates in Kyungnam Province. The going wage rate figures in the first column are their estimates except for engineers and technicians. For these two categories, their estimates appeared to be exceptionally high compared with the national averages in the *Year Book of Labor Statistics* (1973). We opted for the figures in the Year Book which were determined as of April, 1972. See the *Year Book of Labor Statistics* (1973), Office of Labor Affairs, p. 121.

is about 50 per cent of the wage rate of apprentices. For semi-skilled workers we assume a slightly higher percentage (60 per cent) than that for apprentices since their skills may to some extent enable them to find productive employment in the domestic manufacturing sector rather than the
rural agricultural sector.

About one third of those in the "clerical and others" category are not
clerical workers and may be considered unskilled. We took a weighted
average of the percentages assumed for skilled workers and apprentices
to get 70 per cent for this type of worker. These assumed percentages give
us the marginal productivity estimates shown in Table 7.

The shadow multiplier for savings appearing in formulas (1) and (2) is
the ratio of the marginal utility of investment to that of present consumption. This ratio will be greater than unity when the saving market is in
the sort of disequilibrium which presumably predominates in developing
countries. Measuring this ratio, therefore, is a formidable task and we
must be content with a very rough guess. We arbitrarily assume that the
time rate of discount on future consumption is 7 per cent and that the
marginal investment yields a stream of future consumption equal to 20
per cent of the initial investment annually for 20 years. This implies a shadow multiplier for savings equal to 2.1. Since this is intended to be only
a rough guess, the reinvestment complication is assumed away.

Empirical evidence shows that the average propensity to consume decreases, in the short-run, as the level of income increases. Table 7 shows
the average wage rate actually paid in the MAFEZ. The rates are slightly
higher than the ones in the domestic manufacturing sector. Our sample
of 231 workers shows that the average propensity to consume is about 90
per cent. Based on these considerations, we assume the following values of
the average propensity to consume of each labor category. By α, we measure the average propensity to consume out of the tax and rental revenue
from the MAFEZ. We arbitrarily assume that it is about 50 per cent.

The shadow wage rates are computed by formulas (1) and (2) and the
results are shown in Table 7. Since any single estimate of the shadow wage
rate is bound to be subject to errors in many respects, we experiment with
three alternative estimates. As the upper bound, we take the going wage
rate in the domestic manufacturing sector (alternative A). The estimates
obtained by formula (2) are close to the estimates of the marginal productivity of labor and taken as the lower bound (alternative C). The third
alternative is the estimates obtained by formula (1) and these lie, except
for the higher wage category, between the upper and lower bounds (alternative B). Finally, we assume that the shadow wage rate does not change

Labor Category	α	β
Clerical & Others	.87	.85
Engineers	.85	.83
Technicians	.87	.85
Skilled Workers	.90	.87
Semi-Skilled Workers	.93	.90
Apprentices	.93	.90

over time, at least for the period we are concerned with.

Foreign Exchange Benefits

The foreign exchange benefit can be measured as the product of net foreign exchange earnings and the excess of the shadow price of foreign exchange over the official exchange rate.

It is expected that the MAFEZ will bring in positive net foreign exchange earnings over the whole period. Foreign exchange may be earned from the following sources; wage payments to domestic workers, sale of raw materials and intermediate inputs, supply of utilities, taxes and rentals, foreign capital investments in cash, and other miscellaneous supporting activities. Sources of foreign exchange outflow include dividend payments on equity held by foreigners, wage payments to foreign employees, and liquidation of foreign equity holdings. From the sale of goods and services, we must subtract the direct and indirect import content to get net earnings in foreign exchange. We assume that the direct and indirect import content of the consumption basket of an average worker, raw materials and intermediate inputs, and utilities are 10, 85, and 90 per cent, respectively.[11]

Rentals and costs of other supporting services are included in the factory and management expenditure account of the MAFEZ firms. We assume that 30 per cent of this expenditure accrues to the domestic sector and hence represents net foreign exchange earnings.

Total foreign investment in operating funds is considered to be a net

---

[11] The percentage assumed here for intermediate inputs and raw materials is much higher than Han's estimate of 44 per cent for an average dollar of exports by Korea in 1968. He did not, however, include indirect import requirements although foreign capital needs were taken into account. For the textile fabrics and electrical machinery industries, which seem to be the relevant ones here, he obtained 71 and 76 per cent respectively. See Han, pp. 112–113.

addition to the foreign exchange holding of the domestic sector. We assume that the MAFEZ firms will realize a 30 per cent rate of profit (before
taxes) on the investments outstanding.[12] Assuming that all profits are paid
out in dividends and that the tax rate, when applicable, on gross profits
is 20 per cent, we get dividend rate of 24 percent after taxes on gross
profits. Of this, 1.1 per cent would be payed to domestic investors with
22.9 per cent flowing out to foreigners.

Let SPFE, R_0, I, and IT denote the shadow price of foreign exchange,
official exchange rate, total commodity imports (at c.i.f. prices), and import tariffs, respectively.

A simple method of estimating SPFE is

$$SPFE = R_0 \left(1 + \frac{IT}{I} \right) \quad\dots\dots\dots\dots\dots\dots\dots\dots\dots\dots(3)$$

This is a method proposed by Schydlowsky. The basic position implicit
in this method is that the SPFE is the marginal utility of foreign exchange
and we may approximate the marginal utility by the domestic demand price of imported goods. Equation (3) assumes that the domestic demand price
equals to the import price plus the tariff. We, of course, wish to incorporate
domestic indirect taxes and other considerations but the task is prohi-
bitively formidable. Using data for 1972, formula (3) yields an SPFE
which exceeds R_0 by 29.2 won. We assume that this differential will be
maintained throughout the period we are concerned.

Rental Revenue

Assuming that the MAFEZ will eventually be fully occupied and know-
ing the size of rentable space and the rental rates, we can estimate the
stream of rental revenue easily and relatively free from error.

Tax Revenue and Returns to Domestic Capital Invested

As previously mentioned, we simply assume an average tax rate of 20
per cent on profits before taxes, which again is assumed to be 30 per cent
of total equity. Profits after taxes will be divided between foreign and
domestic equity holders, if any, according to their equity ratio.

---

[12] Appendix Tables 1 and 2 indicate profit rates of nearly 50 to 60 per cent. We assume that these are overstated.

IV. MEASUREMENT OF THE BENEFIT-COST RATIO

The desirability of a project depends upon its future performance and, therefore, any project evaluation necessarily involves assumptions about future developments. Fortunately, the MAFEZ has been operating since 1971 and its future may be projected from this experience. Our first concern is the number of man-years which will be employed in the MAFEZ. Figure 1 shows the trend of labor employment (number of domestic workers employed) since the MAFEZ started operating. It is immediately clear that this trend could best be approximated by the logistic growth function of the form

$$P_t = \frac{L^*/\bar{L}}{1 + e^{-(a+bt)}} \quad \dots\dots\dots\dots\dots\dots\dots\dots\dots(4)$$

where L^* and $\bar{L}$ are the upper bounds on the actual and potential levels of employment respectively, and P_t is the level of employment achieved in period t as a percentage of $\bar{L}$. Since (4) is nonlinear, we may estimate:

$$log\left[\frac{P_t}{(L^*/\bar{L}) - P_t}\right] = a + bt \quad \dots\dots\dots\dots\dots(5)$$

for alternative ratios of $L^*/\bar{L}$ and choose the one that yields the highest R^2.

To determine $\bar{L}$, we first calculate the planned employment per pyung of committed factory space as of May, 1974. We then assume that the same employment density will apply to the remaining uncommitted rentable factory sites. This method gives us $\bar{L} = 46,174$ man-years of labor for the subdivisions I and II.

We estimated (5) for different ratios of $L^*/\bar{L}$ but the one that gave the closest fit turned out to be rather low. This appears to be due to the oil crisis and the resulting slowdown in the employment growth rate during the last two months of 1973 and the first half of 1974. Thus we assumed $L^*/\bar{L} = 0.85$, a ratio higher than what the data suggests, and estimated (5) to get:

$$log\left(\frac{P_t}{0.85 - P_t}\right) = -4.97 + 0.15t \qquad R^2 = 0.98$$
$$(-66) \qquad (47) \qquad D\text{-}W = 0.32$$

The fit is quite close (the numbers in the parenthesis above are t-ratios). This result enables us to predict the level of employment under the assumption that future foreign investment will not be significantly different in nature from the existing ones. For all practical purposes, the level

Figure 1.

Trend in Labor Employment

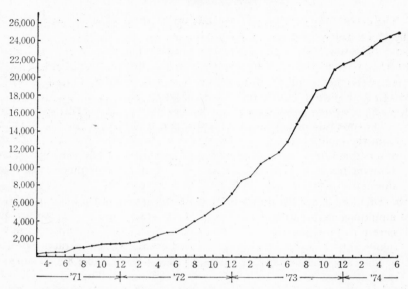

of employment reaches its upper limit in the seventh year. We assume that this level of employment will be maintained from the eighth year on.

The result can be applied to the subdivision II since it would probably be a duplication of the preceding ones. The same method gives us $\bar{L} = 35$, 755. The level of employment can be projected using the results above and assuming that this subdivison will begin its operation, if at all, in 1977.

Exports from the MAFEZ during the observable period lagged the level of employment by about half a year for the initial period, but the lag is reduced to about three months for the later period. It can be seen from Appendix Table 1 that the planned output (export)-labor ratio is about U.S. $8,400 per man-year. Export levels are determined for future years taking into account the lag structure and the output-labor ratio under the assumption that the industry mix and technology will remain basically the same.

Appendix Table 1 also gives requirements per dollar of export for imported raw materials and intermediate inputs, domestically produced raw materials and intermediate inputs, expenditures on public utilities, and factory and management expenditures. In the absence of any relative price changes and any significant change in industry mix and technology, these requirements can also be projected in proportion to the projected level of export.

A benefit-cost ratio will be computed for each of four hypothetical cases;

(1) that subdivision II and the port never materialize and subdivisions I and III operate for 15 years,

(2) the same as (1) but the period of operation is 25 years,

(3) in addition to subdivisions I and III, subdivision II and the port begin operating in 1977. Subdivisions I and III operate for 25 years while subdivision II operates for 19 years,

(4) the same as (3) except that each subdivision operates 5 years longer.

The time rate of discount for future benefits and costs could be deduced from the equilibrium rate of interest in a competitive market. Since the observable rate of interest rarely fulfills this qualification, the appropriate discount rate is hard to determine. We, therefore, experiment with three alternative discount rates of 10, 14, and 16 per cent.

Table 8 shows the estimated benefit-cost ratios under alternative assumptions. They range from a low of 1.17 to a high of 2.35. When the lowest shadow wage rate (C) is assumed, the benefit-cost ratio improves significantly and the MAFEZ appears to be a moderately attractive project in this case with benefit-cost ratios of around two. Table 8 also suggests that there is a real danger of the benefit-cost ratio falling below one. The ratios are more sensitive to the shadow wage rate assumption than to either the discount rate or the terminal year assumption.

Table 8
Benefit-Cost Ratios

Alternative Discount Rate & SWR Assumptions	Case 1	Case 2	Case 3	Case 4
10%—A[1]	1.40	1.61	1.64	1.69
10%—B	1.62	1.85	1.87	1.94
10%—C	1.99	2.26	2.28	2.35
14%—A	1.25	1.39	1.39	1.42
14%—B	1.44	1.60	1.59	1.63
14%—C	1.77	1.96	1.94	1.99
16%—A	1.17	1.29	1.28	1.30
16%—B	1.36	1.49	1.47	1.50
16%—C	1.67	1.83	1.80	1.83

[1]10%-A, for example, denotes the combination of 10% discount rate and shadow wage asssumption A.

We estimated the benefit-cost ratio under the alternative assumption that the domestic sector need not subsidize the MAFEZ firms through export loan. Results are presented in Table 9. Substantial increases in the benefit-cost ratio indicate that the subsidy cost could be significant enough to alter the desirability of the MAFEZ.

The estimated ratios for the cases 3 and 4 give us some indication that addition of subdivision II may not make a substantially better investment than existing ones. Table 10 below shows the estimated marginal benefit-

Table 9

Benefit-Cost Ratios Without the Subsidy Cost

Alternative Discount Rate & SWR Assumptions	Case 1	Case 2	Case 3	Case 4
10% —A	2.37	2.97	3.20	3.40
10% —B	2.74	3.42	3.66	3.89
10% —C	3.36	4.17	4.45	4.72
14% —A	1.95	2.30	2.28	2.36
14% —B	2.26	2.66	2.61	2.70
14% —C	2.78	3.25	3.18	3.25
16% —A	1.78	2.10	2.00	2.06
16% —B	2.07	2.42	2.30	2.36
16% —C	2.54	2.97	2.81	2.88

Table 10

Marginal Benefit-Cost Ratios of Subdivision II

Alternative Discount Rate & SWR Assumptions	B/C Ratios of Subdivisions I & III Combined	Marginal B/C Ratios of Subdivision II
10% — A	1.51	1.72
10% — B	1.75	1.94
10% — C	2.13	2.34
14% — A	1.33	1.41
14% — B	1.53	1.58
14% — C	1.88	1.91
16% — A	1.24	1.27
16% — B	1.44	1.43
16% — C	1.76	1.73

cost ratios of constructing subdivision II and operating it for 19 years. They are compared with the benefit-cost ratios of existing subdivisions when operated for the same number of years.

It can be seen that the marginal ratios are slightly higher than the ratios for existing ones when the discount rate is low, but lower when the discount rate is high and a low shadow wage rate is assumed. It appears that external economies generated by subdivisions I and II are offset, to a large extent, by the high development costs of subdivision II, making it about as desirable an investment opportunity as existing ones.

V. MAXIMIZING BENEFITS FROM THE MAFEZ: CONCLUSION

In view of estimated benefit-cost ratios substantially greater than one in most cases, the MAFEZ does appear to be a viable project as a whole. But this conclusion is contingent on a number of assumptions we made in deriving the estimates. In this section, we will discuss some of these qualifications with a view to ensuring that the MAFEZ be a desirable project.

Obviously, our conclusion depends most critically on the assumptions about the shadow wage rate. Even if the estimated shadow wage rates are correct, it would be reasonable to expect that the gap between the actual and shadow wage rates will disappear gradually as the economy develops and labor becomes scarce. An immediate implication of this is that the benefit-cost ratios we obtained are overstated. On the other hand, although the process will take quite some time, it may not be justified to use too long a time horizon for evaluation of the project. In this sense, cases 3 and 4 seem less appropriate.

Two potentially important aspects have been ignored in this study. One is possible transfer of advanced technology through a free trade zone and the other is environmental pollution. As the MAFEZ now stands, little technological transfer can be expected. Most of the industries and technology are already found in the domestic sector. Thus the MAFEZ might adversely effect domestic export industries. As indicated before, pollution can be a serious problem unless appropriate anti-pollution measures are taken. Since the cost of pollution is likely to be substantial, the MAFEZ may be undesirable if this cost has to be taken into account.

Net benefits seem to depend heavily on the kinds of industries (or the technology used within an industry) admitted to a free trade zone. When labor is abundant, an obvious criterion is to choose those industries (or technologies) that use more labor per unit of factory space. Appendix Tables 1 and 2 indicate the planned and actual labor intensity per pyung by industry. Textile products, electronic and electric products, handicrafts and toys, and optical instruments are ranked high. Food processing, machinery and metals, and "miscellaneous others" are poor in this respect. In terms of wage earnings per pyung, the rankings do not change significantly--optical instruments tops them all, followed by electronic and electric products, textile products, and handicrafts and toys.

Benefits also arise from selling domestic resources to the free trade zone. The planned ratio of domestic resources to total intermediate inputs is high in the food processing and textile industries, while the actual ratio for the latter is rather small. The planned ratios do not differ very much between industries except for textiles and food processing. If we compute the use of domestic resources per pyung, we get more or less the same ranking. Since the benefits to be derived from this source are rather small compared with those of labor employment, it would be unwise to put too much emphasis on this criterion.

Ranking of the industries in terms of foreign exchange earnings per pyung shows that the use of domestic materials is more important than wages. Textiles, food processing, optical instruments, electronic and electric products, and handicrafts and toys are ranked high. If we rank the industries by net benefits per pyung, the ranking does not differ significantly from that according to wage earnings. For maximum benefits, as one would expect, it would be wise to bring in those industries (or technology) that use more labor per pyung.

Since the cost of providing export loans appears to be too much as evidenced by the significant increase in the benefit-cost ratios, the policy certainly needs reconsideration. Other incentives like tax exemption and low rental rates may have to be removed as the size of net benefits shrinks in the future.

Appendix 1. *Planned Full Operation Level of the MAFEZ Firms*

Unit: In Thousand U.S. Dollars

Industry	Investment	Export	Imported Material	Domestic Material	Labor² (man-year)	Total Wage²	Public Utilities	Factory Expenditure	Depreciation Allowance	Management Expenditure	Value Added³
Electronic & Electric(25)¹	26,358	153,375	79,246	32,082	18,932	14,666	1,169	3,613	2,100	6,987	28,178
Machinery & Metal(34)	22,853	86,929	35,864	20,016	8,585	8,020	1,331	2,787	2,398	5,754	18,777
Chemical Products(10)	5,822	19,901	8,120	4,885	4,226	2,618	267	516	312	1,366	4,465
Handicrafts and Toys(8)	958	7,909	4,191	1,637	1,226	722	31	194	49	509	1,298
Textile Products(6)	1,360	8,533	2,307	3,845	1,530	1,045	58	325	87	471	1,440
Food Processing(2)	1,345	15,295	217	9,413	657	411	309	298	413	644	4,001
Optical Instruments(4)	2,074	11,707	4,658	2,046	1,147	1,412	57	742	394	838	2,972
Others(4)	888	5,830	1,699	616	491	474	62	83	223	1,168	1,979
Total (93)	61,658	309,479	136,302	74,540	36,834	29,368	3,284	8,560	5,976	17,737	63,110

Notes: Data from business plans of the individual firms submitted as a part of application for permission. Operation level is on yearly basis. Exchange rates used in converting won into dollars vary slightly depending on the dates the firms applied. Data were collected on Oct. 27, 1973.

¹ Figures in the parenthesis indicate the number of firms included in each category.

² Employment of labor excludes those of foreign technicians and managers. Total wage stands for yearly wage bill of employed labor other than foreigners.

³ Value-added is defined as export value minus imported and domestic materials, public utilities, depreciation allowance, and factory and management expenditures.

Appendix 2. *Performance of the MAFEZ Firms*

Unit: In Thousand U.S. Dollars

Industry	Investment	Export	Imported Material	Domestic Material	Labor² (man-year)	Total Wage³	Public Utilities	Rent	Misc. Expenditure⁴	Value Added⁵
Electronic & Electric(8)¹	3,723	13,494	6,360	1,943	4,260	1,197	221	111	952	3,907
Machinery & Metal(6)	1,239	839	335	9	576	136	18	17	220	240
Chemical Products(4)	606	1,008	432	220	647	192	15	14	115	212
Handicrafts and Toys(6)	440	2,116	962	416	702	169	14	26	76	622
Textile Products(3)	450	2,096	1,291	27	767	346	30	51	209	488
Others(2)	200	639	265	83	253	164	23	8	59	201
Total (29)	6,208	20,192	9,645	2,698	7,205	2,204	321	227	1,631	5,670

Notes:　The survey asked the occupant firms to fill in the cumulated performance record since beginning of operation until June 30, 1973.

[1] Number of firms included in the respective industry.

[2] Number of employed persons outstanding as of June 30, 1973. It excludes all foreigners.

[3] Cumulated wage payment to employees other than foreigners.

[4] Includes depreciation, repairs and maintenance, transportation, and other expenditures.

[5] Value-added defined as export value minus imported and domestic materials, public utilities, rent, and miscellaneous expenditures.

REFERENCES

Bechtel International Corporation, *A Study Report on the MAFEZ,* (Feb. 1972), (UNIDO Contract No. 71/19), Office of the MAFEZ Administration.

Han, K. C., *Policies to Increase Net Foreign Exchange Earnings,* Korea Trade Research Institute, June 1969.

Hong, Wontack, *Optimum Production and Trade Policy through Tax-cum-Subsidy,* Korea Development Institute, 1972.

Jones, R. W., "International Capital Movements and the Theory of Tariffs and Trade," *Quarterly Journal of Economics* (Feb. 1967), pp. 1–38.

Kemp, M. C., *The Pure Theory of International Trade and Investment,* Prentice-Hall, 1969.

Lee, K. S., *The Bruno Production Function, Factor Market Disequilibrium, and Factor Contributions to Growth in the Korean Industrial Sectors,* Korea Development Institute, 1972.

Lee, T. H., *Report on an Economic Analysis of Kaohsiung Export Processing Zone,* (August 1970), the National Taiwan University, Mimeographed in Chinese.

Little, I. M. D. and J. A. Mirrless, *Project Appraisal and Planning for Developing Countries,* Heinemann Educational Books, 1974.

Mundell, R. A., "International Trade and Factor Mobility," *American Economic Review* (June 1957), pp. 321–7.

Office of the MAFEZ Administration, *Monthly Survey of Investments in the MAFEZ,* various issues.

Office of Labor Affairs, *Year Book of Labor Statistics* (1973).

Schydlowsky, D. M., *Project Evaluation in Economies in General Disequilibrium: An Application of Second Best Analysis,* Economic Development Report No. 220 (May 1972), Development Research Group, Harvard University.

Warr, P. G., "Savings Propensities and the Shadow Wage," *Economica* (Nov. 1973), pp. 410–415.